Lecture Notes in Artificial Intelligence 6463

Edited by R. Goebel, J. Siekmann, and W. Wahlster

Subseries of Lecture Notes in Computer Science

Simon Siegler   Nathan Wasser (Eds.)

Verification, Induction, Termination Analysis

Festschrift for Christoph Walther on the Occasion of His 60th Birthday

Springer

Series Editors

Randy Goebel, University of Alberta, Edmonton, Canada
Jörg Siekmann, University of Saarland, Saarbrücken, Germany
Wolfgang Wahlster, DFKI and University of Saarland, Saarbrücken, Germany

Volume Editors

Simon Siegler
Nathan Wasser
Technische Universität Darmstadt, Fachbereich Informatik
Fachgebiet Programmiermethodik
Hochschulstraße 10, 64289 Darmstadt, Germany
E-mail: {siegler, wasser}@informatik.tu-darmstadt.de

Library of Congress Control Number: 2010938599

CR Subject Classification (1998): C.2, D.2, F.3, D.3, H.4, F.4.1

LNCS Sublibrary: SL 7 – Artificial Intelligence

ISSN 0302-9743
ISBN-10 3-642-17171-0 Springer Berlin Heidelberg New York
ISBN-13 978-3-642-17171-0 Springer Berlin Heidelberg New York

springer.com

Printed in Germany

Typesetting: Camera-ready by author, data conversion by Scientific Publishing Services, Chennai, India
Printed on acid-free paper 06/3180

Christoph Walther
(Photo courtesy of Markus Aderhold)

Preface

This Festschrift is dedicated to Christoph Walther on the occasion of his 60th birthday on August 9th, 2010. It consists of articles by some of his colleagues and former students, who, on this momentous occasion, chose to show their appreciation.

In teaching theoretical computer science, Christoph has had a profound influence on many of his former and current students, not least by the introduction of ✓eriFun into the classroom. Outside of his teaching, developing ✓eriFun played a major role in his recent research activities.

When the idea for this Festschrift was first presented to us, it quickly became apparent that Christoph's work in the fields of verification, induction and termination analysis would be mirrored in the contributions, leading us to refer to this project as "VITA".

Since many of the authors have known Christoph for much longer than we have, we feel that the contributions themselves give a better insight into his former and present work than we possibly could. On that note, we hope Christoph enjoys reading this Festschrift and wish him all the best for his future.

The editors would like to thank everyone who showed interest in this project, especially the authors for their contributions and the organisers of the colloquium. Furthermore we would like to thank Kai Sachs for his work in coordinating this Festschrift with Springer. Last, but certainly not least, Veronika Weber has earned our heartfelt gratitude with her constant guidance and helpful advice.

September 2010

Simon Siegler
Nathan Wasser

Karsten Weihe on the Joint Celebration of the 60th Birthdays of Alejandro P. Buchmann, Sorin A. Huss, and Christoph Walther on November 19th, 2010

Honourable Colleague,
Dear Christoph,

Let me first send my congratulations to you as well as to Alejandro Buchmann and Sorin Huss. You jointly celebrate your 60th birthdays this year. I wish you all the best for your future work at TU Darmstadt!

Christoph, among all of your merits, there is one that is particularly connected with my responsibilities as the Head of Department. In those years in which you were the only theoretician in the faculty, you took care and fought hard to ensure that Theory of Computer Science should be considered in all strategic decisions in teaching and research. Our bachelor program in Computer Science and our research landscape would be different, worse in fact, without your permanent engagement.

Besides your extensive and successful research activities, you are particularly deeply engaged in teaching. Generations of students have learned from you, your group, and your tool VeriFun, that formal verification is indeed a very practical issue, and that the formal way is the most profound way of reasoning about software.

You three guys are true institutions of the department (I am tempted to speak of dinosaurs, however, in an absolutely positive sense). You have seen colleagues come and go. Due to your experience and your long time of service in the department, you have become critical nodes of the department's corporate memory network. Your experience has been decisive during many discussions, typically (yet not exclusively ☺) for the better.

I should mention that each of you three guys is equipped with a specific kind of spirit. Your humorous comments, always to the point, have made many meetings amongst colleagues really enjoyable for the audience (well, the meeting chair did not always enjoy them, but that's fine). You have always combined passion with reason, spirit with analysis, vision with rationality.

On behalf of the colleagues, the department, and TU Darmstadt, I hope that you three guys will continue to have a great time together with all of us and an even longer chain of success stories than ever. Happy Birthday!

Table of Contents

Programming Inductive Proofs
A New Approach Based on Contextual Types

Brigitte Pientka

McGill University, Montreal, Canada
bpientka@cs.mcgill.ca

Abstract. In this paper, we present an overview to programming with proofs in the reasoning framework, Beluga. Beluga supports the specification of formal systems given by axioms and inference rules within the logical framework LF. It also supports implementing proofs about formal systems as dependently typed recursive functions. What distinguishes Beluga from other frameworks is that it not only represents binders using higher-order abstract syntax, but directly supports reasoning with contexts and contextual objects. Contextual types allows us to characterize precisely hypothetical and parametric derivations, i.e. derivations which depend on variables and assumptions, and lead to a direct and elegant implementation of inductive proofs as recursive functions. Because of the intrinsic support for binders and contexts, one can think of the design of Beluga as the most advanced technology for specifying and prototyping formal systems together with their meta-theory.

1 Introduction

The POPLmark challenge [ABF$^+$05] triggered wide-spread interest in mechanizing the meta-theory of programming languages, and today, knowing how to formalize proofs in a proof assistant is an essential skill. The interest in mechanizing proofs has also gone beyond small toy examples and several large-scale formalizations to verify compilers using proof-assistants are on their way (see for example [Chl10, Chl07, LCH07, Ler09]).

Although mechanizing properties about programming language are nowadays common, this endeavor is unfortunately still plagued by the necessary overhead to manage bureaucratic details. T. Altenkirch [Alt93] remarked about his formalization of the strong normalization proof for system F in Lego in 1993:

> "When doing the formalization, I discovered that the core part of the proof...is fairly straightforward and only requires a good understanding of the paper version. However, in completing the proof I observed that in certain places I had to invest much more work than expected, e.g. proving lemmas about substitution and weakening" [Alt93]

Today, not much has changed. In this paper, we will identify key operations good meta-languages should support to easily and elegantly represent formal

S. Siegler and N. Wasser (Eds.): Walther Festschrift, LNAI 6463, pp. 1–16, 2010.

systems and proofs about them and give a tutorial to programming proofs in the Beluga environment [Pie08, PD08, PD10]. Beluga is a two-level framework for programming with and reasoning about formal systems. The first layer supports the representation of formal systems within the logical framework LF[HHP93]. On top of LF, we provide a functional language that supports analyzing and manipulating LF data via pattern matching.

Beluga's strength and elegance come from supporting encodings based on higher-order abstract syntax (HOAS), in which binders in the object language are represented as binders in LF's meta-language. As a consequence, users can avoid implementing common and tricky routines dealing with variables, such as capture-avoiding substitution, renaming and fresh name generation. In addition, Beluga provides intrinsic support for contexts and contextual reasoning. This is particularly convenient when representing proofs, since in this setting a natural question arises: how to represent hypothetical and parametric derivations? One may of course represent such assumptions explicitly as lists, but as a consequence we would need to enforce properties such as well-formedness, scope, uniqueness of assumptions, weakening, etc. explicitly. In Beluga, contextual objects directly characterize hypothetical and parametric derivations, and hence the user can stay away from the bureaucracy of explicitly managing and reasoning about contexts. This allows a direct and elegant implementation of inductive proofs about hypothetical and parametric derivations as recursive functions over contextual objects. Because of the intrinsic support for binders and contexts, one can think of the design of Beluga as the most advanced technology for specifying and prototyping formal systems together with their meta-theory.

In this paper, we will first revisit the formalization of the simply-typed lambda-calculus together with its type uniqueness proof (Sec. 2). In particular, we will identify and highlight challenges any meta-language used for mechanizing formal systems and proofs must address. Second, we will give a tutorial to Beluga showing how induction proofs can be directly translated into Beluga functions (Sec. 3). Finally, we summarize the theoretical foundation of Beluga and discuss its implementation (Sec. 4) . In particular, we will touch on the issues of type reconstruction for Beluga. Last but not least, we compare Beluga to related frameworks which support higher-order abstract syntax encodings of formal systems and proofs about them (Sec. 5).

2 Revisiting the Simply-Typed Lambda-Calculus

We begin by revisiting the simply-typed lambda-calculus. We introduce the base type nat and function type $\mathsf{arr}\ T_1\ T_2$. The lambda-terms are either variables, abstractions or applications.

$$\begin{array}{llcl} \text{Types } T, S ::= \mathsf{nat} & & \text{Terms } M, N ::= x \\ \quad\quad\quad\quad \mid \mathsf{arr}\ T\ S & & \quad\quad\quad\quad\quad\quad \mid \mathsf{lam}\ x{:}T.M \\ & & \quad\quad\quad\quad\quad\quad \mid \mathsf{app}\ M\ N \end{array}$$

We label the input x in the lambda-abstraction $\mathsf{lam}\ x{:}T.M$ with its type T to ensure that every lambda-term has a unique type.

2.1 Context-Free Formulation of Typing Rules

We give first a context-free formulation of the typing rules following Gentzen's original presentation of the natural deduction calculus [Gen35]. Let us first define the typing judgment more formally:

Typing Judgment: $\mathsf{oft}\ M\ T$ read as "M is of type T"

Next, we give two typing rules, one for abstractions and one for applications and we label the inference rules with their names. Due to the context-free representation of the rules, we do not need a rule for variables, since whenever a variable is encountered when traversing an abstraction, we generate a new variable x together with the assumption u: $\mathsf{oft}\ x\ T$. To indicate the scope of the parameter x and the hypothesis u: $\mathsf{oft}\ x\ T$, we annotate the rule name t_lam with super-scripts x, u.

$$\dfrac{\begin{array}{c}\overline{\mathsf{oft}\ x\ T}\ u\\ \vdots \\ \mathsf{oft}\ M\ S\end{array}}{\mathsf{oft}\ (\mathsf{lam}\ x{:}T.M)\ (\mathsf{arr}\ T\ S)}\ \mathsf{t\_lam}^{x,u} \qquad \dfrac{\mathsf{oft}\ M\ (\mathsf{arr}\ T\ S) \quad \mathsf{oft}\ N\ T}{\mathsf{oft}\ (\mathsf{app}\ M\ N)\ S}\ \mathsf{t\_app}$$

Since our goal is to prove, type uniqueness we also introduce an equality judgement which states that two types are equal if they are identical.

Equality Judgment: $\mathsf{eq}\ S\ T$ read as "S is equal to the type T"

We only have the reflexivity axiom to define equality.

$$\dfrac{}{\mathsf{eq}\ T\ T}\ \mathsf{ref}$$

2.2 Formulation of Typing Rules with Explicit Contexts

While the context-free representation is sufficient and convenient for describing typing derivations, a formulation with explicit contexts to keep track of the assumptions is often used when actually implementing a type-checker based on these typing rules and also when reasoning about the given type system.

Before we give a formulation of the typing rules based on explicit contexts, we define the context more precisely. In particular, we specify that we are introducing the variable x together with the assumption $u{:}\mathsf{oft}\ x\ T$. As a consequence, we know that every variable x will be associated with a typing assumption $u{:}\mathsf{oft}\ x\ T$.

$$\text{Context } \Gamma ::= \cdot \mid \Gamma, x, u{:}\mathsf{oft}\ x\ T$$

We give the typing rules with explicit contexts next. While in the previous context-free formulation no variable rule was present, we now must have a rule which allows us to look up an assumption in the context. This look-up function relies on the fact that every variable in Γ has a typing assumption associated with it. We typically assume that it is associated with a unique typing assumption. This is silently enforced in the typing rule t_lam where we implicitly rename the variable x, if x is already present in Γ, before extending the context Γ with the variable x together with the assumption $\mathsf{oft}\ x\ T$.

$$\frac{x, u : \mathsf{oft}\ x\ T \in \Gamma}{\Gamma \vdash \mathsf{oft}\ x\ T}\ u$$

$$\frac{\Gamma, x, u : \mathsf{oft}\ x\ T \vdash \mathsf{oft}\ M\ S}{\Gamma \vdash \mathsf{oft}\ (\mathsf{lam}\ x{:}T.M)\ (\mathsf{arr}\ T\ S)}\ \mathsf{t\_lam}^{x,u} \qquad \frac{\Gamma \vdash \mathsf{oft}\ M\ (\mathsf{arr}\ T\ S) \quad \Gamma \vdash \mathsf{oft}\ N\ T}{\Gamma \vdash \mathsf{oft}\ (\mathsf{app}\ M\ N)\ S}\ \mathsf{t\_app}$$

2.3 Type Uniqueness

Finally, let us discuss the proof that every lambda-term has a unique type. While this theorem is quite simple, it is still interesting, since its proof relies on various properties of contexts and bound variables.

Theorem 1. *If* $\mathcal{D} : \Gamma \vdash \mathsf{oft}\ M\ T$ *and* $\mathcal{C} : \Gamma \vdash \mathsf{oft}\ M\ S$ *then* $\mathcal{E} : \mathsf{eq}\ T\ S$.

Proof. Induction on first typing derivation $\mathcal{D}$.

Case 1

$$\mathcal{D} = \frac{\overset{\mathcal{D}_1}{\Gamma \vdash \mathsf{oft}\ M\ (\mathsf{arr}\ T\ S)} \quad \overset{\mathcal{D}_2}{\Gamma \vdash \mathsf{oft}\ N\ T}}{\Gamma \vdash \mathsf{oft}\ (\mathsf{app}\ M\ N)\ S}\ \mathsf{t\_app}$$

$$\mathcal{C} = \frac{\overset{\mathcal{C}_1}{\Gamma \vdash \mathsf{oft}\ M\ (\mathsf{arr}\ T'\ S')} \quad \overset{\mathcal{C}_2}{\Gamma \vdash \mathsf{oft}\ N\ T'}}{\Gamma \vdash \mathsf{oft}\ (\mathsf{app}\ M\ N)\ S'}\ \mathsf{t\_app}$$

$\mathcal{E}$: $\mathsf{eq}\ (\mathsf{arr}\ T\ S)\ (\mathsf{arr}\ T'\ S')$ — by i.h. using $\mathcal{D}_1$ and $\mathcal{C}_1$
$\mathcal{E}$: $\mathsf{eq}\ (\mathsf{arr}\ T\ S)\ (\mathsf{arr}\ T\ S)$ and $S = S'$ and $T = T'$ — by inversion on reflexivity

Therefore there is a proof for $\mathsf{eq}\ S\ S'$ by reflexivity (since we know $S = S'$).

Case 2

$$\mathcal{D} = \frac{\overset{\mathcal{D}_1}{\Gamma, x, u{:}\ \mathsf{oft}\ x\ T \vdash \mathsf{oft}\ M\ S}}{\Gamma \vdash \mathsf{oft}\ (\mathsf{lam}\ x{:}T.M)\ (\mathsf{arr}\ T\ S)}\ \mathsf{t\_lam} \qquad \mathcal{C} = \frac{\overset{\mathcal{C}_1}{\Gamma, x, u{:}\ \mathsf{oft}\ x\ T \vdash \mathsf{oft}\ M\ S'}}{\Gamma \vdash \mathsf{oft}\ (\mathsf{lam}\ x{:}T.M)\ (\mathsf{arr}\ T\ S')}\ \mathsf{t\_lam}$$

$\mathcal{E}$: $\mathsf{eq}\ S\ S'$ — by i.h. using $\mathcal{D}_1$ and $\mathcal{C}_1$
$\mathcal{E}$: $\mathsf{eq}\ S\ S$ and $S = S'$ — by inversion using reflexivity

Therefore there is a proof for $\mathsf{eq}\ (\mathsf{arr}\ T\ S)\ (\mathsf{arr}\ T\ S')$ by reflexivity.

Case 3

$$\mathcal{D} = \frac{x, u\colon \mathsf{oft}\ x\ T \in \Gamma}{\Gamma \vdash \mathsf{oft}\ x\ T}\,u \qquad\qquad \mathcal{C} = \frac{x, v\colon \mathsf{oft}\ x\ S \in \Gamma}{\Gamma \vdash \mathsf{oft}\ x\ S}\,v$$

Every variable x is associated with a unique typing assumption (property of the context), hence $v = u$ and $S = T$.

2.4 Requirements for "Good" Meta-languages

"Good" meta-languages should free the user from dealing with tedious and boring bureaucratic details, so s/he is able to concentrate on the essence of a proof or algorithm. Ultimately, this means users can mechanize proofs quicker, since time is not wasted on cumbersome and tedious details, resulting proofs are easier to understand, since it captures the essential steps, and automation of such proofs is more feasible. In this section, we briefly review two important aspects which arise when mechanizing formal systems and their proofs.

Support for schematic variables and bound variables. When inspecting the typing rules, we notice at least two different kinds of variables. In $\mathsf{lam}\ x.M$, we bind all occurrence of the variable x in the term M. Similarly, we rely on α-renaming of bound variables and also rely on substitution for bound variables, when we for example define the reduction semantics for the lambda-calculus. In addition to bound variables, we also have used schematic variables to describe the typing rules. For example, M, N, T, S are schematic variables. When we use the typing rules to construct a concrete typing derivation for some concrete lambda-term, we instantiate these schematic variables appropriately. We will subsequently call the schematic variables M, N, T, and S *meta-variables*. In addition, we also use *context variable* Γ to denote the sequence of assumptions. Finally, we revisit the variable rule

$$\frac{x, u :\ \mathsf{oft}\ x\ T \in \Gamma}{\Gamma \vdash\ \mathsf{oft}\ x\ T}\,u$$

In this rule, the variable x is not a bound variable, but is a special schematic variable; it represents any variable declared in the context Γ. This is in contrast to schematic meta-variables, which represent any concrete lambda-term. We will call x a *parameter variable* standing for concrete variables from a context Γ.

In addition to α-renaming and substitution for bound variables, we hence also have substitutions for context variables, meta-variables and parameter variables.

Support for contexts. Providing intrinsic support for representing contexts and reasoning about them, will ease the mechanization of proofs. In the previous example, we silently assumed that every declaration occurs at most once. In addition, we often rely on weakening, strengthening and substitution lemmas. Managing and reasoning about contexts is an essential part of proofs about formal systems (see also the benchmarks we recently proposed together with A. Felty in [FP]). Supporting such reasoning about contexts simplifies the proof developments, leads to quicker prototyping, and helps to identify mistakes more easily, since the user can concentrate on the main issues of the proof without being distracted by bookkeeping.

3 Beluga: A Framework for Programming Proofs

3.1 Overview

Beluga is a two-level system. On the first level, it provides an implementation of the logical framework LF [HHP93] similar to the implementation of LF in the Twelf system [PS99]. This supports a compact representation of formal systems and derivations exploiting higher-order abstract syntax and dependent types.

One important characteristic is that our encodings of the object language are adequate, i.e. there is a one-to-one correspondence between the terms in the object language and the terms characterized in the meta-language, namely LF. Consequently, proofs about the typing rules and lambda-terms do not deal with proof obligations which establish that the given derivation is well-formed or that a given derivation is impossible.

On top of LF, we provide a functional language which supports writing recursive functions via pattern matching on LF objects. Taking a fresh look at the proofs-as-programs paradigm, we can identify the following correspondence between on paper proofs and Beluga functions.

On paper proof	Proofs as functions in Beluga
Case analysis	Case analysis and pattern matching
Inversion	Pattern matching using let-expression
Induction Hypothesis	Recursive call

Case analysis on a derivation in the on paper proof will correspond to a case-expression which pattern matches on contextual objects describing the derivation. An inversion step in the informal proof corresponds to a case-expression with one case which can be be written using a let-expression in Beluga. Finally, the appeal to the induction hypothesis corresponds to the recursive call in a Beluga program.

As mentioned earlier, a key feature of Beluga is its support for contextual types to characterize contextual objects. Contextual types characterize contextual objects and thereby directly ensure we are only working with well-scoped derivations. Moreover, we can parameterize programs over contexts using context variables. This is essential when we want to model cases where the context grows as in the proof for type uniqueness when we considered the case which concluded with the typing rule for lambda-abstractions. It also allows us to express fine grained invariants and distinguish between different contexts.

Taken together, Beluga allows for a compact and elegant representation of proofs about formal system.

3.2 Representing Simply-Typed Lambda-Calculus in LF

To represent the simply-typed lambda-calculus in the logical framework LF, we define two LF types: the LF type `tp` for describing the types of our simply-typed lambda-calculus, and the LF type `tm` for characterizing the terms of the lambda-calculus.

```
tp: type .
nat: tp.
arr: tp → tp → tp.
```

```
tm: type .
lam : tp → (tm→tm) → tm.
app : tm → tm → tm.
```

The LF type `tp` has two constructors, `nat` and `arr`, corresponding to the types nat and arr T S respectively. Since `arr` is a constructor which takes in two arguments, its type is `tp → tp → tp`.

The LF type `tm` also has two constructors. The constructor `app` takes as input two objects of type `tm` and allows us to construct an object of type `tm`. The constructor for lambda-terms also takes two arguments as input; it first takes an object of type `tp` for the type annotation and the body of the abstraction is second. We use higher-order abstract syntax to represent the object-level binding of the variable x in the body M. Accordingly, the body of the abstraction is represented by the type `(tm → tm)`. For example, lam x:(arr nat nat) . lam y:nat . app x y is represented by `lam (arr nat nat)` λ`x.lam nat` λ`y.app x y`. This encoding has several well-known advantages: First, the encoding naturally supports α-renaming of bound variables, which is inherited from the logical framework. Second, the encoding elegantly supports substitution for bound variables which reduces to β-reduction in the logical framework LF.

Next, we represent the context-free typing rules given earlier. Following the judgments-as-types principle, we define the type family `oft` which is indexed by terms `tm` and types `tp`. Each inference rule is then represented as a constant of the type `oft M T`. The rule `t_app` encodes the typing rule for applications: from derivations of `oft M (arr T S)` and `oft N T` we obtain a derivation for `oft (app M N) S`. The rule `t_lam` encodes directly the parametric hypothetical derivation "for all x assuming oft x T we can derive oft M S" using the dependent function type `{x:tm} oft x T → oft (M x) S`. While in the on-paper formulation of the rule, we silently assumed that we renamed x appropriately to ensure that x is new, we explicitly rename the bound variables in the representation of this rule in LF. This is achieved by the LF application `M x`.

```
oft: tm → tp → type .

t_app: oft M1 (arr T S) → oft N T
       → oft (app M N) S.
t_lam: ({x:tm} oft x T → oft (M x) S)
       → oft (lam T M) (arr T S).
```

```
eq: tp → tp → type .
ref: eq T T.
```

Finally, we represent the equality judgement as the type family `eq` which is indexed by two objects `tp`. Reflexivity is the only constant inhabiting the type `eq T S`. For a longer introduction on how to represent formal systems in the logical framework LF, we refer the reader to Pfenning's course notes [Pfe97].

3.3 Representing Theorems as Types in Beluga

Due to its support for dependent types and binders, Beluga is an ideal meta-language for representing theorems and proofs. Let us recall the theorem for type uniqueness from the previous section.

Theorem 2. *If* $\mathcal{D} : \Gamma \vdash \mathsf{oft}\, M\; T$ *and* $\mathcal{C} : \Gamma \vdash \mathsf{oft}\, M\; S$ *then* $\mathcal{E} : \mathsf{eq}\, T\; S$.

This statement makes explicit the context Γ containing variables together with their typing assumptions. Before showing how to implement it, we describe more precisely the shape of contexts Γ, using a context schema declaration:

```
schema tctx = some [t:tp] block x:tm. oft x t;
```

The schema `tctx` describes a context containing assumptions `x:tm`, each associated with a typing assumption `oft x t` for some type `t`. Formally, we are using a dependent product Σ (used only in contexts) to tie `x` to `oft x t`. We thus do not need to establish separately that for every variable there is a unique typing assumption: this is inherent in the definition of `tctx`. The schema classifies well-formed contexts and checking whether a context satisfies a schema will be part of type checking. As a consequence, type checking will ensure that we are manipulating only well-formed contexts, that later declarations overshadow previous declarations, and that all declarations are of the specified form.

To illustrate, we show some well-formed and some ill-formed contexts.

Context	Is of schema `tctx`?
`b1:block x:tm.oft x (arr nat nat),` `b2:block y:tm.oft y nat`	yes
`x:tm, u:oft x (arr nat nat)`	no (not grouped in blocks)
`y:tm`	no (typing assumption for `y` is missing)
`b:block x:tm.oft y nat`	no (`y` is free)
`b1:block x:tm.oft x (arr nat nat),` `b2:block y:tm.oft x nat`	no (wrong binding structure)

Let us now show the type of a recursive function in Beluga which corresponds to the type uniqueness theorem.

```
{g:tctx} (oft (M ..) T)[g] → (oft (M ..) S)[g] → (eq T S)[ ]
```

We can read this type as follows: For all context `g` of schema `tctx`, given a derivation for `oft (M ..) T` in the context `g` and a derivation for `oft (M ..) S` in the context `g`, we return a derivation showing that `eq T S` in the empty context. Although we quantified over the context `g` at the outside, it need not be passed explicitely to a function of this type, but Beluga will be able to reconstruct it.

We call the type `(oft (M ..) T)[g]` a contextual type and the object inhabiting it a contextual object. Since the term `M` can depend on the variables declared in the context `g`, we write `(M ..)`. Formally, `M` itself is a contextual object of type `tm[g]` and `..` is the identity substitution which α-renames the bound variables. On the other hand, `T` and `S` stand for closed objects of type `tp` and they cannot refer to declarations from the context `g`. Note that these subtleties were not captured in our original informal statement of the type uniqueness theorem.

3.4 Representing Inductive Proofs as Recursive Programs

We now show the program which corresponds to the inductive proof given in Section 2.3. The proof of type uniqueness proceeds by case analysis on the first derivation. Accordingly, the recursive function pattern-matches on the first derivation d which has type (oft (M ..) T) [g].

```
rec unique : {g:tctx}
             (oft (M ..) T)[g] → (oft (M ..) S)[g] → (eq T S)[ ] =
fn d ⇒ fn f ⇒ case d of
| [g] t_app (D1 ..) (D2 ..) ⇒                       % Application case
  let [g] t_app (F1 ..) (F2 ..) = f in
  let [ ] ref = unique ([g] D1 ..) ([g] F1 ..) in
    [ ] ref

| [g] t_lam (λx.λu. D .. x u) ⇒                     % Abstraction case
  let [g] t_lam (λx.λu. F .. x u) = f in
  let [ ] ref = unique ([g,b:block x:tm.oft x _ ] D .. b.1 b.2)
                      ([g,b] F .. b.1 b.2) in
   [ ] ref

| [g] #q.2 .. ⇒               % d : oft #q.1 T      % Assumption case
  let [g] #r.2 .. = f in      % f : oft #q.1 S
    [ ] ref ;
```

We consider each case individually. Each case in the proof on page 4 will correspond to one case in the case-expression.

Application case. If the first derivation d concludes with t_app, it matches the pattern [g] t_app (D1 ..) (D2 ..), and is a contextual object in the context g of type oft (app (M ..) (N ..)) S. D1 corresponds to the first premise of the typing rule for applications and has the contextual type (oft (M ..) (arr T S)) [g].

Using a let-binding, we invert the second argument, the derivation f which must have type (oft (app (M ..) (N ..)) S') [g]. F1 corresponds to the first premise of the typing rule for applications and has the contextual type (oft (M ..) (arr T' S')) [g]. The appeal to the induction hypothesis using D1 and F1 in the on-paper proof corresponds to the recursive call unique ([g] D1 ..) ([g] F1 ..). Note that while unique's type says it takes a context variable {g:tctx}, we do not pass it explicitly; Beluga infers it from the context in the first argument passed. The result of the recursive call is a contextual object of type (eq (arr T S) (arr T' S')) [ ]. The only rule that could derive such an object is ref, and pattern matching establishes that arr T S = arr T' S' and hence T = T' and S = S'. Therefore, there is a proof of [ ] eq S S' using the rule ref.

Abstraction case. If the first derivation d concludes with t_lam, it matches the pattern [g] t_lam (λx.λu. D .. x u), and is a contextual object in the context g of type oft (lam T (λx. M .. x)) (arr T S). Pattern matching—through a let-binding—serves to invert the second derivation f, which must have been by t_lam with a subderivation F1 ..x u deriving oft (M ..x) S' that can use x, u:oft x T, and assumptions from g.

The use of the induction hypothesis on `D` and `F` in a paper proof corresponds to the recursive call to `unique`. To appeal to the induction hypothesis, we need to extend the context by pairing up `x` and the typing assumption `oft x T`. This is accomplished by creating the declaration `b:block x:tm. oft x T`. In the code, we wrote an underscore _ instead of `T`, which tells Beluga to reconstruct it. (We cannot write `T` there without binding it by explicitly giving the type of `D`, so it is easier to write _.) To retrieve `x` we take the first projection `b.1`, and to retrieve `x`'s typing assumption we take the second projection `b.2`.

Now we can appeal to the induction hypothesis using `D1 ..b.1 b.2` and `F1 ..b.1 b.2` in the context `g,b:block x:tm. oft x T1`. From the i.h. we get a contextual object, a closed derivation of `(equal (arr T S) (arr T S'))[ ]`. The only rule that could derive this is `ref`, and pattern matching establishes that `S` must equal `S'`, since we must have `arr T S` = `arr T1 S'`. Therefore, there is a proof of `[] equal S S'`, and we can finish with the reflexivity rule `ref`.

Assumption case. Here, we must have used an assumption from the context `g` to construct the derivation `d`. Parameter variables allow a generic case that matches a declaration `block x:tm.oft x T` for any `T` in `g`. Since our pattern match proceeds on typing derivations, we want the second component of the parameter `#q`, written as `#q.2`. The pattern match on `d` also establishes that `M = #q.1`. Next, we pattern match on `f`, which has type `oft (#q.1 ..) S` in the context `g`. Clearly, the only possible way to derive `f` is by using an assumption from `g`. We call this assumption `#r`, standing for a declaration `block y:tm. oft y S`, so `#r.2` refers to the second component `oft (#r.1 ..) S`. Pattern matching between `#r.2` and `f` also establishes that `#r.1 = #q.1`. Finally, we observe that `#r.1 = #q.1` only if `#r` is equal to `#q`. We can only instantiate the parameter variables `#r` and `#q` with bound variables from the context or other parameter variables. Consequently, the only solution to establish that `#r.1 = #q.1` is the one where both the parameter variable `#r` and the parameter variable `#q` refer to the same bound variable in the context `g`. Hence, we must have `#r = #q`, and both parameters must have equal types, and `S = S' = T = T'`. (In general, unification in the presence of Σ-types does not yield a unique unifier, but in Beluga only parameter variables and variables from the context can be of Σ type, yielding a unique solution.)

4 Revisiting the Design of Beluga

4.1 Theoretical Foundation

Beluga's foundation rests on the idea of contextual modal type theory which was introduced in detail in [NPP08]. A contextual object $[\Psi]M$ has contextual type $A[\Psi]$ if M has type A in the context Ψ. In the setting of Beluga, we use a contextual type to describe an LF object within a context. By design, variables occuring in M can never extrude their scope. Generalizing ideas in [DPS97] data of type $A[\Psi]$ may be embedded into computations and analyzed via pattern matching. Consequently, different arguments to a computation may have different local contexts and we can distinguish between data of type $A[\,]$ which is closed and open data of type $A[\Psi]$ giving us fine-grained control. Since we want to allow recursion over open data objects and the local context Ψ may grow as we analyze the object M, our foundation supports context variables.

In [Pie08], we presented a simply-typed foundation for Beluga which included a bi-directional type system together with type preservation and progress proofs. Subsequently in [PD08], we extended this work to account for dependent types.

The design of Beluga distunguishes cleanly between bound variables on the LF-level and schematic variables, such as meta-variables, parameter variables and context variables.

4.2 Implementation

Beluga is implemented in OCaml. It provides a re-implementation of the logical framework LF together with LF type reconstruction and LF type checking based on explicit substitutions [ACCL90]. In addition, we designed a palatable source language for writing recursive functions about contextual objects. We list some of the challenges we addressed below.

Type reconstruction for LF. Our LF type reconstruction algorithm is designed around the ideas in [Pfe91] and closely resembles the implementation of LF type reconstruction in the Twelf system [PS99]. The essential principle can be summarized as follows: Process every declaration one at a time. Given a constant declaration, we infer the type of the free variables and any omitted arguments η-expanding variables when necessary. The free variables and the variables occurring in omitted arguments together constitute the implicit arguments of the constant. When subsequently using this constant we must omit passing implicit arguments. To ilustrate, let us briefly revisit the declaration of `t_lam`.

```
t_lam: ({x:tm} oft x T → oft (M x) S)
        → oft (lam T M) (arr T S).
```

Type reconstruction will produce the following type:

```
t_lam: {T:tp}{M:tm -> tm}{S:tp}
       ({x:tm} oft x T → oft (M x) S)
         → oft (lam T (λx. M x)) (arr T S).
```

The variables `T:tp`, `S:tp`, and `M:tm → tm` are called implicit arguments. Note, we also η-expanded `M`, where it was necessary. When we subsequently use the constant `t_lam`, for example within the program `unique` where we pattern match on the shape of the objects of type `(oft (M ..) (T ..))[g]`, we simply write `[g ] t_lam (λx.λu. D .. x u)` and omit passing the arguments for `T:tp`, `S:tp`, and `M:tm → tm`.

However there are a few subtle differences between our implementation and the one found in the Twelf system: Our implementation of the constraint-based unification algorithm [EP91, Pfe91] is more conservative and addresses some known shortcomings [Ree09]. Our surface language is also slightly more restrictive than Twelf's surface language, since we only handle η-expansion and require that the user writes LF objects in β-normal form. This makes the implementation and the theoretical foundation for LF type reconstruction more streamlined. Type reconstruction is, in general, undecidable for LF and our algorithm reports a principal type, a type error, or that the source term needs more type information.

Type reconstruction for Beluga programs. In Beluga, we write recursive programs over contextual LF objects which are embedded within computations. Hence, we first generalized LF type reconstruction so it can be used for contextual LF objects. This is necessary, since these objects may contain context-variables, meta-variables and parameter variables which are absent from the pure logical framework LF. We also extended the unification algorithm to handle parameter variables and Σ-types for variables.

In addition, we extended the general principle behind LF reconstruction to support type reconstruction for computations: given a computation-level type such as for example

```
{g:tctx} (oft (M ..) T)[g] → (oft (M ..) S)[g] → (eq T S)[ ]
```

we first infer the contextual type of `M`, `T` and `S`.

```
{g:tctx}{M::tm[g]}{T::tp[ ]}{S::tp[ ]}
(oft (M ..) T)[g] → (oft (M ..) S)[g] → (eq T S)[ ]
```

In general, the free variables and the variables occurring in omitted arguments together with the context variable constitute the implicit arguments of the function and must be omitted when using the function. In the type of `unique`, we have no omitted arguments and hence the implicit arguments are the context variable `g` and the free variables `T`, `S`, and `M`. When we make a recursive call to `unique` in for example the `t_app` case, we simply write `unique ([g] D1 ..) ([g] F1 ..)` omitting the implicit arguments.

We provide special syntax for declaring that a context must be passed explicitely and will not be reconstructed. In this case, the schema of the context variable we quantify over is wrapped in `(   )*`.

Finally, case-expressions pose unique challenges in the presence of dependent types, since pattern matching on an object may refine the type of the object. In our implementation, we first reconstruct the types of free variables occurring in the pattern itself and insert any omitted arguments. Next, we reconstruct a refinement substitution which is then stored together with the pattern. For example, when we pattern match on `[g] t_lam λx.λu. D .. x u` the scrutinee had type `(oft (M ..) T)[g]` but the pattern has the contextual type `(oft (lam λx. N .. x ) (arr T1 T2))[g]`. Hence, we synthesize the refinement `(lam λx.N .. x) = M ..` and `(arr T1 T2) = T`.

Context subsumption. Beluga also supports context subsumption, so one can provide a contextual object in a context Ψ in place of a contextual object in some other context Φ, provided Ψ can be obtained by weakening Φ. This mechanism, similar to world subsumption in Twelf, is crucial when assembling larger proofs. For example, if we require a context that contains only declarations `tm`, then we can supply a context which contains declarations `block x:tm. oft x nat`.

Totality. Type-checking guarantees local consistency and partial correctness, but does not guarantee that functions are total. For verifying that the implemented function is total and constitutes a valid proof, we need to verify that all cases are covered and that the function is terminating, i.e. all recursive calls are on smaller arguments. Building on the algorithm described in [DP09], Joshua Dunfield recently added a coverage checker to Beluga. The final missing piece to verifying totality is a termination checker which we envision will follow ideas used in the Twelf system [RP96, Pie05] for checking that arguments in recursive calls are indeed smaller.

5 Comparison with Other Systems Supporting HOAS

Encodings based on higher-order abstract syntax represent binders in the object language via binders in the meta-language. As a consequence, they inherit all the properties from the meta-language such as renaming of bound variables and substitution for bound variables. This means the user can avoid implementing tedious and sometimes tricky operations, such as capture-avoiding substitution. However, even in systems supporting HOAS we find different approaches to supporting contexts and the properties about them.

The Hybrid system [MMF08] tries to exploit the advantages of HOAS within the well-understood setting of higher-order logic as implemented by systems such as Isabelle and Coq. Hybrid provides a definitional layer where higher-order abstract syntax representations are compiled to de Bruijn representations, with tools for reasoning about them using tactical theorem proving and principles of (co)induction. This is a flexible approach, but contexts must be defined explicitly and properties about them must be established separately [FM09].

Abella [Gac08] is an interactive theorem prover for reasoning about specifications of formal systems. Its theoretical basis is different, but it supports encodings based on higher-order abstract syntax. However, contexts are not first-class and must be managed explicitly. For example, type uniqueness requires a lemma that each variable has a unique typing assumption, which comes for free in Beluga.

On the other side of spectrum, we find systems such as Twelf, Delphin and Beluga. Twelf is the most mature system and it provides a uniform meta-language for specifying formal systems together with their proofs using HOAS. Proofs are implemented as relations, and one establishes separately that the relation constitutes a total function and Twelf supports both termination and coverage checking. Delphin [PS09] is closest to Beluga. Proofs are implemented as functions (like Beluga) rather than relations, and its implementation uses much of the Twelf infrastructure.

In Twelf and Delphin, contexts are implicitely supported and we can reason about the contexts using world checking. However, the user does not have fine-grained control over the context. In particular we cannot state that a given object is closed while some other object is not. In the statement of the type uniqueness theorem for example, we cannot distinguish between the fact that the typing derivation depends on assumptions from the context while the proof that two types are equal does not depend on the context.

Another difference to Twelf and Delphin lies in the type reconstruction and coverage algorithms for Beluga programs. In the type uniqueness proof for example, Beluga crucially relies on the fact that the type constructor `arr` is injective; given an object of type `eq (arr T S) (arr T S')[ ]` we reason by inversion that the only possible way we could have derived an object of this type is by the rule `ref`. Therefore, type reconstruction will synthesize `S = S'` which is then used to finish the proof. In Twelf and Delphin, we need to prove a lemma stating "if `eq (arr T S) (arr T S')` then `eq S S'`, since the coverage checker will otherwise not accept the proof.

Beluga may be thought of as the most advanced system for reasoning about formal systems, since it provides not only support for binders but also for contexts. Contexts are explicit in the system; we can distinguish between different contexts, reason with them using context subsumption, and even observe their shape by matching on them.

6 Conclusion

Beluga is a powerful programming environment for implementing formal systems together with their meta-theory. Besides the type uniqueness example, our test suite includes standard examples such as the Church-Rosser theorem, cut-admissibility, Natural Deduction to Hilbert-style proof translations, proofs about compiler transformations, and preservation and progress for various ML-like languages. Together with A. Felty, we have proposed a list of simple benchmarks [FP] which highlight the challenges due to representing and managing a context of assumptions. Recently, we also re-implemented part one of the POPLmark challenge [ABF+05], soundness and completeness of algorithmic subtying for System $F_{\mathtt{sub}}$, following the proof pearl in [Pie07] where we exploit a higher-order representation of the assumptions.

Beluga is however not only a reasoning environment, but may also serve as an experimental framework for programming with dependent types and proof objects, useful for certified programming and proof-carrying code [Nec97]. We used Beluga to implement for example type-preserving CPS translations, translations between deBruijn and HOAS representation of terms, certifying type checking algorithms, and type-preserving interpreters.

In the future, we plan to concentrate on automating proofs. Currently, the recursive functions that implement induction proofs must be written by hand. We plan to explore how to enable the user to interactively develop functions in collaboration with theorem provers that can fill in parts of functions (that is, proofs) automatically.

References

[ABF+05] Aydemir, B., Bohannon, A., Fairbairn, M., Foster, J., Pierce, B., Sewell, P., Vytiniotis, D., Washburn, G., Weirich, S., Zdancewic, S.: Mechanized metatheory for the masses: The POPLMark challenge. In: Hurd, J., Melham, T. (eds.) TPHOLs 2005. LNCS, vol. 3603, pp. 50–65. Springer, Heidelberg (2005)

[ACCL90] Abadi, M., Cardelli, L., Curien, P., Lèvy, J.: Explicit substitutions. In: 17th Annual ACM SIGPLAN-SIGACT Symposium on Principles of Programming Languages (POPL 1990), pp. 31–46. ACM Press, New York (1990)

[Alt93] Altenkirch, T.: A formalization of the strong normalization proof for system f in lego. In: Bezem, M., Groote, J.F. (eds.) TLCA 1993. LNCS, vol. 664, pp. 13–28. Springer, Heidelberg (1993)

[Chl07] Chlipala, A.: A certified type-preserving compiler from lambda calculus to assembly language. In: Ferrante, J., McKinley, K.S. (eds.) Proceedings of the ACM SIGPLAN 2007 Conference on Programming Language Design and Implementation (PLDI 2007), pp. 54–65. ACM, New York (2007)

[Chl10] Chlipala, A.: A verified compiler for an impure functional language. In: Hermenegildo, M.V., Palsberg, J. (eds.) 37th Annual ACM SIGPLAN-SIGACT Symposium on Principles of Programming Languages (POPL 2010), pp. 93–106. ACM, New York (2010)

[DP09] Dunfield, J., Pientka, B.: Case analysis of higher-order data. In: International Workshop on Logical Frameworks and Meta-Languages: Theory and Practice (LFMTP 2008). ENTCS, vol. 228, pp. 69–84. Elsevier, Amsterdam (2009)

[DPS97] Despeyroux, J., Pfenning, F., Schürmann, C.: Primitive recursion for higher-order abstract syntax. In: Proceedings of the Third International Conference on Typed Lambda Calculus and Applications (TLCA 1997), pp. 147–163. Springer, Heidelberg (1997)

[EP91] Elliott, C., Pfenning, F.: A semi-functional implementation of a higher-order logic programming language. In: Lee, P. (ed.) Topics in Advanced Language Implementation, pp. 289–325. MIT Press, Cambridge (1991)

[FM09] Felty, A.P., Momigliano, A.: Reasoning with hypothetical judgments and open terms in hybrid. In: 11th ACM SIGPLAN Conference on Principles and Practice of Declarative Programming (PPDP 2009), pp. 83–92. ACM Press, New York (2009)

[FP] Felty, A.P., Pientka, B.: Reasoning with higher-order abstract syntax and contexts: A comparison. In: Kaufmann, M., Paulson, L.C. (eds.) Interactive Theorem Proving. LNCS, vol. 6172, pp. 227–242. Springer, Heidelberg (2010)

[Gac08] Gacek, A.: The Abella interactive theorem prover (system description). In: Armando, A., Baumgartner, P., Dowek, G. (eds.) IJCAR 2008. LNCS (LNAI), vol. 5195, pp. 154–161. Springer, Heidelberg (2008)

[Gen35] Gentzen, G.: Untersuchungen über das logische Schließen. Mathematische Zeitschrift 39, 176–210 (1935)

[HHP93] Harper, R., Honsell, F., Plotkin, G.: A framework for defining logics. Journal of the ACM 40(1), 143–184 (1993)

[LCH07] Lee, D.K., Crary, K., Harper, R.: Towards a Mechanized Metatheory of Standard ML. In: Hofmann, M., Felleisen, M. (eds.) 34th Annual ACM SIGPLAN-SIGACT Symposium on Principles of Programming Languages (POPL 2007), pp. 173–184. ACM Press, New York (2007)

[Ler09] Leroy, X.: A formally verified compiler back-end. J. Autom. Reasoning 43(4), 363–446 (2009)

[MMF08] Momigliano, A., Martin, A.J., Felty, A.P.: Two-Level Hybrid: A system for reasoning using higher-order abstract syntax. In: International Workshop on Logical Frameworks and Meta-Languages: Theory and Practice (LFMTP 2007). ENTCS, vol. 196, pp. 85–93. Elsevier, Amsterdam (2008)

[Nec97] Necula, G.C.: Proof-carrying code. In: 24th Annual Symposium on Principles of Programming Languages (POPL 1997), pp. 106–119. ACM Press, New York (1997)

[NPP08] Nanevski, A., Pfenning, F., Pientka, B.: Contextual modal type theory. ACM Transactions on Computational Logic 9(3), 1–49 (2008)

[PD08] Pientka, B., Dunfield, J.: Programming with proofs and explicit contexts. In: ACM SIGPLAN Symposium on Principles and Practice of Declarative Programming (PPDP 2008), pp. 163–173. ACM Press, New York (July 2008)

[PD10] Pientka, B., Dunfield, J.: Beluga:a Framework for Programming and Reasoning with Deductive Systems (System Description). In: Giesl, J., Hähnle, R. (eds.) Automated Reasoning. LNCS(LNAI), vol. 6173, pp. 15–21. Springer, Heidelberg (2010)

[Pfe91] Pfenning, F.: Logic programming in the LF logical framework. In: Huet, G., Plotkin, G. (eds.) Logical Frameworks, pp. 149–181. Cambridge University Press, Cambridge (1991)

[Pfe97] Pfenning, F.: Computation and Deduction (1997)

[Pie05] Pientka, B.: Verifying termination and reduction properties about higher-order logic programs. Journal of Automated Reasoning 34(2), 179–207 (2005)

[Pie07] Pientka, B.: Proof pearl: The power of higher-order encodings in the logical framework LF. In: Schneider, K., Brandt, J. (eds.) TPHOLs 2007. LNCS, vol. 4732, pp. 246–261. Springer, Heidelberg (2007)

[Pie08] Pientka, B.: A type-theoretic foundation for programming with higher-order abstract syntax and first-class substitutions. In: 35th Annual ACM SIGPLAN-SIGACT Symposium on Principles of Programming Languages (POPL 2008), pp. 371–382. ACM Press, New York (2008)

[PS99] Pfenning, F., Schürmann, C.: System description: Twelf — a meta-logical framework for deductive systems. In: Ganzinger, H. (ed.) CADE 1999. LNCS (LNAI), vol. 1632, pp. 202–206. Springer, Heidelberg (1999)

[PS09] Poswolsky, A., Schürmann, C.: System description: Delphin—a functional programming language for deductive systems. In: International Workshop on Logical Frameworks and Meta-Languages: Theory and Practice (LFMTP 2008). ENTCS, vol. 228, pp. 135–141. Elsevier, Amsterdam (2009)

[Ree09] Reed, J.: Higher-order constraint simplification in dependent type theory. In: Felty, A., Cheney, J. (eds.) International Workshop on Logical Frameworks and Meta-Languages: Theory and Practice, LFMTP 2009 (2009)

[RP96] Rohwedder, E., Pfenning, F.: Mode and termination checking for higher-order logic programs. In: Riis Nielson, H. (ed.) ESOP 1996. LNCS, vol. 1058, pp. 296–310. Springer, Heidelberg (1996)

Termination Graphs for Java Bytecode*

Marc Brockschmidt, Carsten Otto, Christian von Essen, and Jürgen Giesl

LuFG Informatik 2, RWTH Aachen University, Germany

Abstract. To prove termination of Java Bytecode (JBC) automatically, we transform JBC to finite *termination graphs* which represent all possible runs of the program. Afterwards, the graph can be translated into "simple" formalisms like term rewriting and existing tools can be used to prove termination of the resulting term rewrite system (TRS). In this paper we show that termination graphs indeed capture the semantics of JBC correctly. Hence, termination of the TRS resulting from the termination graph implies termination of the original JBC program.

1 Introduction

Termination is an important property of programs. Therefore, techniques to analyze termination automatically have been studied for decades [7,8,20]. While most work focused on *term rewrite systems* or *declarative programming languages*, recently there have also been many results on termination of *imperative programs* (e.g., [2,4,5]). However, these are "stand-alone" methods which do not allow to re-use the many existing termination techniques and tools for TRSs and declarative languages. Therefore, in [15] we presented the first rewriting-based approach for proving termination of a real imperative object-oriented language, viz. Java Bytecode. Related TRS-based approaches had already proved successful for termination analysis of Haskell and Prolog [10,16].

JBC [13] is an assembly-like object-oriented language designed as intermediate format for the execution of Java by a Java Virtual Machine (JVM). While there exist several static analysis techniques for JBC, we are only aware of two other automated methods to analyze termination of JBC, implemented in the tools COSTA [1] and Julia [18]. They transform JBC into a constraint logic program by abstracting every object of a dynamic data type to an integer denoting its path-length (i.e., the length of the maximal path of references obtained by following the fields of objects). While this fixed mapping from objects to integers leads to a very efficient analysis, it also restricts the power of these methods.

In contrast, in our approach from [15], we represent data objects not by integers, but by *terms* which express as much information as possible about the data objects. In this way, we can benefit from the fact that rewrite techniques can automatically generate suitable well-founded orders comparing arbitrary forms of terms. Moreover, by using TRSs with built-in integers [9], our approach is not only powerful for algorithms on user-defined data structures, but also for algorithms on pre-defined data types like integers.

* Supported by the DFG grant GI 274/5-3 and by the G.I.F. grant 966-116.6.

S. Siegler and N. Wasser (Eds.): Walther Festschrift, LNAI 6463, pp. 17–37, 2010.

However, it is not easy to transform JBC to a TRS which is suitable for termination analysis. Therefore, we first transform JBC to so-called *termination graphs* which represent all possible runs of the JBC program. These graphs handle all aspects of the programming language that cannot easily be expressed in term rewriting (e.g., side effects, cyclicity of data objects, object-orientation, etc.). Similar graphs are also used in program optimization techniques [17].

To analyze termination of a set $\mathcal{S}$ of desired initial (concrete) program states, we first represent this set by a suitable *abstract* state. This abstract state is the starting node of the termination graph. Then this state is evaluated symbolically, which leads to its child nodes in the termination graph. This symbolic evaluation is repeated until one reaches states that are *instances* of states that already appeared earlier in the termination graph. So while we perform considerably less abstraction than direct termination tools like [1,18], we also apply suitable abstract interpretations [6] in order to obtain finite representations for all possible forms of the heap at a certain program position.

Afterwards, a TRS is generated from the termination graph whose termination implies termination of the original JBC program for all initial states $\mathcal{S}$. This TRS can then be handled by existing TRS termination techniques and tools.

We implemented this approach in our tool AProVE [11] and in the *International Termination Competitions*,[1] AProVE achieved competitive results compared to Julia and COSTA. So rewriting techniques can indeed be successfully used for termination analysis of imperative object-oriented languages like Java.

However, [15] only introduced termination graphs informally and did not prove that these graphs really represent the semantics of JBC. In the present paper, we give a formal justification for the concept of termination graphs. Since the semantics of JBC is not formally specified, in this paper we do not focus on full JBC, but on JINJA Bytecode [12].[2] JINJA is a small Java-like programming language with a corresponding bytecode. It exhibits the core features of Java, its semantics is formally specified, and the corresponding correctness proofs were performed in the Isabelle/HOL theorem prover [14]. So in the following, "JBC" always refers to "JINJA Bytecode". We present the following new contributions:

- In Sect. 2, we define termination graphs formally and determine how states in these graphs are evaluated symbolically (Def. 6, 7). To this end, we introduce three kinds of edges in termination graphs ($\overset{\text{EVAL}}{\longrightarrow}$, $\overset{\text{INS}}{\longrightarrow}$, $\overset{\text{REF}}{\longrightarrow}$). In contrast to [15], we extend these graphs to handle also method calls and exceptions.
- In Sect. 3, we prove that on *concrete* states, our definition of "symbolic evaluation" is equivalent to evaluation in JBC (Thm. 10). As illustrated in Fig. 1, there is a mapping TRANS from JBC program states to our notion of concrete states. Then, Thm. 10 proves that if a program state j_1 of a JBC program is evaluated to a state j_2 (i.e., $j_1 \overset{jvm}{\longrightarrow} j_2$), then TRANS($j_1$) is

[1] See `http://www.termination-portal.org/wiki/Termination_Competition`

[2] For the same reason, the correctness proof for the termination technique of [18] also regarded a simplified instruction set similar to JINJA instead of full JBC.

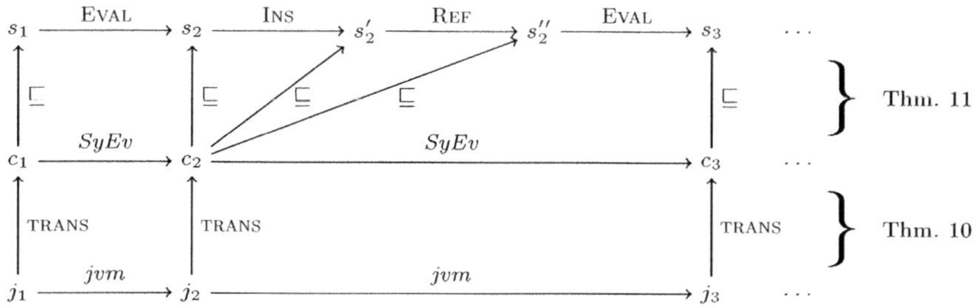

Fig. 1. Relation between evaluation in JBC and paths in the termination graph

evaluated to TRANS(j_2) using our definitions of "states" and of "symbolic evaluation" from Sect. 2 (i.e., TRANS(j_1) $\stackrel{SyEv}{\longrightarrow}$ TRANS(j_2)).

- In Sect. 4, we prove that our notion of symbolic evaluation for *abstract* states correctly simulates the evaluation of concrete states. More precisely, let c_1 be a concrete state which can be evaluated to the concrete state c_2 (i.e., $c_1 \stackrel{SyEv}{\longrightarrow} c_2$). Then Thm. 11 states that if the termination graph contains an abstract state s_1 which represents c_1 (i.e., c_1 is an *instance* of s_1, denoted $c_1 \sqsubseteq s_1$), then there is a path from s_1 to another abstract state s_2 in the termination graph such that s_2 represents c_2 (i.e., $c_2 \sqsubseteq s_2$).

Note that Thm. 10 and 11 imply the "soundness" of termination graphs, cf. Cor. 12: Suppose there is an infinite JBC-computation $j_1 \stackrel{jvm}{\longrightarrow} j_2 \stackrel{jvm}{\longrightarrow} \ldots$ where j_1 is represented in the termination graph (i.e., there is a state s_1 in the termination graph with TRANS(j_1) $= c_1 \sqsubseteq s_1$). Then by Thm. 10 there is an infinite symbolic evaluation $c_1 \stackrel{SyEv}{\longrightarrow} c_2 \stackrel{SyEv}{\longrightarrow} \ldots$, where TRANS($j_i$) $= c_i$ for all i. Hence, Thm. 11 implies that there is an infinite so-called computation path in the termination graph starting with the node s_1. As shown in [15, Thm. 3.7], then the TRS resulting from the termination graph is not terminating.

2 Constructing Termination Graphs

To illustrate termination graphs, we regard the method `create` in Fig. 2. `List` is a data type whose `next` field points to the next list element and we omitted the fields for the values of list elements to ease readability. The constructor `List(n)` creates a new list object with `n` as its tail. The method `create(x)` first ensures that `x` is at least 1. Then it creates a list of length `x`. In the end, the list is made cyclic by letting the `next` field of the last list element point to the start of the list. The method `create` terminates as `x` is decreased until it is 1.

After introducing our notion of *states* in Sect. 2.1, we describe the construction of termination graphs in Sect. 2.2 and explain the JBC program of Fig. 2 in parallel. Sect. 2.3 formally defines symbolic evaluation and termination graphs.

```
public class List {
 public List next;

 public List(List n) {
    this.next = n;
 }

 public static
 List create(int x) {

   List last;
   List cur;
   if (x <= 0) {
    return null;
   }
   cur = new List(null);
   last = cur;
   while (x != 1) {
    x--;
    cur = new List(cur);
   }
   last.next = cur;
   return cur;

 }
}
```

```
public static List create(int);
     ...                    // return null for x <= 0
     New       List         // create List object
     Push      null         // load null reference
     Invoke    <init> 2     // call constructor
     Store     "cur"        // store into cur
     Load      "cur"        // load cur to opstack
     Store     "last"       // store into last
hd:  Load      "x"          // load x to opstack
     Push      1            // load 1 to opstack
     CmpEq                  // compare x and 1
     IfFalse   "bd"         // jump to bd if x != 1
     Load      "last"       // load last to opstack
     Load      "cur"        // load cur to opstack
     Putfield  next         // set last.next = cur
     Load      "cur"        // load cur to opstack
     Return                 // return cur
bd:  Load      "x"          // load x to opstack
     Push      -1           // load -1 to opstack
     IAdd                   // add x and -1
     Store     "x"          // store result in x
     New       List         // create List object
     Load      "cur"        // load cur to opstack
     Invoke    <init> 2     // call constructor
     Store     "cur"        // store into cur
     Goto      "hd"         // jump to loop condition
```

Fig. 2. Java Code and a corresponding JINJA Bytecode for the method create

2.1 States

The nodes of the termination graph are *abstract states* which represent *sets* of concrete states, using a formalization which is especially suitable for a translation into TRSs. Our approach is restricted to verified sequential JBC programs without recursion. To simplify the presentation in the paper, as in JINJA, we exclude floating point arithmetic, arrays, and static class fields. However, our approach can easily be extended to such constructs and indeed, our implementation also handles such programs. We define the set of all states as

$$\begin{aligned}\textsc{States} = {} & (\textsc{ProgPos} \times \textsc{LocVar} \times \textsc{OpStack})^* \times \\ & (\{\bot\} \cup \textsc{References}) \times \textsc{Heap} \times \textsc{Annotations}\,.\end{aligned}$$

$\texttt{CmpEq} \mid \texttt{x}{:}i_1, \texttt{l}{:}o_1, \texttt{c}{:}o_1 \mid i_2, i_1$
$i_1 = [1,\infty)\ \ i_2 = [1,1]$
$o_1 = \texttt{List}(\texttt{next} = \texttt{null})$

Fig. 3. Abstract state

Consider the state in Fig. 3. Its first component is the program position (from ProgPos). In the examples, we represent it by the next program instruction to be executed (e.g., "CmpEq").

The second component are the local variables that have a defined value at the current program position, i.e., $\textsc{LocVar} = \textsc{References}^*$. References are addresses in the heap, where we also have $\texttt{null} \in \textsc{References}$. In our representation, we do not store primitive values directly, but indirectly using references to the heap.

In examples we denote local variables by names instead of numbers. Thus, "$\texttt{x}{:}i_1, \texttt{l}{:}o_1, \texttt{c}{:}o_1$" means that the value of the 0th local variable x is a reference i_1 for integers and the 1st and 2nd local variables l and c both reference the address o_1. So different local variables can point to the same address.

The third component is the operand stack that JBC instructions operate on, i.e., $\textsc{OpStack} = \textsc{References}^*$. The empty operand stack is denoted "ε" and "i_2, i_1" denotes a stack with top element i_2 and bottom element i_1.

In contrast to [15], we allow *several* method calls and a triple from ($\textsc{ProgPos} \times \textsc{LocVar} \times \textsc{OpStack}$) is just one *frame* of the *call stack*. Thus, an abstract state may contain a sequence of such triples. If a method calls another method, then a new frame is put on top of the call stack. This frame has its own program counter, local variables, and operand stack. Consider the state in Fig. 4, where the `List` constructor was called. Hence, the top frame on the call stack corresponds to the first statement of this constructor method. The lower frame corresponds to the statement `Store "cur"` in the method `create`. It will be executed when the constructor in the top frame has finished.

`Load "this"` | `t`:o_1,`n`:`null` | ε
`Store "cur"` | `x`:i_1 | ε
$i_1 = [1, \infty)$
$o_1 =$ `List(next = null)`

Fig. 4. State with 2 frames

The component from $(\{\bot\} \cup \textsc{References})$ in the definition of $\textsc{States}$ is used for exceptions and will be explained at the end of Sect. 2.2. Here, $\bot$ means that no exception was thrown (we omit $\bot$ in examples to ease readability).

We write the first three components of a state in the first line and separate them by "|". The fourth component $\textsc{Heap}$ is written in the lines below. It contains information about the values of $\textsc{References}$. We represent it by a partial function, i.e., $\textsc{Heap} = \textsc{References} \rightarrow \textsc{Unknown} \cup \textsc{Integers} \cup \textsc{Instances}$.

The values in $\textsc{Unknown} = \textsc{Classnames} \times \{?\}$ represent tree-shaped (and thus acyclic) objects where we have no information except the type. $\textsc{Classnames}$ are the names of all classes and interfaces. For example, "$o_3 =$ `List`(?)" means that the object at address o_3 is `null` or of type `List` (or a subtype of `List`).

We represent integers as possibly unbounded intervals, i.e. $\textsc{Integers} = \{\{x \in \mathbb{Z} \mid a \leq x \leq b\} \mid a \in \mathbb{Z} \cup \{-\infty\}, b \in \mathbb{Z} \cup \{\infty\}, a \leq b\}$. So $i_1 = [1, \infty)$ means that any positive integer can be at the address i_1. Since current TRS termination tools cannot handle 32-bit `int`-numbers as in real Java, we treat `int` as the infinite set of all integers (this is done in JINJA as well).

To represent $\textsc{Instances}$ (i.e., objects) of some class, we describe the values of their fields, i.e., $\textsc{Instances} = \textsc{Classnames} \times (\textsc{FieldIDs} \rightarrow \textsc{References})$. To prevent ambiguities, in general the $\textsc{FieldIDs}$ also contain the respective class names. So "$o_1 =$ `List(next = null)`" means that at the address o_1, there is a `List` object and the value of its field `next` is `null`. For all $(cl, f) \in \textsc{Instances}$, the function f is defined for all fields of the class cl and all of its superclasses.

All sharing information must be explicitly represented. If an abstract state s contains the non-`null` references o_1, o_2 and does not mention that they could be sharing, then s only represents concrete states where o_1 and the references reachable from o_1 are disjoint from o_2 and the references reachable from o_2.

Sharing or aliasing for *concrete* objects can of course be represented easily, e.g., we could have $o_2 =$ `List(next =` o_1`)` which means that o_1 and o_2 do not point to disjoint parts of the heap h (i.e., they *join*). But to represent such concepts for *unknown* objects, we use three kinds of *annotations*. Annotations are only built for references $o \neq \texttt{null}$ with $h(o) \notin$ INTEGERS.

Equality annotations like "$o_1 \ =^? \ o_2$" mean that the addresses o_1 and o_2 could be equal. Here the value of at least one of o_1 and o_2 must be UNKNOWN. To represent states where two objects "*may join*", we use *joinability annotations* "$o_1 \searrow\!\swarrow o_2$". We say that o' is a *direct successor* of o in a state s (denoted $o \to_s o'$) iff the object at address o has a field whose value is o'. Then "$o_1 \searrow\!\swarrow o_2$" means that if the value of o_1 is UNKNOWN, then there could be an o with $o_1 \to_s^+ o$ and $o_2 \to_s^* o$, i.e., o is a proper successor of o_1 and a (possibly non-proper) successor of o_2. Note that $\searrow\!\swarrow$ is symmetric,[3] so "$o_1 \searrow\!\swarrow o_2$" also means that if o_2 is UNKNOWN, then there could be an o' with $o_1 \to_s^* o'$ and $o_2 \to_s^+ o'$. Finally, we use *cyclicity annotations* "$o!$" to denote that the object at address o is not necessarily tree-shaped (so in particular, it could be cyclic).[4]

2.2 Termination Graphs, Refinements, and Instances

To build termination graphs, we begin with an abstract state describing all concrete initial states. In our example, we want to know whether all calls of `create` terminate. So in the corresponding initial abstract state, the value of `x` is not an actual integer, but $(-\infty, \infty)$. After symbolically executing the first JBC instructions, one reaches the instruction "`New List`". This corresponds to state A in Fig. 5 where the value of `x` is from $[1, \infty)$.

We can evaluate "`New List`" without further information about `x` and reach the node B via an *evaluation edge*. Here, a new `List` instance was created at address o_1 in the heap and o_1 was pushed on the operand stack. "`New List`" does not execute the constructor yet, but just allocates the needed memory and sets all fields to default values. Thus, the `next` field of the new object is set to `null`.

"`Push null`" pushes `null` on the operand stack. The elements `null` and o_1 on the stack are the arguments for the constructor `<init>` 2 that is invoked, where "2" means that the constructor with two parameters (`n` and `this`) is used.

This leads to D, cf. Fig. 4. In the top frame, the local variables `this` (abbreviated `t`) and `n` have the values o_1 and `null`. In the second frame, the arguments that were passed to the constructor were removed from the operand stack.

We did not depict the evaluation of the constructor and continue with state E, where the control flow has returned to `create`. So dotted arrows abbreviate several steps. Our implementation of `<init>` returns the newly created object as its result. Therefore, o_1 has been pushed on the operand stack in E.

Evaluation continues to node F, storing o_1 in the local variables `cur` and `last` (abbreviated `c` and `l`). In F one starts with checking the condition of the `while`

[3] Since both "$=^?$" and "$\searrow\!\swarrow$" are symmetric, we do not distinguish between "$o_1 \ =^? \ o_2$" and "$o_2 \ =^? \ o_1$" and we also do not distinguish between "$o_1 \searrow\!\swarrow o_2$" and "$o_2 \searrow\!\swarrow o_1$".

[4] It is also possible to use an extended notion of annotations which also include sets of FIELDIDS. Then one can express properties like "o may join o' by using only the field `next`" or "o may only have a non-tree structure if one uses *both* fields `next` and `prev`" (such annotations can be helpful to analyze algorithms on doubly-linked lists).

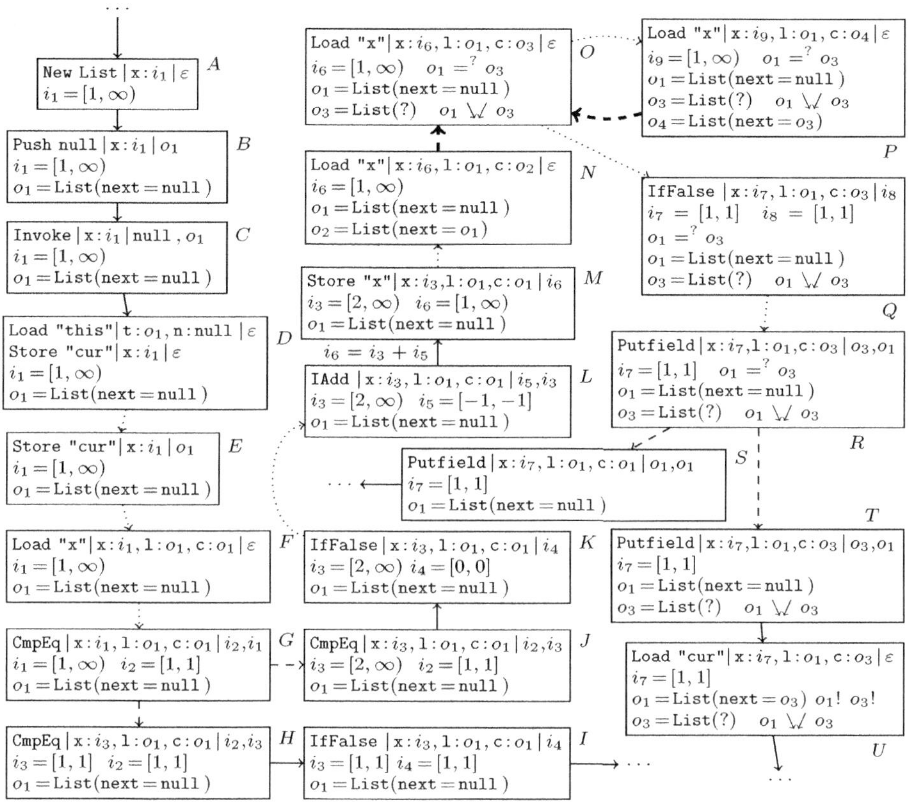

Fig. 5. Termination graph for `create`

loop. To this end, x and the number 1 are pushed on the operand stack and the instruction CmpEq in state G compares them, cf. Fig. 3.

We cannot directly continue the symbolic evaluation, because the control flow depends on the value of the number i_1 in the variable x. So we *refine* the information by an appropriate case analysis. This leads to the states H and J where x's value is from $[1,1]$ resp. $[2,\infty)$. We call this step *integer refinement* and G is connected to H and J by *refinement edges* (denoted by dashed edges in Fig. 5).

To define integer refinements, for any $s \in$ STATES, let $s[o/o']$ be the state obtained from s by replacing all occurrences of the reference o in instance fields, the exception component, local variables, and on the operand stacks by o'. By $s+\{o \mapsto vl\}$ we denote a state which results from s by removing any information about o and instead the heap now maps o to the value vl. So in Fig. 5, J is $(G + \{i_3 \mapsto [2,\infty)\})[i_1/i_3]$. We only keep information on those references in the heap that are reachable from the local variables and the operand stacks.

Definition 1 (Integer refinement). *Let $s \in$ STATES where h is the heap of s and let $o \in$ REFERENCES with $h(o) = V \subseteq \mathbb{Z}$. Let $V_1, \ldots, V_n$ be a partition of V*

(i.e., $V_1 \cup \ldots \cup V_n = V$) with $V_i \in$ Integers*. Moreover, $s_i = (s + \{o_i \mapsto V_i\})[o/o_i]$ for fresh references o_i. Then $\{s_1, \ldots, s_n\}$ is an* integer refinement *of s.*

In Fig. 5, evaluation of `CmpEq` continues and we push `True` resp. `False` on the operand stack leading to the nodes I and K. To simplify the presentation, in the paper we represent the Booleans `True` and `False` by the integers 1 and 0. In I and K, we can then evaluate the `IfFalse` instruction.

From K on, we continue the evaluation by loading the value of `x` and the constant -1 on the operand stack. In L, `IAdd` adds the two topmost stack elements. To keep track of this, we create a new reference i_6 for the result and label the edge from L to M by the relation between i_6, i_3, and i_5. Such labels are used when constructing rewrite rules from the termination graph [15]. Then, the value of i_6 is stored in `x` and the rest of the loop is executed. Afterwards in state N, `cur` points to a list (at address o_2) where a new element was added in front of the original list at o_1. Then the program jumps back to the instruction `Load "x"` at the label "`hd`" in the program, where the loop condition is evaluated.

However, evaluation had already reached this instruction in state F. So the new state N is a repetition in the control flow. The difference between F and N is that in F, `l` and `c` are the same, while in N, `l` refers to o_1 and `c` refers to o_2, where the list at o_1 is the direct successor (or "tail") of the list at o_2.

To obtain *finite* termination graphs, whenever the evaluation reaches a program position for the second time, we "merge" the two corresponding states (like F and N). This widening result is displayed in node O. Here, the annotation "$o_1 =^? o_3$" allows the equality of the references in `l` and `c`, as in J. But O also contains "$o_1 \searrow\!\!\!\!\swarrow o_3$". So `l` may be a successor of `c`, as in N. We connect N to O by an *instance edge* (depicted by a thick dashed line), since the concrete states described by N are a subset of the concrete states described by O. Moreover, we could also connect F to O by an instance edge and discard the states G-N which were only needed to obtain the suitably generalized state O. Note that in this way we maintain the essential invariant of termination graphs, viz. that a node "is terminating" whenever all of its children are terminating.

To define "*instance*", we first define all positions π of references in a state s, where $s|_\pi$ is the reference at position π. A position π is Exc or a sequence starting with $\text{LV}_{i,j}$ or $\text{OS}_{i,j}$ for $i, j \in \mathbb{N}$ (indicating the jth reference in the local variable array or the operand stack of the ith frame), followed by zero or more FieldIDs.

Definition 2 (State positions SPos). *Let $s = (\langle fr_0, \ldots, fr_n \rangle, e, h, a)$ be a state where each stack frame fr_i has the form (pp_i, lv_i, os_i). Then* SPos(s) *is the smallest set containing all the following sequences π:*

- $\pi = \text{LV}_{i,j}$ *where* $0 \le i \le n$, $lv_i = o_{i,0}, \ldots, o_{i,m_i}$, $0 \le j \le m_i$. *Then* $s|_\pi$ *is* $o_{i,j}$.
- $\pi = \text{OS}_{i,j}$ *where* $0 \le i \le n$, $os_i = o'_{i,0}, \ldots, o'_{i,k_i}$, $0 \le j \le k_i$. *Then* $s|_\pi$ *is* $o'_{i,j}$.
- $\pi = \text{Exc}$ *if* $e \ne \bot$. *Then* $s|_\pi$ *is* e.
- $\pi = \pi' v$ *for some* $v \in$ FieldIDs *and some* $\pi' \in$ SPos(s) *where* $h(s|_{\pi'}) = (cl, f) \in$ Instances *and where* $f(v)$ *is defined. Then* $s|_\pi$ *is* $f(v)$.

For any position π, let $\overline{\pi}_s$ denote the maximal prefix of π such that $\overline{\pi}_s \in$ SPos(s)*. We write $\overline{\pi}$ if s is clear from the context.*

In Fig. 5, $F|_{\mathrm{LV}_{0,0}} = i_1, F|_{\mathrm{LV}_{0,1}} = F|_{\mathrm{LV}_{0,2}} = o_1$. If h is F's heap, then $h(o_1) = (\texttt{List}, f) \in \textsc{Instances}$, where $f(\texttt{next}) = \texttt{null}$. So $F|_{\mathrm{LV}_{0,1}\,\texttt{next}} = F|_{\mathrm{LV}_{0,2}\,\texttt{next}} = \texttt{null}$.

Intuitively, a state s' is an instance of a state s if they correspond to the same program position and whenever there is a reference $s'|_\pi$, then either the values represented by $s'|_\pi$ in the heap of s' are a subset of the values represented by $s|_\pi$ in the heap of s or else, π is no position in s. Moreover, shared parts of the heap in s' must also be shared in s. Note that since s and s' correspond to the same position in a *verified* JBC program, s and s' have the same number of local variables and their operand stacks have the same size. In Def. 3, the conditions (a)-(d) handle $\textsc{Integers}$, null, $\textsc{Unknown}$, and $\textsc{Instances}$, whereas the remaining conditions concern equality and annotations. Here, the conditions (e)-(g) handle the case where two positions π, π' of s' are also in $\mathrm{SPos}(s)$.

Definition 3 (Instance). *Let* $s' = (\langle fr'_0, \ldots, fr'_n\rangle, e', h', a')$ *and* $s = (\langle fr_0, \ldots, fr_n\rangle, e, h, a)$, *where* $fr'_i = (pp'_i, lv'_i, os'_i)$ *and* $fr_i = (pp_i, lv_i, os_i)$. *We call* s' *an* instance *of* s *(denoted* $s' \sqsubseteq s$*) iff* $pp_i = pp'_i$ *for all* i *and for all* $\pi, \pi' \in \mathrm{SPos}(s')$:

(a) if $h'(s'|_\pi) \in \textsc{Integers}$ *and* $\pi \in \mathrm{SPos}(s)$, *then* $h'(s'|_\pi) \subseteq h(s|_\pi) \in \textsc{Integers}$.
(b) if $s'|_\pi = \texttt{null}$ *and* $\pi \in \mathrm{SPos}(s)$, *then* $s|_\pi = \texttt{null}$ *or* $h(s|_\pi) \in \textsc{Unknown}$.
(c) if $h'(s'|_\pi) = (cl', ?) \in \textsc{Unknown}$ *and* $\pi \in \mathrm{SPos}(s)$, *then* $h(s|_\pi) = (cl, ?) \in \textsc{Unknown}$ *and* cl' *is* cl *or a subtype of* cl.
(d) if $h'(s'|_\pi) = (cl', f') \in \textsc{Instances}$ *and* $\pi \in \mathrm{SPos}(s)$, *then* $h(s|_\pi) = (cl, ?)$ *or* $h(s|_\pi) = (cl', f) \in \textsc{Instances}$, *where* cl' *must be* cl *or a subtype of* cl.
(e) if $s'|_\pi \neq s'|_{\pi'}$ *and* $\pi, \pi' \in \mathrm{SPos}(s)$, *then* $s|_\pi \neq s|_{\pi'}$.
(f) if $s'|_\pi = s'|_{\pi'}$ *and* $\pi, \pi' \in \mathrm{SPos}(s)$ *where* $h'(s'|_\pi) \in \textsc{Instances} \cup \textsc{Unknown}$, *then* $s|_\pi = s|_{\pi'}$ *or* $s|_\pi =^? s|_{\pi'}$.[5]
(g) if $s'|_\pi =^? s'|_{\pi'}$ *and* $\pi, \pi' \in \mathrm{SPos}(s)$, *then* $s|_\pi =^? s|_{\pi'}$.
(h) if $\big(s'|_\pi = s'|_{\pi'}$ or $s'|_\pi =^? s'|_{\pi'}$ where $h'(s'|_\pi) \in \textsc{Instances} \cup \textsc{Unknown}\big)$ *and* $\{\pi, \pi'\} \not\subseteq \mathrm{SPos}(s)$ *with* $\pi \neq \pi'$, *then* $s|_{\overline{\pi}} \searrow\!\!\swarrow s|_{\overline{\pi'}}$.
(i) if $s'|_\pi \searrow\!\!\swarrow s'|_{\pi'}$, *then* $s|_{\overline{\pi}} \searrow\!\!\swarrow s|_{\overline{\pi'}}$.
(j) if $s'|_\pi!$ *holds, then* $s|_{\overline{\pi}}!$.
(k) if there exist $\rho, \rho' \in \textsc{FieldIDs}^*$ *without common prefix where* $\rho \neq \rho'$, $s'|_{\pi\rho} = s'|_{\pi\rho'}$, $h'(s'|_{\pi\rho}) \in \textsc{Instances} \cup \textsc{Unknown}$, *and* $(\{\pi\rho, \pi\rho'\} \not\subseteq \mathrm{SPos}(s)$ *or* $s|_{\pi\rho} =^? s|_{\pi\rho'})$, *then* $s|_{\overline{\pi}}!$.

In Fig. 5, we have $F \sqsubseteq O$ and $N \sqsubseteq O$. Symbolic evaluation can continue in the new generalized state O. It again leads to a node like G, where an integer refinement is needed to continue. If the value in x is still not 1, eventually one has to evaluate the loop condition again (in node P). Since $P \sqsubseteq O$, we draw an instance edge from P to O and can "close" this part of the termination graph.[6]

[5] For annotations concerning $s|_\pi$ with $\pi \in \mathrm{SPos}(s)$, we usually do not mention that they are from the $\textsc{Annotations}$ component of s, since s is clear from the context.

[6] If P had not been an instance of O, we would have performed another widening step and created a new node which is more general than O and P. By a suitably aggressive widening strategy, one can ensure that after finitely many widening steps, one always reaches a "fixpoint". Then all states that result from further symbolic evaluation are instances of states that already occurred earlier. In this way, we can automatically generate a finite termination graph for any non-recursive JBC program.

If the value in x is 1 (which is checked in state Q), we reach state R. Here, the references o_1 and o_3 in `l` and `c` have been loaded on the operand stack and one now has to execute the `Putfield` instruction which sets the `next` field of the object at the address o_1 to o_3. To find out which references are affected by this operation, we need to decide whether $o_1 = o_3$ holds. To this end, we perform an *equality refinement* according to the annotation "$o_1 =^? o_3$".

Definition 4 (Equality refinement). *Let $s \in$ STATES where h is the heap of s and where s contains "$o =^? o'$". Hence, $h(o) \in$ UNKNOWN or $h(o') \in$ UNKNOWN. W.l.o.g. let $h(o) \in$ UNKNOWN. Let $s_= = s[o/o']$ and let $s_{\neq}$ result from s by removing "$o =^? o'$". Then $\{s_=, s_{\neq}\}$ is an* equality refinement *of s.*

In Fig. 5, equality refinement of R results in S (where $o_1 = o_3$) and T (where $o_1 \neq o_3$ and thus, "$o_1 =^? o_3$" was removed). In T's successor U, the `next` field of o_1 has been set to o_3. However, o_1 and o_3 may join due to "$o_1 \searrow\!\!\swarrow o_3$". So in particular, T also represents states where $o_3 \to^+ o_1$. Thus, writing o_3 to a field of o_1 could create a cyclic data object. Therefore, all non-concrete elements in the abstracted object must be annotated with !. Consequently, our symbolic evaluation has to extend our state with "$o_1!$" and "$o_3!$". From U on, the graph construction can be finished directly by evaluating the remaining instructions.

From the termination graph, one could generate the following 1-rule TRS which describes the operations on the cycle of the termination graph.

$$\mathsf{f}_O(i_6, \mathsf{List}(\mathsf{null}), o_3) \to \mathsf{f}_O(i_6 - 1, \mathsf{List}(\mathsf{null}), \mathsf{List}(o_3)) \mid i_6 > 0 \wedge i_6 \neq 1 \qquad (1)$$

Here we also took the condition from the states before O into account which ensures that the loop is only executed for numbers x that are greater than 0.

As mentioned in Sect. 1, we regard TRSs where the integers and operations like "$-$", "$>$", "$\neq$" are built in [9] and we represent objects by terms. So essentially, for any class `C` with n fields we introduce an n-ary function symbol C whose arguments correspond to the fields of `C`. Hence, the object `List(next = null)` is represented by the term $\mathsf{List}(\mathsf{null})$. A state like O is translated into a term $\mathsf{f}_O(\ldots)$ whose direct subterms correspond to the exception component (if it is not $\perp$), the local variables, and the entries of the operand stack. Hence, Rule (1) describes that in each loop iteration, the value of the 0th local variable decreases from i_6 to $i_6 - 1$, the value of the 1st variable remains $\mathsf{List}(\mathsf{null})$, and the value of the 2nd variable increases from o_3 to $\mathsf{List}(o_3)$. Termination of this TRS is easy to show and indeed, AProVE proves termination of `create` automatically.

Finally, we have a third kind of refinement. This *instance refinement* is used if we need information about the existence or the type of an UNKNOWN instance. Consider Fig. 6, where in state A we want to access the `next` field of the `List` object in o_1. However, we cannot evaluate `Getfield`, as the instance in o_1 is UNKNOWN. To refine o_1, we create a successor B where the instance exists and is exactly of type `List` and a state C where o_1 is `null`.

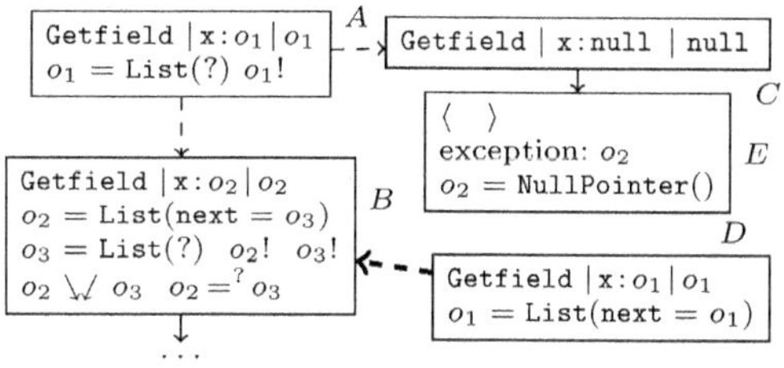

Fig. 6. Instance refinement and exceptions

In A the instance may be cyclic, indicated by $o_1!$. For this reason, the instance refinement has to add appropriate annotations to B. For example, state D (where o_1 is a concrete cyclic list) is an instance of B.

In C, evaluation of `Getfield` throws a `NullPointer` exception. If an exception handler for this type is defined, evaluation would continue there and a reference to the `NullPointer` object is pushed to the operand stack. But here, no such handler exists and E reaches a program end. Here, the call stack is empty and the exception component e is no longer $\bot$, but an object o_2 of type `NullPointer`.

Definition 5 (Instance refinement). *Let $s \in$ STATES where h is the heap of s and $h(o) = (cl, ?)$. Let $cl_1, \ldots, cl_n$ be all non-abstract (not necessarily proper) subtypes of cl. Then $\{s_{\texttt{null}}, s_1, \ldots, s_n\}$ is an* instance refinement *of s. Here, $s_{\texttt{null}} = s[o/\texttt{null}]$ and in s_i, we replace o by a fresh reference o_i pointing to an object of type cl_i. For all fields $v_{i,1} \ldots v_{i,m_i}$ of cl_i (where $v_{i,j}$ has type $cl_{i,j}$), a new reference $o_{i,j}$ is generated which points to the most general value $vl_{i,j}$ of type $cl_{i,j}$, i.e., $(-\infty, \infty)$ for integers and $cl_{i,j}(?)$ for reference types. Then s_i is $(s + \{o_i \mapsto (cl_i, f_i), o_{i,1} \mapsto vl_{i,1}, \ldots, o_{i,m_i} \mapsto vl_{i,m_i}\})[o/o_i]$, where $f_i(v_{i,j}) = o_{i,j}$ for all j. Moreover, new annotations are added in s_i: If s contained $o' \curlyvee o$, we add $o' =^? o_{i,j}$ and $o' \curlyvee o_{i,j}$ for all j.[7] If we had $o!$, we also add $o_{i,j}!$, $o_i =^? o_{i,j}$, $o_i \curlyvee o_{i,j}$, $o_{i,j} =^? o_{i,j'}$, and $o_{i,j} \curlyvee o_{i,j'}$ for all j, j' with $j \neq j'$.*

2.3 Defining Symbolic Evaluation and Termination Graphs

To define symbolic evaluation formally, for every JINJA instruction, we formulate a corresponding inference rule for symbolic evaluation of our abstract states. This is straightforward for all JINJA instructions except `Putfield`. Thus, in Def. 6 we only present the rules corresponding to a simple JINJA Bytecode instruction (`Load`) and to `Putfield`. We will show in Sect. 3 that on non-abstract states, our inference rules indeed simulate the semantics of JINJA.

For a state s whose topmost frame has m local variables with values $o_0, \ldots, o_m$, "`Load` b" pushes the value o_b of the bth local variable to the operand stack. Executing "`Putfield` v" in a state with the operand stack $o_0, o_1, \ldots, o_k$ means that one wants to write o_0 to the field v of the object at address o_1. This is only allowed if there is no annotation "$o_1 =^? o$" for any o. Then the function f that maps every field of o_1 to its value is updated such that v is now mapped to o_0.

[7] Of course, if $cl_{i,j}$ and the type of o' have no common subtype or one of them is `int`, then $o' =^? o_{i,j}$ does not need to be added.

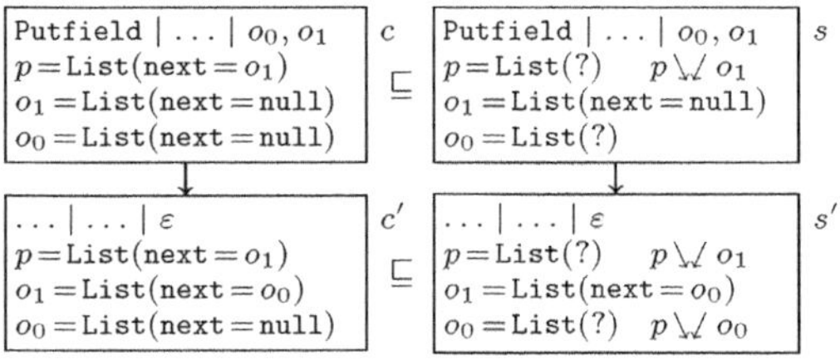

Fig. 7. `Putfield` and annotations

However, we may also have to update annotations when evaluating `Putfield`. Consider the concrete state c and the abstract state s in Fig. 7. We have $c \sqsubseteq s$, as the connection between p and o_1 in c (i.e., $p \to_c^* o_1$) was replaced by "$p \bigvee o_1$" in s. In both states, we consider a `Putfield` instruction which writes o_0 into the field `next` of o_1. For c, we obtain the state c' where we we now also have $p \to_{c'}^* o_0$. However, to evaluate `Putfield` in the abstract state s, it is not sufficient to just write o_0 to the field `next` of o_1. Then c' would not be an instance of the resulting state s', since s' would not represent the connection between p and o_0. Therefore, we have to add "$p \bigvee o_0$" in s'. Now $c' \sqsubseteq s'$ indeed holds. A similar problem was discussed for node U of Fig. 5, where we had to add "!" annotations after evaluating `Putfield`.

To specify when we need such additional annotations, for any state s let $o \sim_s o'$ denote that "$o =^? o'$" or "$o \bigvee o'$" is contained in s. Then we define $\leadsto_s$ as $\to_s^* \circ (= \cup \sim_s)$, i.e., $o \leadsto_s o''$ iff there is an o' with $o \to_s^* o'$, where $o' = o''$ or $o' \sim_s o''$. We drop the index "s" if s is clear from the context. For example, in Fig. 7, we have $p \to_{c'}^* o_1$, $p \to_{c'}^* o_0$ and $p \leadsto_{s'} o_1$, $p \leadsto_{s'} o_0$.

Consider a `Putfield` instruction which writes the reference o_0 into the instance referenced by o_1. After evaluation, o_1 may reach any reference q that could be reached by o_0 up to now. Moreover, q cannot only be reached from o_1, but from every reference p that could possibly reach o_1 up to now. Therefore, we must add "$p \bigvee q$" for all p, q with $p \sim o_1$ and $o_0 \leadsto q$.

Moreover, `Putfield` may create new non-tree shaped objects if there is a reference p that can reach a reference q in several ways after the evaluation. This can only happen if $p \leadsto q$ and $p \leadsto o_1$ held before (otherwise p would not be influenced by `Putfield`). If the new field content o_0 could also reach q ($o_0 \leadsto q$), a second connection from p over o_0 to q may be created by the evaluation. Then we have to add "p!" for all p for which a q exists such that $p \leadsto q$, $p \leadsto o_1$, and $o_0 \leadsto q$.[8] It suffices to do this for references p where the paths from p to o_1 and from p to q do not have a common non-empty prefix.

Finally, o_0 could have reached a non-tree shaped object or a reference q marked with !. In this case, we have to add "p!" for all p with $p \sim o_1$.

In Def. 6, for any mapping h, let $h + \{k \mapsto d\}$ be the function that maps k to d and every $k' \neq k$ to $h(k')$. For $pp \in$ ProgPos, let $pp + 1$ be the position of the next instruction. Moreover, $instr(pp)$ is the instruction at position pp.

[8] This happened in state T of Fig. 5 where o_3 was written to the field of o_1. We already had $o_1 \leadsto_T o_3$ and $o_3 \leadsto_T o_1$, since T contained the annotation "$o_1 \bigvee o_3$". Hence, in the successor state U of T, we had to add the annotations "o_1!" and "o_3!".

Definition 6 (Symbolic evaluation $\overset{SyEv}{\longrightarrow}$). *For every JINJA instruction, we define a corresponding inference rule for symbolic evaluation of states. We write $s \overset{SyEv}{\longrightarrow} s'$ if s is transformed to s' by one of these rules. Below, we give the rules for* `Load` *and* `Putfield` *(in the case where no exception was thrown). The rules for the other instructions are analogous.*

$$\frac{\begin{array}{c} s = (\langle (pp, lv, os), fr_1, \ldots, fr_n \rangle, \bot, h, a) \\ instr(pp) = \texttt{Load}\ b \qquad lv = o_0, \ldots, o_m \qquad os = o'_0, \ldots, o'_k \end{array}}{s' = (\langle (pp+1, lv, os'), fr_1, \ldots, fr_n \rangle, \bot, h, a) \qquad os' = o_b, o'_0, \ldots, o'_k}$$

$$\frac{\begin{array}{c} s = (\langle (pp, lv, os), fr_1, \ldots, fr_n \rangle, \bot, h, a) \\ instr(pp) = \texttt{Putfield}\ v \qquad os = o_0, o_1, o_2, \ldots, o_k \\ h(o_1) = (cl, f) \in \text{INSTANCES} \qquad a \text{ contains no annotation } o_1 =^? o \end{array}}{\begin{array}{c} s' = (\langle (pp+1, lv, os'), fr_1, \ldots, fr_n \rangle, \bot, h', a') \qquad os' = o_2, \ldots, o_k \\ h' = h + (o_1 \mapsto (cl, f')) \qquad f' = f + (v \mapsto o_0) \end{array}}$$

In the rule for `Putfield`, *a' contains all annotations in a, and in addition:*

- *a' contains "$p \bigvee q$" for all p, q with $p \sim_s o_1$ and $o_0 \rightsquigarrow_s q$*
- *a' contains "$p!$" for all p where $p \rightsquigarrow_s q$, $p \rightsquigarrow_s o_1$, $o_0 \rightsquigarrow_s q$ for some q, and where the paths from p to o_1 and p to q have no common non-empty prefix.*
- *if a contains "$q!$" for some q with $o_0 \rightarrow_s^* q$ or if there are π, ρ, ρ' with $\rho \neq \rho'$ where $s|_\pi = o_0$ and $s|_{\pi\rho} = s|_{\pi\rho'}$, then a' contains "$p!$" for all p with $p \sim_s o_1$.*

Finally, we define termination graphs formally. As illustrated, termination graphs are constructed by repeatedly expanding those leaves that do not correspond to program ends (i.e., where the call stack is not empty). Whenever possible, we evaluate the abstract state in a leaf (resulting in an *evaluation edge* $\overset{\text{EVAL}}{\longrightarrow}$). If evaluation is not possible, we use a refinement to perform a case analysis (resulting in *refinement edges* $\overset{\text{REF}}{\longrightarrow}$). To obtain a finite graph, we introduce more general states whenever a program position is visited a second time in our symbolic evaluation and add appropriate *instance edges* $\overset{\text{INS}}{\longrightarrow}$. However, we require all cycles of the termination graph to contain at least one evaluation edge.

Definition 7 (Termination graph). *A graph (N, E) with $N \subseteq \text{STATES}$ and $E \subseteq N \times \{\text{EVAL}, \text{REF}, \text{INS}\} \times N$ is a* termination graph *if every cycle contains at least one edge labelled with* EVAL *and one of the following holds for each $s \in N$:*

- *s has just one outgoing edge (s, EVAL, s') and $s \overset{SyEv}{\longrightarrow} s'$.*
- *There is a refinement $\{s_1, \ldots, s_n\}$ of s according to Def. 1, 4, or 5, and the outgoing edges of s are $(s, \text{REF}, s_1), \ldots, (s, \text{REF}, s_n)$.*
- *s has just one outgoing edge (s, INS, s') and $s \sqsubseteq s'$.*
- *s has no outgoing edge and $s = (\varepsilon, e, h, a)$.*

3 Simulating JBC by Concrete States

In this section we show that if one only regards *concrete* states, the rules for symbolic evaluation in Def. 6 correspond to the operational semantics of JINJA.

Definition 8 (Concrete states). *Let* $c \in \text{STATES}$ *and let* h *be the heap of* c. *We call* c concrete *iff* c *contains no annotations and for all* $\pi \in \text{SPOS}(c)$, *either* $c|_\pi = \texttt{null}$ *or* $h(c|_\pi) \in \text{INSTANCES} \cup \{[z,z] \mid z \in \mathbb{Z}\}$.

Def. 9 recapitulates the definition of JINJA states from [12] in a formulation that is similar to our states. However, integers are not represented by references, there are no integer intervals, no unknown values, and no annotations.

Definition 9 (JINJA states). *Let* $\text{VAL} = \mathbb{Z} \cup \text{REFERENCES}$. *Then we define:*

$$\begin{array}{ll}
\text{JINJASTATES} = & (\text{PROGPOS} \times \text{JINJALOCVAR} \times \text{JINJAOPSTACK})^* \times \\
& (\{\bot\} \cup \text{REFERENCES}) \times \text{JINJAHEAP} \\
\text{JINJALOCVAR} = & \text{VAL}^* \\
\text{JINJAOPSTACK} = & \text{VAL}^* \\
\text{JINJAHEAP} = & \text{REFERENCES} \to \text{JINJAINSTANCES} \\
\text{JINJAINSTANCES} = & \text{CLASSNAMES} \times (\text{FIELDIDS} \to \text{VAL})
\end{array}$$

To define a function TRANS which maps each JINJA state to a corresponding concrete state, we first introduce a function $tr_{Val} : \text{VAL} \to \text{REFERENCES}$ with $tr_{Val}(o) = o$ for all $o \in \text{REFERENCES}$. Moreover, tr_{Val} maps every $z \in \mathbb{Z}$ to a fresh reference o_z. Later, the value of o_z in the heap will be the interval $[z,z]$.

Now we define $tr_{Ins} : \text{JINJAINSTANCES} \to \text{INSTANCES}$. For any $f : \text{FIELDIDS} \to \text{VAL}$, let $tr_{Ins}(cl, f) = (cl, \widetilde{f})$, where $\widetilde{f}(v) = tr_{Val}(f(v))$ for all $v \in \text{FIELDIDS}$.

Next we define $tr_{Heap} : \text{JINJAHEAP} \to \text{HEAP}$. For any $h \in \text{JINJAHEAP}$, $tr_{Heap}(h)$ is a function from REFERENCES to INTEGERS $\cup$ INSTANCES. For any $o \in \text{REFERENCES}$, let $tr_{Heap}(h)(o) = tr_{Ins}(h(o))$. Furthermore, we need to add the new references for integers, i.e., $tr_{Heap}(h)(o_z) = [z,z]$ for all $z \in \mathbb{Z}$.

Let $tr_{Frame} : (\text{PROGPOS} \times \text{JINJALOCVAR} \times \text{JINJAOPSTACK}) \to (\text{PROGPOS} \times \text{LOCVAR} \times \text{OPSTACK})$ with $tr_{Frame}(pp, lv, os) = (pp, \widetilde{lv}, \widetilde{os})$. If $lv = o_0, \ldots, o_m$, $os = o'_0, \ldots, o'_k$, then $\widetilde{lv} = tr_{Val}(o_0), \ldots, tr_{Val}(o_m)$, $\widetilde{os} = tr_{Val}(o'_0), \ldots, tr_{Val}(o'_k)$.

Finally we define $\text{TRANS} : \text{JINJASTATES} \to \text{STATES}$. For any $j \in \text{JINJASTATES}$ with $j = (\langle fr_0, \ldots, fr_n \rangle, e, h)$, let $\text{TRANS}(j) = (\langle tr_{Frame}(fr_0), \ldots, tr_{Frame}(fr_n) \rangle, e', tr_{Heap}(h), \varnothing)$, where $e' = \bot$ if $e = \bot$ and $e' = tr_{Val}(e)$ otherwise.

For $j, j' \in \text{JINJASTATES}$, $j \xrightarrow{jvm} j'$ denotes that evaluating j one step according to the semantics of JINJA [12] leads to j'. Thm. 10 shows that $\xrightarrow{jvm}$ can be simulated by the evaluation of concrete states as defined in Def. 6, cf. Fig. 1.

Theorem 10 (Evaluation of concrete states simulates JINJA evaluation). *For all* $j, j' \in \text{JINJASTATES}$, $j \xrightarrow{jvm} j'$ *implies* $\text{TRANS}(j) \xrightarrow{SyEv} \text{TRANS}(j')$.

Proof. We give the proof for the most complex JINJA instruction (i.e., `Putfield` in the case where no exception was thrown). The proof is analogous for the other instructions. Here, $\xrightarrow{jvm}$ is defined by the following inference rule.

$$\frac{\begin{array}{cc} j = (\langle (pp, lv, os), fr_1, \ldots, fr_n\rangle, \bot, h) & instr(pp) = \texttt{Putfield}\ v \\ os = o_0, o_1, o_2, \ldots, o_k & h(o_1) = (cl, f) \in \text{JINJAINSTANCES} \end{array}}{\begin{array}{cc} j' = (\langle (pp+1, lv, os'), fr_1, \ldots, fr_n\rangle, \bot, h') & os' = o_2, \ldots, o_k \\ h' = h + (o_1 \mapsto (cl, f')) & f' = f + (v \mapsto o_0) \end{array}}$$

Let $j \stackrel{jvm}{\longrightarrow} j'$ by the above rule. Then $\text{TRANS}(j) = (\langle (pp, \widetilde{lv}, \widetilde{os}), tr_{Frame}(fr_1), \ldots, tr_{Frame}(fr_n)\rangle, \bot, tr_{Heap}(h), \varnothing)$ with $\widetilde{os} = tr_{Val}(o_0), tr_{Val}(o_1), \ldots, tr_{Val}(o_k)$. Note that $tr_{Val}(o_1) = o_1$. Moreover, $\text{TRANS}(j') = (\langle (pp+1, \widetilde{lv}, \widetilde{os'}), tr_{Frame}(fr_1), \ldots, tr_{Frame}(fr_n)\rangle, \bot, tr_{Heap}(h'), \varnothing)$ with $\widetilde{os'} = tr_{Val}(o_2), \ldots, tr_{Val}(o_k)$.

On the other hand, by Def. 6 for $c = \text{TRANS}(j)$, we have $c \stackrel{SyEv}{\longrightarrow} c'$ with $c' = (\langle (pp+1, \widetilde{lv}, \widetilde{os'}), tr_{Frame}(fr_1), \ldots, tr_{Frame}(fr_n)\rangle, \bot, tr_{Heap}(h)', \varnothing)$. It remains to show that $tr_{Heap}(h') = tr_{Heap}(h)'$. For any new reference o_z for integers, we have $tr_{Heap}(h')(o_z) = [z, z] = tr_{Heap}(h)'(o_z)$. For any $o \in \text{REFERENCES} \setminus \{o_1\}$, we have $tr_{Heap}(h')(o) = tr_{Ins}(h'(o)) = tr_{Ins}(h(o))$ and $tr_{Heap}(h)'(o) = tr_{Heap}(h)(o) = tr_{Ins}(h(o))$. Finally, $tr_{Heap}(h')(o_1) = tr_{Ins}(h'(o_1)) = tr_{Ins}(cl, f') = (cl, \widetilde{f'})$ where $\widetilde{f'}(v) = tr_{Val}(o_0)$ and $\widetilde{f'}(w) = tr_{Val}(f(w))$ for all $w \in \text{FIELDIDS} \setminus \{v\}$. Moreover, $tr_{Heap}(h)'(o_1) = (cl, (\widetilde{f})')$ where $(\widetilde{f})'(v) = tr_{Val}(o_0)$ and $(\widetilde{f})'(w) = \widetilde{f}(w) = tr_{Val}(f(w))$ for all $w \in \text{FIELDIDS} \setminus \{v\}$. □

4 Simulating Concrete States by Abstract States

Now we show that our symbolic evaluation on *abstract* states is indeed consistent with the evaluation of all represented *concrete* states, cf. the upper half of Fig. 1.

Theorem 11 (Evaluation of abstract states simulates evaluation of concrete states). *Let $c, c', s \in \text{STATES}$, where c is concrete, $c \stackrel{SyEv}{\longrightarrow} c'$, $c \sqsubseteq s$, and s occurs in a termination graph G. Then G contains a path $s(\stackrel{\text{INS}}{\longrightarrow} \cup \stackrel{\text{REF}}{\longrightarrow})^* \circ \stackrel{\text{EVAL}}{\longrightarrow} s'$ such that $c' \sqsubseteq s'$.*

Proof. We prove the theorem by induction on the sum of the lengths of all paths from s to the next $\stackrel{\text{EVAL}}{\longrightarrow}$ edge. This sum is always finite, since every cycle of a termination graph contains an evaluation edge, cf. Def. 7. We perform a case analysis on the type of the outgoing edges of s. If there is an edge $s \stackrel{\text{INS}}{\longrightarrow} \tilde{s}$, and hence $s \sqsubseteq \tilde{s}$, we prove transitivity of $\sqsubseteq$ (Lemma 13, Sect. 4.1). Then $c \sqsubseteq s$ implies $c \sqsubseteq \tilde{s}$ and the claim follows from the induction hypothesis.

If the outgoing edges of s are $\stackrel{\text{REF}}{\longrightarrow}$ edges (i.e., $s \stackrel{\text{REF}}{\longrightarrow} s_1, \ldots, s \stackrel{\text{REF}}{\longrightarrow} s_n$), we show that our refinements are "*valid*", i.e., $c \sqsubseteq s$ implies $c \sqsubseteq s_j$ for some s_j (Lemmas 14-16, Sect. 4.2). Again, then the claim follows from the induction hypothesis.

Finally, if the first step is an $\stackrel{\text{EVAL}}{\longrightarrow}$-step (i.e., $s \stackrel{SyEv}{\longrightarrow} s'$), we prove the correctness of the $\stackrel{SyEv}{\longrightarrow}$ relation on abstract states (Lemma 19, Sect. 4.3). □

With Thm. 10 and 11, we can prove the "soundness" of termination graphs.

Corollary 12 (Soundness of termination graphs). *Let* $j_1 \in$ JINJASTATES *have an infinite evaluation* $j_1 \stackrel{jvm}{\longrightarrow} j_2 \stackrel{jvm}{\longrightarrow} \ldots$ *and let* G *be a termination graph with a state* s_1^1 *such that* $\text{TRANS}(j_1) \sqsubseteq s_1^1$. *Then* G *contains an infinite* computation path $s_1^1, \ldots, s_1^{n_1}, s_2^1, \ldots, s_2^{n_2}, \ldots$ *such that* $\text{TRANS}(j_i) \sqsubseteq s_i^1$ *for all* i.

Proof. The corollary follows directly from Thm. 10 and 11, cf. Sect. 1. □

As shown in [15, Thm. 3.7], if the TRS resulting from a termination graph is terminating, then there is no infinite computation path. Thus, Cor. 12 proves the soundness of our approach for automated termination analysis of JBC.

4.1 Transitivity of $\sqsubseteq$

Lemma 13 ($\sqsubseteq$ transitive). *If* $s'' \sqsubseteq s'$ *and* $s' \sqsubseteq s$, *then also* $s'' \sqsubseteq s$.

Proof. We prove the lemma by checking each of the conditions in Def. 3. Here, we only consider Def. 3(a)-(d) and refer to [3] for the (similar) proof of the remaining conditions. Let $\pi \in \text{SPos}(s)$ and let h (h', h'') be the heap of s (s', s''). Note that $\pi \in \text{SPos}(s)$ implies $\pi \in \text{SPos}(s')$ and $\pi \in \text{SPos}(s'')$, cf. [15, Lemma 4.1].

(a) If $h''(s''|_\pi) \in$ INTEGERS, then because of $s'' \sqsubseteq s'$ also $h'(s'|_\pi) \in$ INTEGERS and thus $h(s|_\pi) \in$ INTEGERS. We also have $h''(s''|_\pi) \subseteq h'(s'|_\pi) \subseteq h(s|_\pi)$.

(b) If $s''|_\pi = \texttt{null}$, then by $s'' \sqsubseteq s'$ we have either
$s'|_\pi = \texttt{null}$ and thus, $s|_\pi = \texttt{null}$ or $h(s|_\pi) \in$ UNKNOWN
or $h'(s'|_\pi) \in$ UNKNOWN and thus, $h(s|_\pi) \in$ UNKNOWN.

(c) If $h''(s''|_\pi) = (cl'', ?)$, then $h'(s'|_\pi) = (cl', ?)$ and thus also $h(s|_\pi) = (cl, ?)$. Here, cl'' is cl' or a subtype of cl', and cl' is cl or a subtype of cl. Note that the subtype relation of JBC types is transitive by definition.

(d) If $h''(s''|_\pi) = (cl'', f'') \in$ INSTANCES, then either
$h'(s'|_\pi) = (cl', ?)$ and thus, also $h(s|_\pi) = (cl, ?)$
or $h'(s'|_\pi) = (cl'', f') \in$ INSTANCES and thus,
either $h(s|_\pi) = (cl, ?)$ or $h(s|_\pi) = (cl'', f) \in$ INSTANCES.
Again, cl'' is cl' or a subtype of cl', and cl' is cl or a subtype of cl. □

4.2 Validity of Refinements

We say that a refinement $\rho : \text{STATES} \rightarrow 2^{\text{STATES}}$ is *valid* iff for all $s \in$ STATES and all concrete states c, $c \sqsubseteq s$ implies that there is an $s' \in \rho(s)$ such that $c \sqsubseteq s'$. We now prove the validity of our refinements from Def. 1, 4, and 5.

Lemma 14. *The integer refinement is valid.*

Proof. Let $\{s_1, \ldots, s_n\}$ be an *integer refinement* of s where $s_i = (s + \{o_i \mapsto V_i\})[o/o_i]$ and $h_s(o) = V = V_1 \cup \ldots \cup V_n \subseteq \mathbb{Z}$ for the heap h_s of s.

Let c be a concrete state with heap h_c and $c \sqsubseteq s$. Let $\Pi = \{\pi \in \text{SPos}(s) \mid s|_\pi = o\}$. By Def. 3(e), there is a $z \in \mathbb{Z}$ such that $h_c(c|_\pi) = [z, z]$ for all $\pi \in \Pi$. Let $z \in V_i$ and let h_{s_i} be the heap of s_i. Then $h_{s_i}(s_i|_\pi) = V_i$ for all $\pi \in \Pi$.

To show $c \sqsubseteq s_i$, we only have to check condition Def. 3(a). Let $\tau \in \text{SPos}(c) \cap \text{SPos}(s_i)$ with $h_c(c|_\tau) = [z', z'] \in \text{Integers}$. If $\tau \notin \Pi$, then this position was not affected by the integer refinement and thus, $h_c(c|_\tau) \subseteq h_s(s|_\tau) = h_{s_i}(s_i|_\tau)$. If $\tau \in \Pi$, then we have $z' = z$ and thus $h_c(c|_\tau) \subseteq V_i = h_{s_i}(s_i|_\tau)$. □

Lemma 15. *The equality refinement is valid.*

Proof. Let $\{s_=, s_{\neq}\}$ be an equality refinement of s, using the annotation $o =^? o'$. Let c be a concrete state with $c \sqsubseteq s$. We want to prove that $c \sqsubseteq s_{\neq}$ or $c \sqsubseteq s_=$.

Let $\Pi = \{\tau \in \text{SPos}(s) \mid s|_\tau = o\}$, $\Pi' = \{\tau' \in \text{SPos}(s) \mid s|_{\tau'} = o'\}$. By Def. 3(e) there are o_c and o'_c with $c|_\tau = o_c$ for all $\tau \in \Pi$ and $c|_{\tau'} = o'_c$ for all $\tau' \in \Pi'$.

If $o_c \neq o'_c$, we trivially have $c \sqsubseteq s_{\neq}$, as $s_{\neq}$ differs from s only in the removed annotation "$o =^? o'$" which is not needed when regarding instances like c.

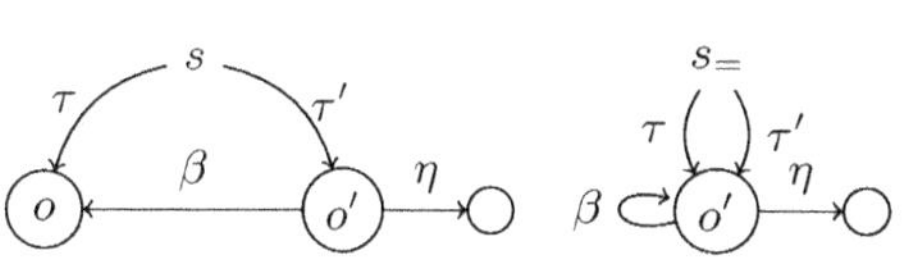

Fig. 8. Illustrating Lemma 15

If $o_c = o'_c$, we prove $c \sqsubseteq s_=$. The only change between s and $s_=$ was on or below positions in Π. Consider Fig. 8, where a state s with $s|_\tau = o$ and $s|_{\tau'} = o'$ is depicted on the left (i.e., $\tau \in \Pi$ and $\tau' \in \Pi'$). When we perform an equality refinement and replace o by o', we reach the state $s_=$ on the right. As illustrated there, we can decompose any position $\pi \in \text{SPos}(s_=)$ with a prefix in Π into $\tau\beta\eta$, where τ is the shortest prefix in Π and $\tau\beta$ is the longest prefix with $s_=|_{\tau\beta} = s_=|_\tau$.

With this decomposition, we have $s_=|_\tau = s|_{\tau'}$ for $\tau' \in \Pi'$ and thus $s_=|_{\tau\beta\eta} = s_=|_{\tau\eta} = s_=|_{\tau'\eta} = s|_{\tau'\eta}$. For $c \sqsubseteq s_=$, we now only have to check the conditions of Def. 3 for any position of $s_=$ of the form $\tau\beta\eta$ as above. Then the claim follows directly, as the conditions of Def. 3 already hold for $\tau'\eta$, since $c \sqsubseteq s$. □

Lemma 16. *The instance refinement is valid.*

Proof. Let $S = \{s_{\texttt{null}}, s_1, \ldots, s_n\}$ be an instance refinement of s on reference o. Let c be concrete with heap h_c and $c \sqsubseteq s$. We prove that $c \sqsubseteq s'$ for some $s' \in S$.

By Def. 5, $h_s(o) = (cl, ?)$, where h_s is the heap of s. Let $\Pi = \{\pi \in \text{SPos}(s) \mid s|_\pi = o\}$. The instance refinement only changed values at positions in Π and below. It may have added annotations for references at other positions, but as annotations only allow *more* sharing effects, we do not have to consider these positions. By Def. 3(e), there is an o_c such that $c|_\pi = o_c$ for all $\pi \in \Pi$. If $o_c = \texttt{null}$, we set $s' = s_{\texttt{null}}$. If $h_c(o_c) = (cl_i, f)$, we set $s' = s_i$, where s_i is obtained by refining the type cl to cl_i. Now one can prove $c \sqsubseteq s'$ by checking all conditions of Def. 3, as in the proof of Lemma 13. For the full proof, see [3]. □

4.3 Correctness of Symbolic Evaluation

Finally, we prove that every evaluation of a concrete state is also represented by the evaluation of the corresponding abstract state. This is trivial for most instructions, since they only affect the values of local variables or the operand stack. The only instruction which changes data objects on the heap is `Putfield`.

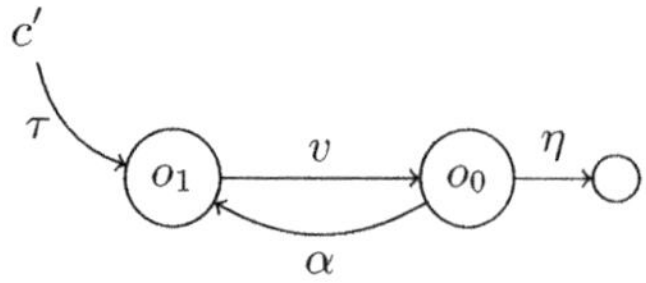

Fig. 9. Illustrating Lemma 17

Consider the evaluation of a concrete state c to another state c' by executing "`Putfield` v" which writes o_0 to the field v of the object at address o_1. Similar to the proof of Lemma 15, every position π of c' where the state was changed can be decomposed into $\pi = \tau\beta\eta$. Here, the first part τ leads to o_1 and it is the longest prefix that is not affected by the evaluation of `Putfield`. Similarly, the last part η is the longest suffix of π that was not changed by evaluating `Putfield`. So in particular, $c'|_{\tau\beta} = o_0$. The middle part β contains those parts that were actually changed in the evaluation step. So usually, β is just the field v. However, if $o_0 \to_c^* o_1$, then the object at o_1 in c' has become cyclic and then β can be more complex. Consider Fig. 9, where $c'|_\tau = o_1$ and regard the position $\pi = \tau v\,\alpha\, v\,\eta$. Here, the position π was influenced twice by the evaluation, as the middle part $\beta = v\,\alpha\, v$ contains a cycle using the field v. In the following, let $\pi_1 < \pi_2$ denote that π_1 is a proper prefix of π_2 and let $\leq$ be the reflexive closure of $<$.

Definition 17 (Change of concrete states by `Putfield`). *Let $c \in$ STATES be concrete with "`Putfield` v" as the next instruction to be evaluated and $c|_{\mathrm{OS}_{0,1}} \neq$ `null`. Let $c \stackrel{SyEv}{\longrightarrow} c'$ (i.e., in c', the object at reference $c|_{\mathrm{OS}_{0,0}}$ has been written to the field v of the object at reference $c|_{\mathrm{OS}_{0,1}}$). Then δ denotes the function that maps positions in c', which has a shorter operand stack than c, to positions in c, i.e., $\delta(w\,\pi) = w\,\pi$ if $w \neq \mathrm{OS}_{0,j}$ and $\delta(w\,\pi) = \mathrm{OS}_{0,j+2}\ \pi$ if $w = \mathrm{OS}_{0,j}$. For any $\pi \in \mathrm{SPos}(c')$ with $c'|_\pi \neq c|_{\delta(\pi)}$, its* Putfield-decomposition *is $\pi = \tau\beta\eta$, where*

- *τ is the shortest prefix of π such that both $c'|_\tau = c|_{\mathrm{OS}_{0,1}}$ and $\tau\, v \leq \pi$,*
- *β is the longest position of the form $\beta = v\,\alpha_1\, v\,\alpha_2\, v \ldots\ v\,\alpha_n\, v$ for some $n \geq 0$ where $\tau\beta \leq \pi$, $c'|_{\tau\, v\,\alpha_j} = c|_{\mathrm{OS}_{0,1}}$, and $c'|_{\tau\, v\,\rho} \neq c|_{\mathrm{OS}_{0,1}}$ for all $\rho < \alpha_j$ and all $1 \leq j \leq n$. Note that this implies $c'|_{\tau\,\beta} = c'|_{\tau\, v} = c|_{\mathrm{OS}_{0,0}}$ and $c'|_\pi = c|_{\mathrm{OS}_{0,0}\ \eta}$.*

We now show that Putfield-decompositions can be lifted to abstract states.

Lemma 18 (Change of abstract states by `Putfield`). *Let $s \in$ STATES with "`Putfield` v" as next instruction and $s|_{\mathrm{OS}_{0,1}} \neq$ `null`. Let $s \stackrel{SyEv}{\longrightarrow} s'$ and let c be concrete with $c \sqsubseteq s$ and $c \stackrel{SyEv}{\longrightarrow} c'$. For any $\pi \in \mathrm{SPos}(s') \cap \mathrm{SPos}(c')$, we have:*

- *If $c'|_\pi = c|_{\delta(\pi)}$, then $s'|_\pi = s|_{\delta(\pi)}$.*
- *If $c'|_\pi \neq c|_{\delta(\pi)}$, then for the corresponding Putfield-decomposition $\pi = \tau\beta\eta$, we have $s'|_\tau = s|_{\mathrm{OS}_{0,1}}$, $s'|_{\tau\beta} = s'|_{\tau\, v} = s|_{\mathrm{OS}_{0,0}}$, and $s'|_\pi = s|_{\mathrm{OS}_{0,0}\ \eta}$.*

Proof. Note that $s|_{\mathrm{OS}_{0,1}} \neq$ `null` also implies $c|_{\mathrm{OS}_{0,1}} \neq$ `null`, since $c \sqsubseteq s$. Hence, $c'|_\pi = c|_{\delta(\pi)}$ means that the position π is not influenced by the `Putfield` instruction. This implies that we also have $s'|_\pi = s|_{\delta(\pi)}$.

Now let $c'|_\pi \neq c|_{\delta(\pi)}$. Since τ is the shortest prefix with $c'|_\tau = c|_{\mathrm{OS}_{0,1}}$ and $\tau\, v \leq \pi$, this path is not affected by the evaluation, i.e., $c'|_\tau = c|_{\delta(\tau)}$ and $s'|_\tau = s|_{\delta(\tau)}$.

Assume that $s'|_\tau \neq s|_{\mathrm{OS}_{0,1}}$. As $s \stackrel{SyEv}{\longrightarrow} s'$, we have $h_s(s|_{\mathrm{OS}_{0,1}}) \in$ INSTANCES, where h_s is the heap of the state s. But then, as $c|_{\delta(\tau)} = c'|_\tau = c|_{\mathrm{OS}_{0,1}}$ and $s|_{\delta(\tau)} = s'|_\tau \neq s|_{\mathrm{OS}_{0,1}}$, $c \sqsubseteq s$ implies $s|_{\delta(\tau)} =^? s|_{\mathrm{OS}_{0,1}}$. This contradicts the definition of $=^?$, which requires that at least one of $h_s(s|_{\delta(\tau)})$ and $h_s(s|_{\mathrm{OS}_{0,1}})$ must be in UNKNOWN. But here, we do not only have $h_s(s|_{\mathrm{OS}_{0,1}}) \in$ INSTANCES, but also $h_s(s|_{\delta(\tau)}) \in$ INSTANCES. The reason for the latter is that since $\pi \in \mathrm{SPos}(s')$ and $\tau < \pi$, we have $h_{s'}(s'|_\tau) \in$ INSTANCES and thus also $h_s(s|_{\delta(\tau)}) \in$ INSTANCES (recall that $s'|_\tau = s|_{\delta(\tau)}$). Thus, we have shown that $s'|_\tau = s|_{\mathrm{OS}_{0,1}}$. The proof for $s'|_{\tau\beta} = s|_{\mathrm{OS}_{0,0}}$ works analogously (see [3] for details). As η was not affected by `Putfield`, $s'|_{\tau\beta} = s|_{\mathrm{OS}_{0,0}}$ implies $s'|_\pi = s|_{\mathrm{OS}_{0,0}\,\eta}$. □

Now we can finally prove the correctness of our evaluation on abstract states.

Lemma 19 (Correctness of evaluation on abstract states). *Let $c, s \in$ STATES with c concrete and $c \sqsubseteq s$. If $c \stackrel{SyEv}{\longrightarrow} c'$ and $s \stackrel{SyEv}{\longrightarrow} s'$, then $c' \sqsubseteq s'$.*

Proof. For all instructions except `Putfield`, the claim is obvious. Therefore, we prove the lemma for "`Putfield` v", which writes the reference $c|_{\mathrm{OS}_{0,0}}$ to the field v of the instance referenced by $c|_{\mathrm{OS}_{0,1}}$. As the case for $c|_{\mathrm{OS}_{0,1}} =$ `null` (leading to an exception) is trivial, we will not consider it here and assume $c|_{\mathrm{OS}_{0,1}} \neq$ `null`. To prove that $c' \sqsubseteq s'$, we consider each of the conditions of Def. 3.

For Def. 3(a), (b), (d), (e), (f), for any $\pi \in \mathrm{SPos}(c')$, there are two possibilities. We either have $c'|_\pi = c|_{\delta(\pi)}$ and therefore also $s'|_\pi = s|_{\delta(\pi)}$ by Lemma 18. Then the condition on $c'|_\pi$ and $s'|_\pi$ that is needed for $c' \sqsubseteq s'$ follows from the respective condition on $c|_{\delta(\pi)}$ and $s|_{\delta(\pi)}$, since $c \sqsubseteq s$. Otherwise, $c'|_\pi \neq c|_{\delta(\pi)}$. By Lemma 18, there is a position η such that $c'|_\pi = c|_{\mathrm{OS}_{0,0}\,\eta}$ and $s'|_\pi = s|_{\mathrm{OS}_{0,0}\,\eta}$. Now the condition on $c'|_\pi$ and $s'|_\pi$ that is needed for $c' \sqsubseteq s'$ follows from the respective condition on $c|_{\mathrm{OS}_{0,0}\,\eta}$ and $s|_{\mathrm{OS}_{0,0}\,\eta}$, since we have $c \sqsubseteq s$.

Def. 3 (c), (g), (i), (j) are not applicable, since c is a concrete state. It remains to consider (h) and (k). We only give the proof for (h), since the proof for (k) is analogous. Let $h_c, h_{c'}, h_s, h_{s'}$ be the heaps of c, c', s, and s'. We have $c'|_\pi = c'|_{\pi'}$ and $\{\pi, \pi'\} \not\subseteq \mathrm{SPos}(s')$. We only handle the case where $\pi \notin \mathrm{SPos}(s')$ and $\pi' \in \mathrm{SPos}(s')$ and where both $\pi, \pi' \notin \mathrm{SPos}(s')$. The remaining case is analogous to the first. We now have four possibilities (1)-(4):

(1) $c'|_\pi = c|_{\delta(\pi)}$ and $c'|_{\pi'} = c|_{\delta(\pi')}$, i.e., neither π nor π' were affected by the `Putfield` operation. Then $\{\delta(\pi), \delta(\pi')\} \not\subseteq \mathrm{SPos}(s)$ and thus due to $c \sqsubseteq s$, we have $s|_{\overline{\delta(\pi)}} \mathrel{\bigvee\!\!\!\!/} s|_{\overline{\delta(\pi')}}$ and thus also $s'|_{\overline{\pi}} \mathrel{\bigvee\!\!\!\!/} s'|_{\overline{\pi'}}$.

(2) $c'|_\pi \neq c|_{\delta(\pi)}$ and $c'|_{\pi'} = c|_{\delta(\pi')}$, i.e., only π was affected by `Putfield`. Let $\pi = \tau\beta\eta$ be the Putfield-decomposition. We can then distinguish three subcases:

  (2.1) $\tau\beta \in \mathrm{SPos}(s')$ and $\pi = \tau\beta\eta \notin \mathrm{SPos}(s')$. Then also $\mathrm{OS}_{0,0}\,\eta \notin \mathrm{SPos}(s)$, because otherwise the object at position $h_s(s|_{\mathrm{OS}_{0,0}\,\eta})$ would have been written to position $\pi = \tau\beta\eta$ in s'. We have $c|_{\delta(\pi')} = c'|_{\pi'} = c'|_\pi = c|_{\mathrm{OS}_{0,0}\,\eta}$ and as $c \sqsubseteq s$, we have $s|_{\overline{\delta(\pi')}} \mathrel{\bigvee\!\!\!\!/} s|_{\overline{\mathrm{OS}_{0,0}\,\eta}}$. Note that $\overline{\mathrm{OS}_{0,0}\,\eta} = \mathrm{OS}_{0,0}\,\widetilde{\eta}$ for some $\widetilde{\eta} \leq \eta$. Thus also $s'|_{\overline{\pi'}} \mathrel{\bigvee\!\!\!\!/} s'|_{\tau\beta\widetilde{\eta}}$ and hence, $s'|_{\overline{\pi'}} \mathrel{\bigvee\!\!\!\!/} s'|_{\overline{\pi}}$.

(2.2) $\tau \in \mathrm{SPos}(s')$ and $\tau\beta \notin \mathrm{SPos}(s')$. Then for $\beta = v\,\alpha_1\,v\,\alpha_2\,v \ldots \alpha_n\,v$, there is a minimal j with $\tau\,v\,\alpha_1 \ldots v\,\alpha_j \notin \mathrm{SPos}(s')$. We then also have $\mathrm{os}_{0,0}\,\alpha_j \notin \mathrm{SPos}(s)$. As $c|_{\mathrm{os}_{0,1}} = c|_{\mathrm{os}_{0,0}\,\alpha_j}$ by construction of the decomposition and as $c \sqsubseteq s$, we have $s|_{\mathrm{os}_{0,1}} \mathrel{\searrow\!\!\!\swarrow} s|_{\mathrm{os}_{0,0}\,\widetilde{\alpha_j}}$ for some $\widetilde{\alpha_j} \leq \alpha_j$. If $\{\delta(\pi'), \mathrm{os}_{0,0}\,\eta\} \subseteq \mathrm{SPos}(s)$, by $c \sqsubseteq s$, we have $s|_{\delta(\pi')} = s|_{\mathrm{os}_{0,0}\,\eta}$ or $s|_{\delta(\pi')} =^? s|_{\mathrm{os}_{0,0}\,\eta}$. If $\{\delta(\pi'), \mathrm{os}_{0,0}\,\eta\} \not\subseteq \mathrm{SPos}(s)$, by $c \sqsubseteq s$, we have $s|_{\overline{\delta(\pi')}} \mathrel{\searrow\!\!\!\swarrow} s|_{\mathrm{os}_{0,0}\,\widetilde{\eta}}$ for some $\widetilde{\eta} \leq \eta$. Both cases imply $s|_{\mathrm{os}_{0,0}} \leadsto s|_{\overline{\delta(\pi')}}$. As we have $s|_{\mathrm{os}_{0,0}\,\widetilde{\alpha_j}} \sim s|_{\mathrm{os}_{0,1}}$ and $s|_{\mathrm{os}_{0,0}} \leadsto s|_{\overline{\delta(\pi')}}$, the first rule for the annotation additions (from Def. 6) requires $s'|_{\tau\,v\,\widetilde{\alpha_j}} \mathrel{\searrow\!\!\!\swarrow} s'|_{\overline{\pi'}}$. Hence, $s'|_{\tau\,v\,\alpha_1 \ldots v\,\widetilde{\alpha_j}} \mathrel{\searrow\!\!\!\swarrow} s'|_{\overline{\pi'}}$ and thus, $s'|_{\overline{\pi}} \mathrel{\searrow\!\!\!\swarrow} s'|_{\overline{\pi'}}$.

(2.3) $\tau \notin \mathrm{SPos}(s')$. Then also $\delta(\tau) \notin \mathrm{SPos}(s)$ and as $c|_{\delta(\tau)} = c|_{\mathrm{os}_{0,1}}$ and $c \sqsubseteq s$, we have $s|_{\overline{\delta(\tau)}} \mathrel{\searrow\!\!\!\swarrow} s|_{\mathrm{os}_{0,1}}$. We also have $c|_{\mathrm{os}_{0,0}\,\eta} = c|_{\delta(\pi')}$ and thus either $s|_{\mathrm{os}_{0,0}\,\widetilde{\eta}} = s|_{\overline{\delta(\pi')}}$, $s|_{\mathrm{os}_{0,0}\,\widetilde{\eta}} =^? s|_{\overline{\delta(\pi')}}$, or $s|_{\mathrm{os}_{0,0}\,\widetilde{\eta}} \mathrel{\searrow\!\!\!\swarrow} s|_{\overline{\delta(\pi')}}$ for $\widetilde{\eta} \leq \eta$. In all cases, $s|_{\mathrm{os}_{0,0}} \leadsto s|_{\overline{\delta(\pi')}}$. Together with $s|_{\overline{\delta(\tau)}} \sim s|_{\mathrm{os}_{0,1}}$, the first rule for the annotation additions requires $s'|_{\overline{\tau}} \mathrel{\searrow\!\!\!\swarrow} s'|_{\overline{\pi'}}$ and hence, $s'|_{\overline{\pi}} \mathrel{\searrow\!\!\!\swarrow} s'|_{\overline{\pi'}}$.

(3) $c'|_{\pi} = c|_{\delta(\pi)}$ and $c'|_{\pi'} \neq c|_{\delta(\pi')}$, i.e., only π' was affected by the `Putfield` operation. This is analogous to Case (2).

(4) $c'|_{\pi} \neq c|_{\delta(\pi)}$ and $c'|_{\pi'} \neq c|_{\delta(\pi')}$, i.e., both π, π' were affected by `Putfield`. This is proved by a case analysis similar to Case (2) (see [3] for details). □

5 Conclusion

In this paper, we have shown that termination graphs correctly simulate the evaluation of JBC. To this end, we first gave a formal definition of termination graphs (Sect. 2). Then we showed that our notion of symbolic evaluation in these graphs corresponds to the operational semantics of JINJA Bytecode, as long as we are restricted to concrete states (Sect. 3). Afterwards, we proved that every evaluation of concrete states is simulated by a path on abstract states in the termination graph (Sect. 4). Together with the results of [15], this proves the soundness of our approach for automated termination analysis of JBC. Here, JBC is first transformed into termination graphs. Afterwards, one generates TRSs from these graphs and uses existing tools to prove their termination.

The result of the current paper (i.e., the proof that every JBC evaluation is represented by the termination graph) is also useful outside of termination analysis, since termination graphs could also be used for analysis of nullness, sharing, exceptions, etc. Compared to other static analysis techniques, termination graphs perform less abstraction and therefore, while the analysis may be more time-consuming, it can be more precise. Developing such other analyses that build upon termination graphs is the subject of future work.

Acknowledgement. J. Giesl wants to thank C. Walther for having introduced him to many of the research areas that are relevant for this paper (e.g., induction and symbolic evaluation [19], termination [20], and semantics [21]).

References

1. Albert, E., Arenas, P., Codish, M., Genaim, S., Puebla, G., Zanardini, D.: Termination analysis of Java Bytecode. In: Barthe, G., de Boer, F.S. (eds.) FMOODS 2008. LNCS, vol. 5051, pp. 2–18. Springer, Heidelberg (2008)
2. Berdine, J., Cook, B., Distefano, D., O'Hearn, P.: Automatic termination proofs for programs with shape-shifting heaps. In: Ball, T., Jones, R.B. (eds.) CAV 2006. LNCS, vol. 4144, pp. 386–400. Springer, Heidelberg (2006)
3. Brockschmidt, M., Otto, C., von Essen, C., Giesl, J.: Termination graphs for Java Bytecode. Technical Report AIB-2010-15, RWTH Aachen (2010), `http://aib.informatik.rwth-aachen.de`
4. Colón, M., Sipma, H.: Practical methods for proving program termination. In: Brinksma, E., Larsen, K.G. (eds.) CAV 2002. LNCS, vol. 2404, pp. 442–454. Springer, Heidelberg (2002)
5. Cook, B., Podelski, A., Rybalchenko, A.: Termination proofs for systems code. In: Schwartzbach, M.I., Ball, T. (eds.) PLDI 2006, pp. 415–426. ACM Press, New York (2006)
6. Cousot, P., Cousot, R.: Abstract interpretation: A unified lattice model for static analysis of programs by construction or approximation of fixpoints. In: Proc. POPL 1977, pp. 238–252. ACM Press, New York (1977)
7. De Schreye, D., Decorte, S.: Termination of logic programs: The never-ending story. Journal of Logic Programming 19-20, 199–260 (1994)
8. Dershowitz, N.: Termination of rewriting. J. Symb. Comp. 3(1-2), 69–116 (1987)
9. Fuhs, C., Giesl, J., Plücker, M., Schneider-Kamp, P., Falke, S.: Proving termination of integer term rewriting. In: Treinen, R. (ed.) RTA 2009. LNCS, vol. 5595, pp. 32–47. Springer, Heidelberg (2009)
10. Giesl, J., Raffelsieper, M., Schneider-Kamp, P., Swiderski, S., Thiemann, R.: Automated termination proofs for Haskell by term rewriting. ACM TOPLAS (to appear)
11. Giesl, J., Schneider-Kamp, P., Thiemann, R.: AProVE 1.2: Automatic termination proofs in the DP framework. In: Furbach, U., Shankar, N. (eds.) IJCAR 2006. LNCS (LNAI), vol. 4130, pp. 281–286. Springer, Heidelberg (2006)
12. Klein, G., Nipkow, T.: A machine-checked model for a Java-like language, virtual machine and compiler. ACM TOPLAS 28(4), 619–695 (2006)
13. Lindholm, T., Yellin, F.: Java Virtual Machine Specification. Prentice-Hall, Englewood Cliffs (1999)
14. Nipkow, T., Paulson, L.C., Wenzel, M.: Isabelle/HOL — A Proof Assistant for Higher-Order Logic. LNCS, vol. 2283. Springer, Heidelberg (2002)
15. Otto, C., Brockschmidt, M., von Essen, C., Giesl, J.: Automated termination analysis of Java Bytecode by term rewriting. In: Lynch,C. (ed.) RTA 2010 LIPIcs, vol. 6, pp. 259–276. Dagstuhl Publishing (2010)
16. Schneider-Kamp, P., Giesl, J., Serebrenik, A., Thiemann, R.: Automated termination proofs for logic programs by term rewriting. ACM TOCL 11(1) (2009)
17. Sørensen, M.H., Glück, R.: An algorithm of generalization in positive supercompilation. In: Lloyd, J.W. (ed.) ILPS 1995, pp. 465–479. MIT Press, Cambridge (1995)
18. Spoto, F., Mesnard, F., Payet, É.: A termination analyser for Java Bytecode based on path-length. ACM TOPLAS 32(3) (2010)
19. Walther, C.: Mathematical induction. In: Handbook of Logic in Artificial Intelligence and Logic Programming, vol. 2, pp. 127–227. Oxford University Press, Oxford (1994)
20. Walther, C.: On proving the termination of algorithms by machine. Artificial Intelligence 71(1), 101–157 (1994)
21. Walther, C.: Semantik und Programmverifikation. Teubner-Wiley, Chichester (2001)

Specifying and Verifying Organizational Security Properties in First-Order Logic

Christoph Brandt[1], Jens Otten[2], Christoph Kreitz[2], and Wolfgang Bibel[3]

[1] Université du Luxembourg
christoph.brandt@uni.lu
[2] University of Potsdam
{jeotten,kreitz}@cs.uni-potsdam.de
[3] Darmstadt University of Technology
bibel@gmx.net

Abstract. In certain critical cases the data flow between business departments in banking organizations has to respect security policies known as Chinese Wall or Bell–La Padula. We show that these policies can be represented by formal requirements and constraints in first-order logic. By additionally providing a formal model for the flow of data between business departments we demonstrate how security policies can be applied to a concrete organizational setting and checked with a first-order theorem prover. Our approach can be applied without requiring a deep formal expertise and it therefore promises a high potential of usability in the business.

Keywords: theorem proving, first-order-logic, Chinese Wall, Bell–La Padula, organizational data-flow, security, leanCoP.

1 Introduction

One of the primary interests of a banking organization is maintaining its reputation. Among other issues this involves avoiding any kind of violation of its mandatory security policies. Due to a lack of precise security models that can be applied in practice, security is primarily implemented as a risk management activity, which is informal in nature and uses rather fuzzy guidelines. Although these practices seem to imply a sound measurement of risks from a methodological point of view, only rough qualitative statements can be made, which do not lead to truly reliable security guarantees.

In this paper we will demonstrate that the shortcomings of the "best-practices" can be overcome in a way that is sound, efficient and usable. We will describe how formal models for security policies and IT landscapes can be built in a way that makes it possible to integrate them in a way transparent to people in the business. We will also show how formal methods can be used to verify security properties within specific IT landscapes. We use first-order logic as the language for representing the formal models and the first-order theorem prover leanCoP [26,24] as the formal verification tool.

Specifically, we will discuss two security policies, the Chinese Wall and the Bell–La Padula policy, in the context of a formally modeled IT landscape that needs to be secured. We will focus on a small example of an IT landscape derived from a concrete

S. Siegler and N. Wasser (Eds.): Walther Festschrift, LNAI 6463, pp. 38–53, 2010.

scenario at Credit Suisse. It consists of two business departments and the data-flow between them. It is assumed that the data-flow represents the email traffic between the departments, which fits the organizational reality at major banking organizations.

The novelty presented in this paper is an engineering-like approach to addressing a real-world problem with the help of formal methods, their implementations and corresponding formal models. Our approach makes it possible to add further security policies and different IT landscapes as separate modules and to combine them in a plug-and-play manner whenever this makes sense. This compositional nature fits well the expectations of people in the business, because it enables them to use the full power of implemented formal methods in an encapsulated way without requiring them to have a deep formal expertise.

The paper is organized as follows. Section 2 describes our approach to assuring security policies in a given IT landscape that enables us to check such policies against different organizational settings. In Sections 3 and 4 we will explain and formally specify the Chinese Wall and Bell–La Padula security policies. Section 5 presents a formal model of a simplified IT landscape, which provides a basis for automated security checks. Section 6 introduces the formal methods and tools that are used in a case study in Section 7, where we check that a concrete set of security constraints implements the Chinese Wall policy in the scenario of Section 4. Section 8 discusses related work and in Section 9 we will draw final conclusions and discuss possibilities for future work.

2 A Generic Approach to Assuring Security

The purpose of this paper is to show how security policies and IT landscapes can be integrated in a formal model that enables practitioners to verify organizational security properties. In the real world, banking organizations run different service landscapes that need to respect a multiplicity of security policies. As a consequence, there is a need for a set of small, well focused, and composable models that can be handled by existing formal tools. As service landscapes and security policies are usually specified in a complementary fashion, the respective modeling processes must be independent and lead to orthogonal models that can be soundly integrated. Obviously, the same formal methods should be used in both activities in order to make a combination of the results possible.

According to Hartel, van Eck, Etalle, and Wieringa [15], security policies like the Chinese Wall are rules that constrain the behavior of a system in order to accomplish a certain security principle, such as "information about a customer must not leak to other customers". Thus a well-defined security principle can be formally checked if a formal specification of the system and the organizational security policy is given. In [15], this verification task is described by the following statement.

$$(\mathit{system} \parallel \mathit{security\ policy}) \models \mathit{security\ principle}\ . \tag{1}$$

Statement (1) can be verified using a formal tool, using an appropriate representation of the system, the security policy, and the security principle in the formal language of that tool. If the verification fails, Hartel, van Eck, Etalle, and Wieringa propose to adjust either the system or the security policy to prove the given security principle.

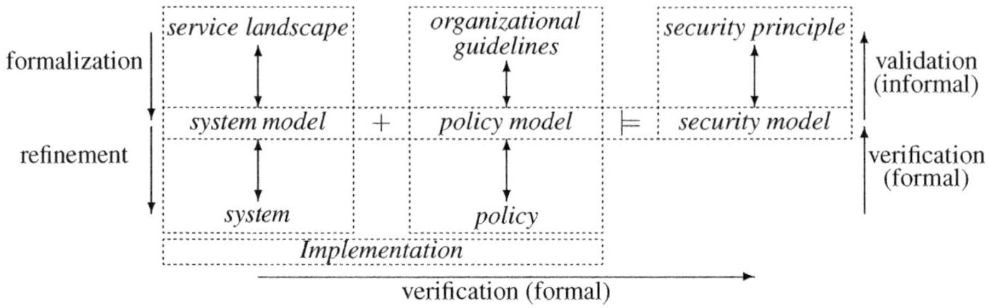

Fig. 1. Generic approach to verifying security properties

In the real world, however, security policies often come as textual documents describing organizational guidelines that have to be refined into a formal policy model. Since organizational policy documents cannot be formalized automatically, generating a formal policy model requires interpreting the meaning of informal organizational guidelines in a way that can easily be validated by security experts. This view is inspired by the work of Freeman, Neely, and Heckard, who have developed a validated security policy modeling approach [12] that can be applied to many types of systems, including networks and distributed systems. Their approach is driven by security requirements and by system architecture and supports working with orthogonal models that can be combined easily and checked automatically. As a consequence, two statements have to be validated in addition to statement (1).

$$\textit{organizational guidelines} \leftrightarrow \textit{policy model} \tag{2}$$

$$\textit{security principle} \leftrightarrow \textit{security model} \tag{3}$$

Our approach will go even one step further. Since banking organizations may use different service landscapes, different policies, and different implementations of the same policy (or landscape), we will use high-level abstractions of system models, policy models, and security models in a verification and link these to the low level representations of the actual system and the policy enforcement code, as illustrated in Figure 1.

This makes it possible to verify abstract properties of a variety of service landscapes and security policies with the same formal tool without being burdened by details of a specific implementation. Verifying that the models are fulfilled by their respective implementations will have to be done separately and, if successfully carried out, will then automatically prove that the concrete systems and policy enforcement mechanisms satisfy the desired security principle. As a consequence, one can combine multiple service landscapes, security policies, and realizations of these in a plug-and-play fashion and provide security guarantees with the help of a formal tool. This makes our approach flexible enough to cope with the dynamic nature of business while keeping the implementation of the formal methods fixed. It is cost effective because modules can be exchanged and reused in other contexts and verified automatically. It is mathematically sound and promises a high potential for being used by people in the business. The reuse potential of the formal models is an important reason to justify possible upfront investments for building them.

In their work on reasoning about security policies Halpern and Weissman [14] show that a formalism used for this purpose must not only be expressive and usable by non-logicians, but also be sufficiently tractable, since otherwise verification tools may not scale well and thus become useless in practice. According to these authors another important issue is identifying and resolving conflicts that may occur when different policy sets are merged, which is often the case in business scenarios.

In consequence of all these conceptual deliberations, our approach will use first-order logic to specify the system and policy models in an orthogonal fashion that allows for a later integration. Relevant aspects of a service landscape as well as the organizational guidelines of the security policy will be represented in the form of first-order axioms. The security principle to be verified must be formulated as a theorem in first-order logic. Then using a first-order theorem prover to derive the theorem from the set of axioms will verify that the security principle holds in the given service landscape and for the given security policy. Finally, formalizing the system and the policy enforcement mechanisms as first-order axioms as well will enable the theorem prover to verify their correctness with respect to the models and thus prove that the security principle is satisfied by the implementation of the system and of the security policy.

3 The Chinese Wall Model

A Chinese Wall, also known as Brewer and Nash Model [8], is most commonly employed in investment banks between the corporate-advisory area and the brokering department in order to separate those giving corporate advice on takeovers from those advising clients about buying shares. The " wall" shall prevent leaks of corporate inside information, which could influence the advice given to clients making investments, but allow staff to take advantage of facts that are not yet known to the general public.

Maintaining client confidentiality is crucial to any firm, but particularly to large multi-service businesses. If a firm provides a wide range of services, clients must be able to trust that information about themselves will not be exploited for the benefit of other clients. Therefore clients must be able to trust in Chinese Walls. In recent years, however, some Wall Street scandals have made people doubt the effectiveness of Chinese Walls, as executives of respectable firms have traded illegally on inside information for their own benefit.

The term Chinese Wall was popularized in the United States following the stock market crash of 1929, when the U.S. government legislated information separation between investment bankers and brokerage firms, in order to limit the conflict of interest between objective analysis of companies and the desire for successful initial public offerings. Rather than forbidding one firm from engaging in both businesses, the regulation permitted the implementation of Chinese Wall procedures.

Our formalization of the Chinese Wall policy is built upon the legal specifications, which are expressed by three security requirements. These requirements are mapped onto formal constraints that have to be proved in order to verify an implementation of the Chinese Wall policy. We use the general notion of a log file (l) to record actions (get, new, $drop$, put) of subjects (s) who send data objects (ob) to each other at certain points in time (t).

Requirement CW 1. *Once a subject has accessed an object the only other objects accessible by that subject lie within the same company data set or within a different conflict of interest class.*

The formalization of this requirement in first-order logic states that if an entry $\mathit{element}(s, \mathtt{get}, \mathit{ob}, t)$ of the log file l shows that a subject s gets an object ob at some time t (or creates a new one) and if s does not drop the object again at some time t', then the subject can get another object ob' at some time t'' afterward if and only if ob and ob' are not in a conflict of interest class. No restrictions apply if the new object carries sanitized information.

Requirement CW 2. *A subject can access at most one company data set in each conflict of interest class.*

More precisely, if a subject s gets an object ob and doesn't drop it again, it cannot get an object ob' from a different owner in the same class of conflict. This restriction does not apply to objects carrying sanitized information.

The following two first-order formulas reflect the intentions expressed by the first and the second requirement. Since the two requirements partly overlap, the formulas do not formalize them in a one-to-one fashion, but reorganize the underlying conditions in a way that helps keep the formalizations as simple as possible.

$$\begin{array}{c} \forall s\ \forall \mathit{ob}\ \forall \mathit{ob}'\ \forall i\ \forall t\ \forall t'\ \forall t''\ \forall l \\ (((\mathit{member}(\mathit{element}(s, \mathtt{get}, \mathit{ob}, t), l) \vee \mathit{member}(\mathit{element}(s, \mathtt{new}, \mathit{ob}, t), l)) \\ \wedge \neg \mathit{member}(\mathit{element}(s, \mathtt{drop}, \mathit{ob}, t'), l) \wedge t<t' \wedge\ t' \leq t'' \wedge \\ (\mathit{info}(i, \mathit{ob}') \wedge \mathit{sanitized}(i)) \vee \neg \mathit{conflict}(\mathit{ob}, \mathit{ob}')) \\ \Rightarrow\ \mathit{permitted}(s, \mathit{get}(\mathit{ob}', t'', l))) \end{array} \tag{4}$$

$$\begin{array}{c} \forall s\ \forall \mathit{ob}\ \forall \mathit{ob}'\ \forall i\ \forall t\ \forall t'\ \forall t''\ \forall l \\ (((\mathit{member}(\mathit{element}(s, \mathtt{get}, \mathit{ob}, t), l) \vee \mathit{member}(\mathit{element}(s, \mathtt{new}, \mathit{ob}, t), l)) \\ \wedge \neg \mathit{member}(\mathit{element}(s, \mathtt{drop}, \mathit{ob}, t'), l) \wedge t<t' \wedge\ t' \leq t'' \wedge \\ \mathit{info}(i, \mathit{ob}') \wedge \neg \mathit{sanitized}(i) \wedge \mathit{conflict}(\mathit{ob}, \mathit{ob}')) \\ \Rightarrow\ \neg \mathit{permitted}(s, \mathit{get}(\mathit{ob}', t'', l))) \end{array} \tag{5}$$

Requirement CW 3. *The flow of unsanitized information is confined to its own company data set; sanitized information may however flow freely throughout the system.*

If a subject s gets an object ob (and doesn't drop it again) and creates a new object ob' afterwords then the new object is allowed to be put back if and only it has the same ownership as the first one or any information shared by the two objects is sanitized.

We use two formulas to represent the "if" and the "only if" parts separately, as this simplifies the verification process.

$$\begin{array}{c} \forall s\ \forall \mathit{ob}\ \forall \mathit{ob}'\ \forall i\ \forall i'\ \forall t\ \forall t'\ \forall t''\ \forall t'''\ \forall t''''\ \forall l \\ ((\mathit{member}(\mathit{element}(s, \mathtt{get}, \mathit{ob}, t), l) \wedge \neg \mathit{member}(\mathit{element}(s, \mathtt{drop}, \mathit{ob}, t'), l) \\ \wedge\ \mathit{member}(\mathit{element}(s, \mathtt{new}, \mathit{ob}', t''), l) \wedge \neg \mathit{member}(\mathit{element}(s, \mathtt{drop}, \mathit{ob}', t'''), l) \\ \wedge\ t<t' \wedge t' \leq t'' \wedge\ t''<t''' \wedge\ t''' \leq t'''' \wedge\ \mathit{ob} \neq \mathit{ob}' \wedge\ \mathit{info}(i, \mathit{ob}) \wedge\ \mathit{info}(i', \mathit{ob}') \\ \wedge\ (\mathit{sameowner}(\mathit{ob}, \mathit{ob}') \vee \mathit{sanitized}(i') \vee i \neq i')) \\ \Rightarrow\ \mathit{permitted}(s, \mathit{put}(\mathit{ob}', t'''', l))) \end{array} \tag{6}$$

$$\begin{array}{c}\forall s\, \forall ob\, \forall ob'\, \forall i\, \forall i'\, \forall t\, \forall t'\, \forall t''\, \forall t'''\, \forall t''''\, \forall l \\ ((\mathit{member}(\mathit{element}(s, \mathtt{get}, ob, t), l) \wedge \neg \mathit{member}(\mathit{element}(s, \mathtt{drop}, ob, t'), l) \\ \wedge\ \mathit{member}(\mathit{element}(s, \mathtt{new}, ob', t''), l) \wedge \neg \mathit{member}(\mathit{element}(s, \mathtt{drop}, ob', t'''), l) \\ \wedge\ t{<}t' \wedge\ t'{\leq}t'' \wedge\ t''{<}t''' \wedge\ t'''{\leq}t'''' \wedge\ ob{\neq}ob' \wedge\ \mathit{info}(i, ob) \wedge\ \mathit{info}(i', ob') \\ \wedge\ \neg \mathit{sameowner}(ob, ob') \wedge\ \neg \mathit{sanitized}(i') \wedge\ i{=}i') \\ \Rightarrow\ \neg \mathit{permitted}(s, \mathit{put}(ob', t'''', l)))\end{array} \tag{7}$$

4 The Bell–La Padula Model

The Bell–La Padula security policy aims at securing the confidentiality of information. Its underlying idea is to prevent subjects with a given security level from reading data with a higher security level than their own. This is called the *no read-up principle*. It also prevents a subject from writing to any object of a security level lower than its own (*no write-down principle*). Finally, it specifies the discretionary access control through an access matrix (*need-to-know principle*). Later, lattice- or compartment-based models were introduced to realize horizontal and vertical data segments.

The Bell–La Padula security policy dates back to 1973 when David Elliot Bell and Leonard J. La Padula were working on a security model on behalf of the US Air Force with the intention to protect confidential data [4]. Formally, the model is based on the concept of a state machine representing a set of allowable states in a computer network system. The model divides entities into subjects and objects and defines the notion of a secure state. It has been shown that state transitions preserve the security properties by moving from secure states to secure states.

A system state is defined to be secure if the only permitted access modes of subjects to objects are in accordance with the Bell–La Padula policy. To determine whether a specific access mode is permitted, the clearance level of a subject is compared to the classification of the object. The clearance scheme is expressed in terms of a lattice. The no read-up and the no write-down principle define two mandatory access control (MAC) rules, and the access matrix realizes a discretionary access control (DAC) rule.

Information may be transferred from a classified document to an unclassified one by the use of trusted subjects. Trusted subjects are not restricted by the no write-down principle, but untrusted subjects are. The latter can only create content at or above their own security level and they can only view content at or below their own security level.

It is instructive to compare the Chinese Wall and the Bell–La Padula security policy using similar terms as used by Brewer and Nash, who argue that the Bell–La Padula model is not able to simulate the Chinese Wall model. Brewer and Nash point out, for example, that in the real world management may suddenly require user A to have access to a company data-set X if user B is unavailable. However, it is not possible to change the need-to-know of user A to the one of user B unless user A has had no access to another conflicting company data-set before. Otherwise, the Chinese Wall security policy would be violated. Brewer and Nash argue that the Bell–La Padula model is not able to provide the necessary information to answer this question. They also argue that the Bell–La Padula security policy only works under the assumption that subjects are not given the freedom to choose which company data-set they wish to access. In Brewer and Nash's formalization of the Bell–La Padula policy the freedom of choice can only be restored at the expense of failing to express the mandatory controls. As a consequence, the Bell–La Padula model can be used to model either the mandatory part or the free of choice part of the Chinese Wall security policy, but not both at the same time. As the Brewer and Nash model cannot simulate all aspects of the Bell–La Padula security policy, both security policies need to be treated independently but applied simultaneously in case they have to be enforced together in a given scenario.

By using one common formalization for both security policies we can represent the Bell–La Padula properties by two formal constraints on a service landscape, which again can be checked by a first-order theorem prover.

Requirement BLP 1 (Simple security). *Access is granted only if the subject's clearance is greater than the object's classification and the subject's need-to-know includes the object's category(ies).*

This requirement can be translated immediately into two first-order formulas.

$$\begin{gathered}\forall s\ \forall ob\ \forall c\ \forall l \\ ((seclevel(ob) \leq seclevel(s) \wedge needtoknow(ob, s) \\ \wedge\ (category(c, ob) \Rightarrow category(c, s))) \\ \Rightarrow\ permitted(s, get(ob, t, l)))\end{gathered} \tag{8}$$

$$\begin{gathered}\forall s\ \forall ob\ \forall c\ \forall l \\ ((seclevel(ob) > seclevel(s) \vee \neg needtoknow(ob, s) \\ \vee\ \neg(category(c, ob) \Rightarrow category(c, s))) \\ \Rightarrow\ \neg permitted(s, get(ob, t, l)))\end{gathered} \tag{9}$$

Requirement BLP 2 (∗-property). *Write access is granted only if the output object's classification is greater or equal to the classification of all input objects, and its category includes the category(ies) of all input objects.*

If a subject s gets or creates an object ob (and doesn't drop it again) and later creates a new object ob' that shares information with ob then the new object is allowed to be put back if and only if its security level is greater or equal to the one of ob and if its category includes the category of ob. Again, we use two formulas to represent this requirement.

$$\begin{gathered}\forall s\ \forall ob\ \forall ob'\ \forall c\ \forall i\ \forall i'\ \forall t\ \forall t'\ \forall t''\ \forall t'''\ \forall t''''\ \forall l \\ (((member(element(s, \mathtt{get}, ob, t), l) \vee member(element(s, \mathtt{new}, ob, t), l)) \\ \wedge \neg member(element(s, \mathtt{drop}, ob, t'), l) \wedge member(element(s, \mathtt{new}, ob', t''), l) \\ \wedge\ \neg member(element(s, \mathtt{drop}, ob', t'''), l) \\ \wedge\ t < t' \wedge\ t' \leq t'' \wedge\ t'' < t''' \wedge\ t''' \leq t'''' \wedge\ info(i, ob) \wedge info(i', ob') \wedge\ (i \neq i' \\ \vee\ (i = i' \wedge\ seclevel(ob) \leq seclevel(ob') \wedge (category(c, ob) \Rightarrow category(c, ob')))) \\ \Rightarrow\ permitted(s, put(ob', t'''', l)))\end{gathered} \tag{10}$$

$$\begin{gathered}\forall s\ \forall ob\ \forall ob'\ \forall c\ \forall i\ \forall i'\ \forall t\ \forall t'\ \forall t''\ \forall t'''\ \forall t''''\ \forall l \\ (((member(element(s, \mathtt{get}, ob, t), l) \vee member(element(s, \mathtt{new}, ob, t), l)) \\ \wedge \neg member(element(s, \mathtt{drop}, ob, t'), l) \wedge member(element(s, \mathtt{new}, ob', t''), l) \\ \wedge\ \neg member(element(s, \mathtt{drop}, ob', t'''), l) \\ \wedge\ t < t' \wedge t' \leq t'' \wedge\ t'' < t''' \wedge\ t''' \leq t'''' \wedge\ info(i, ob) \wedge info(i', ob') \wedge\ (i = i') \\ \wedge\ (seclevel(ob) > seclevel(ob') \vee\ \neg(category(c, ob) \Rightarrow category(c, s))) \\ \Rightarrow\ \neg permitted(s, put(ob', t'''', l)))\end{gathered} \tag{11}$$

5 The Service Landscape Model

In [2], F. Arbab introduces the notion of abstract behavior types (ABT) and Reo connectors as a model for system components and their composition. ABTs provide a well-defined semantics based on constraint automata and are therefore suited to automatic model checking. On the other hand they can be used in a very intuitive way by the people in the field. The model supports exogenous coordination and synchronous communication by abstracting away the internal implementation of components, focusing only on their observable outside behavior. Hence, formally pre-defined connectors and components can be simply clicked together as graphical objects conforming a formal graph grammar for this domain-specific modeling language.

ABTs can be seen as a high-level alternative to abstract data types. They define an abstract behavior as a relation among a set of timed-data-streams without specifying the operations or data types that may be used to implement such a behavior. Therefore, ABT models allow for a much looser coupling of components than ADTs and support formal models of a message driven service landscape that fit the Chinese Wall policy's conceptual understanding of messages being sent between different subjects.

The example IT landscape that we will formalize here is a simplified version of a concrete scenario at Credit Suisse. There are two departments, A and B, which are able to send data objects to each other by separate connectors. For instance, department A is the corporate-advisory area and department B is the brokering department. The data-flow between the two departments is realized by two separate Reo connectors as shown in Figure 2.

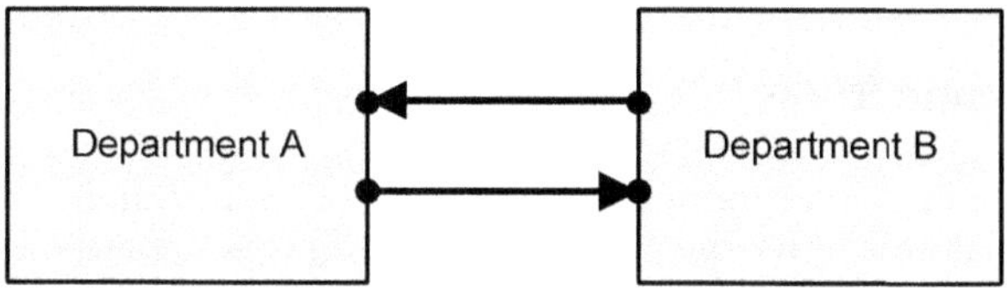

Fig. 2. Data-flow between department A and B

In our model, the different departments are represented by their separate abstract behavior types shown as blocks in Figure 2. Formally, the Reo channels conform to $Sync$ channels, realized as a $Sync$ ABT, and the abstract behavior types representing the two departments are realized as *department-A* ABT and *department-B* ABT. The operational semantics of a $Sync$ ABT is defined as $\langle \alpha, a \rangle Sync \langle \beta, b \rangle \equiv \langle \alpha, a \rangle = \langle \beta, b \rangle$, where, as shown in [2], the $Sync$ ABT represents the behavior of any entity that (1) produces an output data stream identical to its input data stream ($\alpha = \beta$), and (2) produces every element in its output at the same time as its respective input element is consumed ($a = b$). The operational semantics of a *department-A* ABT is defined as

department-A $ABT(\langle \alpha_i, a_i \rangle; \langle \alpha_o, a_o \rangle) \equiv (a_i < a_i') \wedge (a_o < a_o') \wedge (a_i \neq a_o)$,

which means that there is an input and an output timed-data stream representing put and get operations at a certain point in time. Operations are atomic. They happen sequentially and do not overlap. As we focus on the behavior, the concrete data

(α_i, α_o) is not specified further. The operational semantics of *department-B* is defined analogously.

This specification fits well with our formal specification of the Chinese Wall policy. To describe which agent is able to get data-objects from another one based on the given ABT/Reo model, we introduce two first-order axioms, which specify that it is possible for data-objects to be sent between both departments.

Axiom 1. *If department A has created a new object that still has not been dropped or put elsewhere, department B can get it, assuming that department A can send objects to department B as shown in Figure 2.*

$$\begin{array}{c} \forall ob\ \forall t\ \forall t'_1\ \forall t'_2\ \forall t'' \\ ((member(element(A, \mathtt{new}, ob, t), l) \wedge \neg member(element(A, \mathtt{drop}, ob, t'_1), l) \\ \wedge\ \neg member(element(A, \mathtt{put}, ob, t'_2), l)\ \wedge\ t{<}t'_1 \wedge\ t'_1{\leq}t'' \wedge\ t{<}t'_2 \wedge\ t'_2{\leq}t'') \\ \Rightarrow\ possible(B, get(ob, t'', l))) \end{array} \tag{12}$$

Axiom 2. *If department B has created a new object that still has not been dropped or put elsewhere, department A can get it, assuming that department B can send objects to department A as shown in Figure 2.*

$$\begin{array}{c} \forall ob\ \forall t\ \forall t'_1\ \forall t'_2\ \forall t'' \\ ((member(element(B, \mathtt{new}, ob, t), l) \wedge \neg member(element(B, \mathtt{drop}, ob, t'_1), l) \\ \wedge\ \neg member(element(B, \mathtt{put}, ob, t'_2), l)\ \wedge\ t{<}t'_1 \wedge\ t'_1{\leq}t'' \wedge\ t{<}t'_2 \wedge\ t'_2{\leq}t'') \\ \Rightarrow\ possible(A, get(ob, t'', l))) \end{array} \tag{13}$$

6 Methods and Tools

In order to prove first-order formulas that occur in our verification process we will use the automated theorem prover leanCoP. leanCoP is a very compact implementation of the connection calculus, a popular proof search method for first-order logic.

6.1 The Connection Calculus

There are several proof search calculi to automate formal reasoning in first-order logic; see [11] for an introduction. Connection calculi [5,6,20] are particularly successful due to the goal-oriented proof search. Their main inference step connects an atomic formula of the conjecture, or an atomic formula of the proof derivation, to a new atomic formula with the same predicate symbol but different polarity. This pair of atomic formulas $\{A, \neg A\}$ is called a connection and corresponds to a closed branch in the tableau framework [11] or an axiom in the sequent calculus [13].

The standard version of the connection calculus requires the input formula to be in disjunctive normal form or *clausal form*, i.e. of the form $C_1 \vee \ldots \vee C_n$ where C_i is a clause of the form $L_1 \wedge \ldots \wedge L_n$, L_i is a literal of the form A or $\neg A$ where A is an atomic formula. A formula in clausal form can be written as a set of clauses $\{C_1, \ldots, C_n\}$ and is called a *matrix*. In the graphical representation of a matrix, its clauses are arranged horizontally, while the literals of each clause are arranged vertically.

Example 1. Let $(((\exists x\, Q(x) \vee \neg Q(c)) \Rightarrow P) \wedge (P \Rightarrow (\exists y\, Q(y) \wedge R))) \Rightarrow (P \wedge R)$ be a (first-order) formula. Its equivalent clausal form, in which y is replaced by the Skolem term b, is $(P \wedge R) \vee (\neg P \wedge Q(x)) \vee (\neg Q(b) \wedge P) \vee (\neg Q(c) \wedge \neg P) \vee (P \wedge \neg R)$. The matrix of this formula is

$$M_1 = \{\{P, R\}, \{\neg P, Qx\}, \{\neg Qb, P\}, \{\neg Qc, \neg P\}, \{P, \neg R\}\}$$

where some parentheses are omitted for simplicity. It consists of five clauses and has the following two-dimensional graphical representation:

$$\begin{bmatrix} P & \neg P & \neg Qb & \neg Qc & P \\ R & Qx & P & \neg P & \neg R \end{bmatrix}.$$

A *connection* contains two literals of the form $\{A, \neg A\}$. A *path* through a matrix $M = \{C_1, \ldots, C_n\}$ is a set that contains one literal from each clause, i.e. $\cup_{i=1}^{n} \{L_i'\}$ with $L_i' \in C_i$. A *first-order substitution* σ is a mapping from the set of first-order variables to the set of terms. In $\sigma(L)$ all variables of the literal L are substituted according to the substitution σ.

Example 2. In the matrix M_1 of Example 1 the sets $\{P, \neg P\}$, $\{R, \neg R\}$, $\{Qx, \neg Qb\}$ and $\{Qx, \neg Qc\}$ are connections. $\{P, \neg P, \neg Qb, \neg Qc, \neg R\}$ and $\{R, Qx, \neg Qb, \neg Qc, P\}$ are, e.g., paths through the matrix M_1. $\sigma(x) = c$ is, e.g., a first-order substitution.

According to the *deduction theorem*, a (conjecture) formula C is a logical consequence of a set of (axiom) formulas $\{A_1, \ldots, A_n\}$ if and only if the formula $(A_1 \wedge \ldots \wedge A_n) \Rightarrow C$ is logically valid. Hence, we can use logical calculi, such as the connection calculus, in order to determine if a given first-order formula is logically valid.

The *matrix characterization* [6] of classical validity can be seen as the underlying basis of the connection calculus. This characterization can be extended to some non-classical logics as well [18,34]. Let M^μ be the matrix M, in which copies of clauses have been added according to the *multiplicity* $\mu : M \rightarrow I\!N$.

Matrix characterization. *A matrix M is valid iff there exists a multiplicity μ, a first-order substitution σ and a set of connections $\mathcal{C}$, such that every path through M^μ contains a complementary connection of $\mathcal{C}$, i.e. a connection $\{A_1, \neg A_2\} \in \mathcal{C}$ with $\sigma(A_1) = \sigma(A_2)$.*

The connection calculus uses a *connection-driven* search strategy in order to calculate an appropriate set of connections $\mathcal{C}$. In each inference step a connection is identified along an active (sub-)path and only paths not containing the active path and this connection will be considered afterward. See [5,6,25] for more details. Proof search in the connection calculus is carried out by first applying the *start rule* and then repeatedly applying the *reduction* or the *extension rule*. The latter rules identify a connection $\{A_1, \neg A_2\}$ with $\sigma(A_1) = \sigma(A_2)$. An unification algorithm for calculating the first-order substitution σ is given in, e.g., [21].

Example 3. A proof in the connection calculus for the matrix M_1 of Example 1, using the graphical matrix representation, is given in Figure 3. It illustrates the seven proof steps required for a proof of M_1. The literals of each connection are connected with a line. The literals of the active path are boxed. While the extension steps connect a literal to a new clause (step 1, 2, 4, 5, and 6), the reduction steps connect to literals of the active path (step 3 and 7). With the first-order substitution $\sigma(x') = \sigma(x'') = c$ all paths through M_1 contain a complementary connection. Hence, the matrix M_1 and the original formula given in Example 1 are valid.

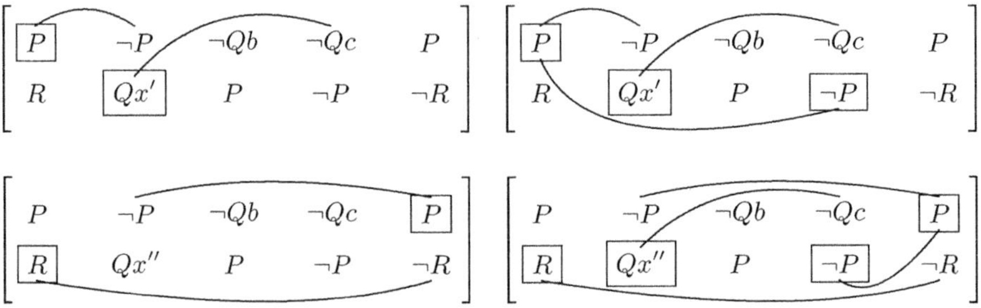

Fig. 3. A (graphical) proof in the connection calculus

6.2 The Automated Theorem Prover leanCoP

leanCoP [26,24] is an automated theorem prover for classical first-order logic with equality[1]. It is a very compact implementation of the connection calculus. The reduction rule of the connection calculus is applied before the extension rule. Open branches are selected depth-first and iterative deepening on the proof depth is performed in order to achieve completeness. Additional inference rules include regularity and lemmata [20], as well as restricted backtracking [25]. leanCoP uses an optimized structure-preserving transformation into clausal form and a fixed strategy scheduling [25].

leanCoP is implemented in Prolog and uses Prolog's built-in indexing mechanism to find connections quickly. Although the source code of the core proof search algorithm consists of only one Prolog predicate that is a few lines long, leanCoP shows a strong performance and is currently the fastest implementation of a connection calculus [25]. leanCoP has won several prizes at the CADE System Competition (CASC), a yearly competition for fully automatic theorem provers for first-order logic. E.g., at this years CASC-J5, leanCoP-Ω, an extended version of leanCoP, won the new TFA division that contains problems in first-order logic with arithmetic [31].

leanCoP can read input formulas in leanCoP syntax as well as in TPTP syntax [30]. Equality axioms are automatically added if required. The leanCoP core prover returns a very compact connection proof, which is translated into a readable proof. Several output formats are available. Version 2.2 of leanCoP supports the output of proofs in the new TPTP syntax for representing derivations in connection calculi [27]. SETHEO [19] and KoMeT [7] are other high-performance implementations of the connection calculus. SETHEO was, e.g., successfully used to verify large software systems [28].

[1] The leanCoP theorem prover is available under the GNU general public license. It can be downloaded from the leanCoP web site at `http://www.leancop.de`

7 The Case

In the following we will use the formal specification of the Chinese Wall policy and prove that the first-order formulas defining its operational semantics are in line with the expected high level behavior of the policy as stated in Section 3. For our case we will choose formula (4) of Requirement CW 2 of the Chinese Wall specification. We will give a brief overview of the used predicates, explain the implementation of this requirement in the corresponding leanCoP format, present certain actions we took to optimize the proof search and discuss the obtained result.

The operational semantics has been specified in 97 first-order formulas. The predicates used are `admissibleL`, `eappend`, `emember`, `info`, `sanitized`, `conflict` and `permitted`. `admissibleL` plays the role of a type guard. It makes sure that, in case the second parameter is set to `yes`, every log file `L` is well-formed according to the rules of the Chinese Wall policy. The predicate `eappend` is used to append two log files and takes into account that log files contain only elements that have a certain structure. Correspondingly, the predicate `emember` is true if a log file contains a given element when the third parameter is set to `yes`. When the third parameter is set to `no`, the predicate `emember` is true if a given log file does *not* contain the specified element. Using the additional parameter `yes`/`no`, instead of using the logical negation, ensures better control when using the predicate within other definitions. The predicate `info` defines the relation between concrete *information* and *data*-objects carrying it. The predicate `sanitized` is true if the given information is sanitized; otherwise it is false. The predicate `conflict` implements the conflict behavior between any two data objects that can be created, sent and received in a Chinese Wall scenario by the different subjects. It is true if there is a conflict between two data objects; otherwise it is false. The predicate `permitted` is true if, for a given log file, it is permitted to add the given element describing a specific operation.

Formula (4) of Requirement CW 2 in leanCoP format is presented in Figure 4. It can be decomposed into three different parts. The first part contains one `admissibleL` and two `eappend` predicates and ensures that the log file is well-formed. The second part

```
all OB: all OB1: all I: all T: all T1: all T2: all L:
all TT1: all TT2: all TT3: all L1:
all OPT1: all OPT2: all OBB1: all OBB2: all HEAD: all TAIL:
( ( (T1<=T2), (TT1<TT2), (TT2<=T2), admissibleL(L,yes),
    eappend([element(OPT1,OBB1,TT1)],L1,L),
    eappend(HEAD,[element(OPT2,OBB2,TT3)|TAIL],L),
    ( emember(element(new,OB,T),L,yes), (T<T1) ;
      emember(element(get,OB,T),L,yes), (T<T1) ),
    emember(element(drop,OB,T1),L,no),
    ( (info(I,OB1), sanitized(I)) ; ~ conflict(OB,OB1) )
  ) => permitted(get,OB1,T2,L,yes)
)
```

Fig. 4. Chinese Wall requirement of formula (4) in leanCoP format

specifies that the log file contains an element with a `new` operation or an element with a `get` operation regarding an object `OB`. It further states that there was no `drop` operation of this object since then. The third part of the formula ensures that there is no conflict between the object `OB` and another object `OB1`. This is true if the other object carries sanitized information only, or if there is no direct conflict between the two objects. Compared to the original formula (4) in Section 3, the order of some predicates have been changed in order to optimize the proof search. For the same reason the current formalization considers only one subject s.

The formula shown in Figure 4 has been proved fully automatically using the automated theorem prover leanCoP. The translated input formula consists of 185 clauses. leanCoP finds a proof in 80 seconds, performing more than 10 million inference steps during the proof search. The final proof consists of 148 proof steps and is output in a readable form. The proof is non-trivial and shows that fully automated tools are necessary in order to find proofs for these kinds of problems. Table 1 contains a summary of the statistics for the proof found by leanCoP.

By default leanCoP uses a fixed strategy scheduling, where different proof search strategies are consecutively invoked in order to increase the chance to find a proof. If the given formulas have a specific form, specific strategies can be switched on or off in order to speed up the proof process. It turned out that for our formulas the strategy "`[def,conj,cut]`" is the most successful one (see [24] for details). It uses a definitional transformation into clausal form, starts the proof search with the conjecture clauses, and uses restricted backtracking, a technique that restricts the search space in a very effective way [25]. Hence, these settings were also used to find the proof for the requirement given in Figure 4.

During the development of the formal specification many adjustment were necessary, in order to ensure correctness of the given specification. This process is probably as difficult as the proof process itself. But once the formal specification is done, it can be used to prove similar requirements with only little additional effort.

Table 1. Some statistics about the proof found by leanCoP

Number of formal axioms	97
Number of input clauses	185
Number of required inference steps	10.687.197
Number of proof steps in final proof	148
Time required to find the proof	80 seconds

The obtained result is an example of a formal verification of a part of the policy model based on the given policy as introduced in Figure 1. It helps to countercheck the top-down development of the policy by a bottom-up verification.

8 Related Work

Although it has been long established in the scientific community that integrated models and tools are needed to address security issues [9], research solutions often have focused on technical issues. There is no holistic approach taking care of the interplay between the

IT and the business universe. Besides a generic interest in integrating different models, there is the claim that different concerns should be covered by specific models [12] to reduce the overall complexity for each single model. As a result, architectural models and security requirements are usually handled separately, even if there might be an integrated view at the end. In order to be useful in practice, models have usually been required to be suitable to model checking and simulation [17], which allows for an automatic evaluation of their security properties. Therefore models often have to reduce the level of details that are available to the formal analysis [33]. There are only few examples where first-order reasoning is used to deal with issues of real-world business applications [29].

Regarding the universe of models there are suggestions to look at the physical, logical and business layer in a separate way and to differentiate between a static build-time and a dynamic run-time view [10,22]. Regarding the IT landscape there are suggestions to look at the security issues of components and the ones of the overall system in a separate way [16] or to separate the handling of policies and security principles [1]. In addition to classical logic used to reason about security models, fuzzy reasoning and fuzzy measurement can be used to cover additional aspects in the security domain [35]. From an architectural point of view there are proposals to extract security functionality out of single applications making it available as general security services [3].

In today's security research literature and in the practical field, there is a strong focus on basic technical issues like authentication, authorization, confidentiality and accountability. However, there is not much regarding the semantic or pragmatic aspects of security. Semantics comes into play when, for example, customer data and deposit data are not allowed to be displayed on the same screen at a time. Encryption does not help here, nor do authentication, authorization, confidentiality or accounting. Pragmatics show up when executing single operations of IT or business services is completely legal. However, a certain combination or thread of such operations might produce a situation that is not compliant with legal regulations. For example, opening a set of accounts to transfer money between them, which is a thread of business operations to fog the history of money's origin, might produce such a violation. The pragmatic aspect can be seen as a certain property of a material business dialog happening between a bank's employee and an IT service that is used [36]. The sound interplay between the business and IT universe is likewise not sufficiently elaborated yet [32].

9 Conclusion

The global financial crisis of the past few years has many different aspects which have been analyzed in a rapidly growing literature. With a few exceptions [23] the role of the IT systems involved in the financial business practices was thereby neglected despite the fact that the lack of transparency of those systems was not helpful in monitoring business policy issues that showed up as one of many reasons leading to this crisis.

International politics is now discussing the introduction of regulatory rules to prevent a future crisis of such a dimension. However, the way IT technology is used to automate business processes in the banking industry is currently very product-oriented. A methodological view is often neglected because of high operational pressures. By addressing methodological questions in a way that could lead to solutions highly usable by people in the field we have shown that the benefits of using formal tools enforcing business policies as well as legal policies become compelling. As a consequence the presented approach will help to lead to new opportunities that support the implementation of legal regulations in the banking industry.

Our approach is a first proof of concept demonstrating how fully implemented formal methods may support the enforcement of policies in a way that is integrated with the ongoing business. As such, it will help addressing some accountability, risk and security issues that cannot be handled successfully today. Therefore, it will support the reduction of risk factors that have shown to be of some importance in the context of the current crisis. Our contribution is just a first step into this direction. There is a lot more that needs to be done, such as providing the remaining horizontal and vertical verifications from Figure 1 for the Chinese Wall policy, verifying other security policies and IT landscapes, and finally creating a verification infrastructure that could be used by skilled people in the business. Nevertheless, our contribution built on top of first-order logic might be a step towards opening the door into such a future development of the financial system, because the methodology underlying our approach does have the full potential for the realization of a future development of this kind.

References

1. Al-Shaer, E.S., Hamed, H.H.: Management and translation of filtering security policies. In: IEEE International Conference on Communications, vol. 1, pp. 256–260 (2003)
2. Arbab, F.: Abstract Behavior Types: A Foundation. Model for Components and Their Composition. Science of Computer Programming 55(1-3), 3–52 (2005)
3. Baltatu, M., Lioy, A., Mazzicchi, D.: Security policy system: status and perspective. In: IEEE International Conference on Networks, pp. 278–284 (2000)
4. Bell, D., La Padula, L.: Secure Computer Systems: Unified Exposition and Multics Interpretation. MTR-2997, The MITRE Corporation, Bedford, MA (1975)
5. Bibel, W.: Matings in Matrices. Communications of the ACM 26, 844–852 (1983)
6. Bibel, W.: Automated Theorem Proving. Vieweg (1987)
7. Bibel, W., Brüning, S., Egly, U., Rath, T.: KoMeT. In: Bundy, A. (ed.) CADE 1994. LNCS(LNAI), vol. 814, pp. 783–787. Springer, Heidelberg (1994)
8. Brewer, D., Nash, M.: The Chinese Wall Security Policy. In: IEEE Symposium on Security and Privacy, pp. 206–214 (1989)
9. Cuppens, F., Saurel, C.: Specifying a security policy: a case study. In: 9th IEEE Computer Security Foundations Workshop, pp. 123–134 (1996)
10. Deswarte, Y., Blain, L., Fabre, J.-C.: Intrusion tolerance in distributed computing systems. In: IEEE Computer Society Symposium on Research in Security and Privacy, pp. 110–121 (1991)
11. Fitting, M.: First-Order Logic and Automated Theorem Proving. Springer, Heidelberg (1990)
12. Freeman, J.W., Neely, R.B., Heckard, M.A.: A validated security policy modeling approach. In: 10th Annual Computer Security Applications Conference, pp. 189–200 (1994)
13. Gentzen, G.: Untersuchungen über das logische Schließen. Mathematische Zeitschrift 39, 176–210, 405–431 (1935)
14. Halpern, J., Weissman, V.: Using First-Order Logic to Reason about Policies. ACM Transactions on Information and System Security 11(4), 21–41 (2008)
15. Hartel, P., van Eck, P., Etalle, S., Wieringa, R.: Modelling mobility aspects of security policies. In: Barthe, G., Burdy, L., Huisman, M., Lanet, J.-L., Muntean, T. (eds.) CASSIS 2004. LNCS, vol. 3362, pp. 172–191. Springer, Heidelberg (2005)

16. Ko, C., Fink, G., Levitt, K.: Automated detection of vulnerabilities in privileged programs by execution monitoring. In: 10th Annual Computer Security Applications Conference, pp. 134–144 (1994)
17. Kotenko, I.: Active vulnerability assessment of computer networks by simulation of complex remote attacks. In: International Conference on Computer Networks and Mobile Computing, pp. 40–47 (2003)
18. Kreitz, C., Otten, J.: Connection-based Theorem Proving in Classical and Non-classical Logics. Journal of Universal Computer Science 5, 88–112 (1999)
19. Letz, R., Schumann, J., Bayerl, S., Bibel, W.: Setheo: A High-performance Theorem Prover. Journal of Automated Reasoning 8, 183–212 (1992)
20. Letz, R., Stenz, G.: Model Elimination and Connection Tableau Procedures. In: Robinson, A., Voronkov, A. (eds.) Handbook of Automated Reasoning, pp. 2015–2114. Elsevier, Amsterdam (2001)
21. Martelli, A., Montanari, U.: An Efficient Unification Algorithm. ACM Transactions on Programming Languages and Systems 4, 258–282 (1982)
22. Menezes, R., Ford, R., Ondi, A.: Swarming computer security: an experiment in policy distribution. In: Swarm Intelligence Symposium, pp. 436–439 (2005)
23. Müller, G., Accorsi, R., Höhn, S., Sackmann, S.: Sichere Nutzungskontrolle für mehr Transparenz in Finanzmärkten. Informatik Spektrum 33(1), 3–13 (2010)
24. Otten, J.: leanCoP 2.0 and ileanCoP 1.2: High Performance Lean Theorem Proving in Classical and Intuitionistic Logic. In: Armando, A., Baumgartner, P., Dowek, G. (eds.) IJCAR 2008. LNCS (LNAI), vol. 5195, pp. 283–291. Springer, Heidelberg (2008)
25. Otten, J.: Restricting Backtracking in Connection Calculi. AI Communications 23(2-3), 159–182 (2010)
26. Otten, J., Bibel, W.: leanCoP: Lean Connection-Based Theorem Proving. Journal of Symbolic Computation 36(1-2), 139–161 (2003)
27. Otten, J., Sutcliffe, G.: Using the TPTP Language for Representing Derivations in Tableau and Connection Calculi. In: Konev, B., Schmidt, R., Schulz, S. (eds.) Workshop on Practical Aspects of Automated Reasoning, Edinburgh, UK (2010)
28. Schumann, J.: Automated Theorem Proving in Software Engineering. Springer, Heidelberg (2002)
29. Stolzenburg, F., Thomas, B.: Analyzing Rule Sets for the Calculation of Banking Fees by a Theorem Prover with Constraints. In: Bibel, W., Schmitt, P.H. (eds.) Automated Deduction - A Basis for Applications, vol. III, pp. 243–264. Kluwer, Dordrecht (1998)
30. Sutcliffe, G.: The TPTP Problem Library and Associated Infrastructure. The FOF and CNF Parts, v3.5.0. Journal of Automated Reasoning 43(4), 337–362 (2009)
31. Sutcliffe, G.: The 5th IJCAR Automated Theorem Proving System Competition. AI Communications (to appear 2011)
32. Tatsubori, M., Imamura, T., Nakamura, Y.: Best-practice patterns and tool support for configuring secure web services messaging. In: IEEE International Conference on Web Services, pp. 244–251 (2004)
33. Trcek, D.: Security policy management for networked information systems. In: Network Operations and Management Symposium, pp. 817–830 (2000)
34. Waaler, A.: Connections in Nonclassical Logics. In: Robinson, A., Voronkov, A. (eds.) Handbook of Automated Reasoning, pp. 1487–1578. Elsevier, Amsterdam (2001)
35. Xie, W., Ma, H.: A policy-based security model for web system. In: IEEE International Conference on Communication Technology, vol. 1, pp. 187–191 (2003)
36. Yu, C.-F.: Access control and authorization plan for customer control of network services. In: IEEE Global Telecommunications Conference, vol. 2, pp. 862–869 (1989)

Change Management for Heterogeneous Development Graphs*

Serge Autexier, Dieter Hutter, and Till Mossakowski

German Research Center for Artificial Intelligence (DFKI GmbH)
Bremen, Germany

Abstract. The error-prone process of formal specification and verification of large systems requires an efficient, evolutionary formal development approach. Development graphs have been designed to support such an approach. They can formally represent the actual state of a software development comprising specification and verification work in a structured way and assist the user in her evolutionary development by the incorporated change management support. In this paper we extend this work with respect to heterogeneous development graphs allowing one to make use of different institutions, i.e. logics, for specifying and verifying large developments. We also push forward the idea of stringent locality of definitions by introducing pre-signatures and pre-signature morphisms, which allow us to build up signatures in an incremental and parametric way.

1 Introduction

Industrial applications of Formal Methods revealed that an efficient, evolutionary formal development approach is absolutely indispensable as it was hardly ever the case that the development steps were correctly designed in the first attempt. The search for formally correct software and the corresponding proofs is more like a formal reflection of partial developments rather than just a way to assure and prove more or less evident facts. Hence there is a need for computer-aided management of the many types of documents involved in the development of highly dependable systems and thus a need for an approach that keeps track of the various dependencies in and between such documents to provide efficient change management.

Development graphs are designed to encode an actual state of a software development in terms of a specification (represented by the nodes and the definition links of the graph) and of its verification (represented by theorem links and the attached proofs). Proof obligations, such as the requirement that a specification satisfies a security policy or that an implementation satisfies a requirement specification, can be represented as (global) theorem links connecting the corresponding theories.

Since software development is an incremental process, development graphs evolve over time. Changes in the specification are reflected by changes of the nodes and the definition links while improvements in the verification work are

* Research supported by BMBF under research grant 01 IW 07002 *FormalSafe*, and DFG under research grant Hu737/3-1 *OMoC*.

S. Siegler and N. Wasser (Eds.): Walther Festschrift, LNAI 6463, pp. 54–80, 2010.

reflected by additional theorem links and attached proofs to justify proposed requirements of the system. Specification and verification activities are intertwined resulting in the need for re-justification of existing proofs once the specification has changed.

In previous work we developed a management of change for formal specifications and proofs to save as much verification work as possible upon changing the specification [9,2,1]. That work exploited the hierarchical structure of logical dependencies between theories and established theory inclusion relationships, to devise a procedure computing non-interference properties of changes in logical theories and established relationships. In this paper we extend this work with respect to heterogeneous development graphs [13] allowing one to make use of different institutions, i.e. logics, for specifying and verifying large developments. In Section 2 we start with a brief overview on the notions of institutions and their (co-)morphisms. A guiding principle of designing development graphs is the stringent locality of specifications. In Section 3 we introduce pre-signatures and pre-signature morphisms allowing us to build up signatures in an incremental and parametric way and in Section 4 we extend this notion to (co-)morphisms between institutions. Based on this foundation we redefine the framework of heterogeneous development graphs in terms of pre-signatures in Section 5 and provide the proof rules for the verification in the large in Section 6. Section 7 is devoted to an analysis of how changes in the specification will affect the applicability of proof rules as well as their results in order to implement a smart replay of proofs in a changed environment.

2 Institutions and Their (Co)Morphisms

Institutions [7] formally capture the notion of logical systems, abstracting away from the details of vocabularies (signatures), sentences, models, and satisfaction (of sentences in models). When working with heterogeneous formal specifications, also mappings between institutions are important.

Definition 1. *An* institution $\mathcal{I}$ *consists of:*

- *a category* $\mathbf{Sign}_\mathcal{I}$ *of* signatures*;*
- *a functor* $\mathbf{Sen}_\mathcal{I}\colon \mathbf{Sign}_\mathcal{I} \to \mathbf{Set}$*,giving a set* $\mathbf{Sen}(\Sigma)$ *of* Σ-sentences *for each signature* $\Sigma \in |\mathbf{Sign}_\mathcal{I}|$*, and a function* $\mathbf{Sen}(\sigma)\colon \mathbf{Sen}(\Sigma) \to \mathbf{Sen}(\Sigma')$ *that yields* σ-translation *of* Σ*-sentences to* Σ'*-sentences for each signature morphism* $\sigma\colon \Sigma \to \Sigma'$*;*
- *a functor* $\mathbf{Mod}_\mathcal{I}\colon \mathbf{Sign}_\mathcal{I}^{op} \to \mathbf{Set}$*,giving a set* $\mathbf{Mod}(\Sigma)$ *of* Σ-models *for each signature* $\Sigma \in |\mathbf{Sign}_\mathcal{I}|$*, and a functor* $\mathbf{Mod}(\sigma)\colon \mathbf{Mod}(\Sigma') \to \mathbf{Mod}(\Sigma)$*, denoted by* $\_|_\sigma$*, that yields* σ-reducts *of* Σ'*-models for each signature morphism* $\sigma\colon \Sigma \to \Sigma'$*; and*
- *for each* $\Sigma \in |\mathbf{Sign}_\mathcal{I}|$*, a* satisfaction relation $\models_{\mathcal{I},\Sigma}\ \subseteq \mathbf{Mod}_\mathcal{I}(\Sigma) \times \mathbf{Sen}_\mathcal{I}(\Sigma)$

such that for any signature morphism $\sigma\colon \Sigma \to \Sigma'$*,* Σ*-sentence* $\varphi \in \mathbf{Sen}_\mathcal{I}(\Sigma)$ *and* Σ'*-model* $M' \in \mathbf{Mod}_\mathcal{I}(\Sigma')$*:*

$$M' \models_{\mathcal{I},\Sigma'} \sigma(\varphi) \iff M'|_\sigma \models_{\mathcal{I},\Sigma} \varphi \qquad [\textit{Satisfaction condition}]$$

The next concept we need is a mapping between institutions. We concentrate here on *institution morphisms* [7] and on *institution comorphisms* (named so in [6]; see "plain maps of institutions" in [11] and "institution representations" in [20,21]).

Definition 2. *Let $\mathcal{I}$ and $\mathcal{I}'$ be institutions. An* institution morphism $\mu\colon \mathcal{I} \to \mathcal{I}'$ *consists of:*

- *a functor $\mu^{Sign}\colon \mathbf{Sign} \to \mathbf{Sign}'$;*
- *a natural transformation $\mu^{Sen}\colon \mathbf{Sen}' \circ \mu^{Sign} \to \mathbf{Sen}$, that is, a family of functions $\mu^{Sen}_\Sigma\colon \mathbf{Sen}'(\mu^{Sign}(\Sigma)) \to \mathbf{Sen}(\Sigma)$, natural in $\Sigma \in |\mathbf{Sign}|$; and*
- *a natural transformation $\mu^{Mod}\colon \mathbf{Mod} \to \mathbf{Mod}' \circ (\mu^{Sign})^{op}$, that is, a family of functions $\mu^{Mod}_\Sigma\colon \mathbf{Mod}(\Sigma) \to \mathbf{Mod}'(\mu^{Sign}(\Sigma))$, natural in $\Sigma \in |\mathbf{Sign}|$,*

such that for any signature $\Sigma \in |\mathbf{Sign}|$, the translations $\mu^{Sen}_\Sigma\colon \mathbf{Sen}'(\rho^{Sign}(\Sigma)) \to \mathbf{Sen}(\Sigma)$ of sentences and $\mu^{Mod}_\Sigma\colon \mathbf{Mod}(\Sigma) \to \mathbf{Mod}'(\rho^{Sign}(\Sigma))$ of models preserve the satisfaction relation, i.e., for any $\varphi' \in \mathbf{Sen}'(\mu^{Sign}(\Sigma))$ and $M \in \mathbf{Mod}(\Sigma)$:

$$M \models_\Sigma \mu^{Sen}_\Sigma(\varphi') \iff \mu^{Mod}_\Sigma(M) \models'_{\mu^{Sign}(\Sigma)} \varphi' \qquad [\textit{Satisfaction condition}]$$

Institution morphisms compose in the obvious, component-wise manner.

An institution comorphism $\rho\colon \mathcal{I} \to \mathcal{I}'$ *consists of:*

- *a functor $\rho^{Sign}\colon \mathbf{Sign} \to \mathbf{Sign}'$;*
- *a natural transformation $\rho^{Sen}\colon \mathbf{Sen} \to \mathbf{Sen}' \circ \rho^{Sign}$, that is, a family of functions $\rho^{Sen}_\Sigma\colon \mathbf{Sen}(\Sigma) \to \mathbf{Sen}'(\rho^{Sign}(\Sigma))$, natural in $\Sigma \in |\mathbf{Sign}|$; and*
- *a natural transformation $\rho^{Mod}\colon \mathbf{Mod}' \circ (\rho^{Sign})^{op} \to \mathbf{Mod}$, that is, a family of functions $\rho^{Mod}_\Sigma\colon \mathbf{Mod}'(\rho^{Sign}(\Sigma)) \to \mathbf{Mod}(\Sigma)$, natural in $\Sigma \in |\mathbf{Sign}|$,*

such that for any $\Sigma \in |\mathbf{Sign}|$, the translations $\rho^{Sen}_\Sigma\colon \mathbf{Sen}(\Sigma) \to \mathbf{Sen}'(\rho^{Sign}(\Sigma))$ of sentences and $\rho^{Mod}_\Sigma\colon \mathbf{Mod}'(\rho^{Sign}(\Sigma)) \to \mathbf{Mod}(\Sigma)$ of models preserve the satisfaction relation, i.e., for any $\varphi \in \mathbf{Sen}(\Sigma)$ and $M' \in \mathbf{Mod}'(\rho^{Sign}(\Sigma))$:

$$M' \models'_{\rho^{Sign}(\Sigma)} \rho^{Sen}_\Sigma(\varphi) \iff \rho^{Mod}_\Sigma(M') \models_\Sigma \varphi \qquad [\textit{Satisfaction condition}]$$

Institution comorphisms compose in the obvious, component-wise manner.

Even though the only essential difference between institution morphisms and comorphisms is in the direction of sentence and model translations wrt. signature translation, the intuition they capture is quite different. Very informally, an institution morphism $\mu\colon \mathcal{I} \to \mathcal{I}'$ shows how a "richer" institution $\mathcal{I}$ is "projected" onto a "poorer" institution $\mathcal{I}'$ (by removing some parts of signatures and models of $\mathcal{I}$ to obtain the simpler signatures and models of $\mathcal{I}'$, and by embedding simpler $\mathcal{I}'$-sentences into more powerful $\mathcal{I}$-sentences). Then, an institution comorphism $\mathcal{I} \to \mathcal{I}'$ shows how a "simpler" institution $\mathcal{I}$ is represented in a "more complex" institution $\mathcal{I}'$ (by representing the simpler signatures and sentences of

$\mathcal{I}$ as signatures and sentences of $\mathcal{I}'$, and extracting simpler $\mathcal{I}$-models from more complex $\mathcal{I}'$-models).[1]

Definition 3. *Institution comorphisms can induce institution morphisms via natural transformations: let* $\rho\colon \mathcal{I} \to \mathcal{I}'$ *be an institution comorphism, let* $\mu^{Sign}\colon \mathbf{Sign}' \to \mathbf{Sign}$ *be a functor and* $\varepsilon\colon \rho^{Sign} \circ \mu^{Sign} \to id_{\mathbf{Sign}'}$ *a natural transformation. Then* ρ ε*-induces the institution morphism* $\mu = \langle \mu^{Sign}, \mu^{Sen}, \mu^{Mod} \rangle\colon \mathcal{I}' \to \mathcal{I}$, *where for* $\Sigma' \in |\mathbf{Sign}'|$, $\mu^{Sen}_{\Sigma'} = \mathbf{Sen}'(\varepsilon_{\Sigma'}) \circ \rho^{Sen}_{\mu^{Sign}(\Sigma')}$ *and* $\mu^{Mod}_{\Sigma} = \rho^{Mod}_{\mu^{Sign}(\Sigma')} \circ \mathbf{Mod}'(\varepsilon_{\Sigma'})$. *Given such an institution morphism* μ, *we denote the corresponding institution comorphism* ρ *by* $CoM(\mu)$.

3 Institutions with Pre-signatures

The abstractness of the signatures in the definition of institution (they are just a category) makes it difficult to develop a change management, which is based on manipulation of individual symbols that constitute a signature. Hence, we need to equip institutions with additional structure such that signatures behave more set-like. There are several approaches in this vein in the literature [19,8,12]. Most of these approaches formalize the fact that signatures are sets with some structure. Here we follow a radical approach by requiring that signatures in a sense *are* sets (more precisely, can be embedded into sets), such that from a set, we can go back to the corresponding signature in a unique way. This ensures that we can unite signatures, intersect them, etc. Of course, only *some* sets are signatures, while in general, such operations only deliver *pre-signatures.*

Definition 4. *An* institution with pre-signatures *is an institution equipped with an embedding* $|\_|\colon \mathbf{Sign} \to \mathbf{Set}$, *the* symbol functor, *and a map* $sym\colon \bigcup_{\Sigma \in |\mathbf{Sign}|} \mathbf{Sen}(\Sigma) \to |\mathbf{Set}|$, *such that*

$$\varphi \in \mathbf{Sen}(\Sigma) \text{ iff } sym(\varphi) \subseteq |\Sigma|$$

for all $\varphi \in \bigcup_{\Sigma \in |\mathbf{Sign}|} \mathbf{Sen}(\Sigma)$. *The map sym gives the set of symbols used in a sentence, and sentences are uniform in the sense that a well-formed sentence is well-formed over a certain signature iff its symbols belong to that signature. Moreover, we require that any inclusion* $\iota\colon |\Sigma_1| \hookrightarrow |\Sigma_2|$ *is a signature morphism (i.e., is in the image of* $|\_|$*).*

In the sequel, we fix an arbitrary institution with pre-signatures. A *pre-signature* Σ is a set, and a *pre-signature morphism* $\bar{\sigma}$ consists of a right-unique set of pairs $graph(\bar{\sigma})$ and a set $dom(\bar{\sigma})$, subject to the requirement that $dom(\bar{\sigma}) \subseteq def(\bar{\sigma})$, where $def(\bar{\sigma}) = \{x | \exists y.\ (x,y) \in graph(\bar{\sigma})\}$. We also define $codef(\bar{\sigma}) = \{y | \exists x.\ (x,y) \in graph(\bar{\sigma})\}$. We write $\bar{\sigma}(x) = y$ iff $(x,y) \in graph(\bar{\sigma})$, and $\bar{\sigma}(x) =$

[1] Variants of comorphisms are also used to encode "more complex" institutions into "simpler" ones: e.g. in [6], a so-called simple theoroidal comorphism is used to code first-order logic with equality in first-order logic without equality. See also [16] for discussion of relative strength of logical systems in a similar context.

$\perp$ iff $x \notin \mathit{def}(\bar{\sigma})$. Pre-signature morphisms will be later related to signature morphisms, and the intuition is that the symbols in $\mathit{dom}(\bar{\sigma})$ must be mapped by the signature morphism, while the symbols in $\mathit{def}(\bar{\sigma}) \setminus \mathit{dom}(\bar{\sigma})$ may be mapped. Given a pre-signature morphism $\bar{\sigma}$ and a pre-signature Σ, define the induced function as

$$\mathit{fun}_{\Sigma}(\bar{\sigma}) = \mathit{graph}(\bar{\sigma})|_{|\Sigma|} \cup \mathit{Id}_{|\Sigma| \setminus \mathit{def}(\bar{\sigma}|_{|\Sigma|})},$$

where $\mathit{graph}(\bar{\sigma})$ is construed as a function and $\bar{\sigma}|_X$ denotes the restriction of $\bar{\sigma}$ to X.

A pre-signature morphism $\bar{\sigma}$ is *well-formed* wrt. a source signature Σ_1 and a target signature Σ_2, if $\mathit{dom}(\bar{\sigma}) \subseteq |\Sigma_1|$ and there exists a signature morphism $\sigma\colon \Sigma_1 \to \Sigma_2$ with $|\sigma| = \mathit{fun}_{|\Sigma_1|}(\bar{\sigma})$. In this case, σ is unique and is called *the signature morphism from Σ_1 to Σ_2 induced by $\bar{\sigma}$* and we will not distinguish between the σ and $\bar{\sigma}$ if Σ_1 and Σ_2 are clear from the context.

Composition of pre-signature morphisms is defined by

$$\bar{\sigma}_2 \circ \bar{\sigma}_1(x) := \begin{cases} \bar{\sigma}_2(\bar{\sigma}_1(x)) & \text{if } x \in \mathit{def}(\bar{\sigma}_1) \text{ and } \bar{\sigma}_1(x) \in \mathit{def}(\bar{\sigma}_2) \\ \bar{\sigma}_1(x) & \text{if } x \in \mathit{def}(\bar{\sigma}_1) \text{ and } \bar{\sigma}_1(x) \notin \mathit{def}(\bar{\sigma}_2) \\ \bar{\sigma}_2(x) & \text{if } x \notin \mathit{def}(\bar{\sigma}_1) \text{ and } x \in \mathit{def}(\bar{\sigma}_2) \\ \perp & \text{otherwise} \end{cases}$$
$$\mathit{dom}(\bar{\sigma}_2 \circ \bar{\sigma}_1) := \mathit{dom}(\bar{\sigma}_1)$$

The following is straightforward:

Proposition 5. *Composition of pre-signature morphisms is associative.*

The definition of composition ensures the following property:

Proposition 6. *If $\mathit{codef}(\mathit{fun}_{\Sigma_1}(\bar{\sigma}_1)) \subseteq |\Sigma_2|$, then*

$$\mathit{fun}_{\Sigma_2}(\bar{\sigma}_2) \circ \mathit{fun}_{\Sigma_1}(\bar{\sigma}_1) = \mathit{fun}_{\Sigma_1}(\bar{\sigma}_2 \circ \bar{\sigma}_1)$$

Proof. Both sides of the equation, when applied to $x \in |\Sigma_1|$, yield

$$\bar{\sigma}_2 \circ \bar{\sigma}_1(x) := \begin{cases} \bar{\sigma}_2(\bar{\sigma}_1(x)) & \text{if } x \in \mathit{def}(\bar{\sigma}_1) \text{ and } \bar{\sigma}_1(x) \in \mathit{def}(\bar{\sigma}_2) \\ \bar{\sigma}_1(x) & \text{if } x \in \mathit{def}(\bar{\sigma}_1) \text{ and } \bar{\sigma}_1(x) \notin \mathit{def}(\bar{\sigma}_2) \\ \bar{\sigma}_2(x) & \text{if } x \notin \mathit{def}(\bar{\sigma}_1) \text{ and } x \in \mathit{def}(\bar{\sigma}_2) \\ x & \text{otherwise} \end{cases}$$

□

A pre-signature $\bar{\Sigma}$ is *well-formed*, if there exists a signature Σ with $|\Sigma| = \bar{\Sigma}$. Since $|\_|$ is an embedding, if Σ exists, it is uniquely determined by $\bar{\Sigma}$. Hence, in the sequel, we often will not distinguish between (a well-formed) $\bar{\Sigma}$ and Σ. In particular, the usual set-theoretic operations become available on signatures, the result being in some cases a (well-formed) signature and in some cases only a non-well-formed pre-signature. (Similar for signature morphisms: e.g. a signature morphism σ is an inclusion if $|\sigma|$ is.) Moreover, we will use pre-signatures also in the role of partial signatures, that is, we will work with pre-signatures that are well-formed only after union with a given (base) pre-signature. A similar remark holds for pre-signature morphisms.

Proposition 7. *Given a pre-signature morphism $\bar{\sigma}$ and three signatures $\Sigma, \Sigma', \Sigma''$ with $\Sigma \subseteq \Sigma'$ and let $\sigma : \Sigma \to \Sigma''$ (resp. $\sigma' : \Sigma' \to \Sigma''$) be the signature morphism induced by $\bar{\sigma}$ from Σ to Σ'' (resp. Σ' to Σ''). Then $\sigma' \circ \iota = \sigma$, where $\iota \colon \Sigma \to \Sigma'$ is the inclusion.*

Every signature morphism $\sigma : \Sigma \to \Sigma'$ induces a pre-signature morphism $\bar{\sigma}$ defined by

$$dom(\bar{\sigma}) := \{x \in \Sigma \mid \sigma(x) \neq x\} \text{ and } \bar{\sigma}(x) := \begin{cases} |\sigma|(x) & \text{if } x \in dom(\bar{\sigma}) \\ \bot & \text{otherwise} \end{cases}$$

Definition 8. *Given two pre-signature morphisms $\bar{\sigma}$ and $\bar{\sigma}'$, we say that $\bar{\sigma} \prec \bar{\sigma}'$ iff $def(\bar{\sigma}) \subseteq def(\bar{\sigma}')$, $dom(\bar{\sigma}) \subseteq dom(\bar{\sigma}')$, and for all $x \in dom(\bar{\sigma})$ $\bar{\sigma}(x) = \bar{\sigma}'(x)$.*

Proposition 9. *$\prec$ is a well-founded partial order on pre-signature morphisms.*

Proposition 10. *Let $\bar{\sigma}$ be a pre-signature morphism and $\sigma : \Sigma \to \Sigma'$ be its induced signature morphism between Σ and Σ'. Then for the pre-signature morphism $\bar{\sigma}'$ induced by σ, it holds that $\bar{\sigma}' \prec \bar{\sigma}$ and the signature morphism from Σ to Σ' induced by $\bar{\sigma}'$ is σ.*

Definition 11. *An institution comorphism $\rho : \mathcal{I} \to \mathcal{I}'$ is* modular *if there is*

- *$\rho^{PreSign}$ mapping pre-signatures to pre-signatures and pre-signature morphisms to pre-signature morphisms*[2] *and*
- *$\rho^{PreSen} \colon \bigcup_{\Sigma \in |\mathbf{Sign}|} \to \bigcup_{\Sigma \in |\mathbf{Sign}'|}$*

satisfying the following conditions:

1. $|\rho^{Sign}(\Sigma)| = \rho^{PreSign}(|\Sigma|)$,
2. $|\rho^{Sign}(\sigma)| = \rho^{PreSign}(|\sigma|)$,
3. $\rho^{PreSign}(fun_\Sigma(\bar{\sigma})) = fun_{\rho(\Sigma)}(\rho^{PreSign}(\bar{\sigma}))$,
4. *for each signature morphism $\sigma : \Sigma_1 \to \Sigma_2$,*

$$|\rho^{Sign}(\Sigma_2)| = |\rho^{Sign}(\sigma)|(|\rho^{Sign}(\Sigma_1)|) \cup \rho^{PreSign}(|\Sigma_2| \setminus |\sigma|(|\Sigma_1|))$$

5. $\rho^{Sen}_\Sigma(\varphi) = \rho^{PreSen}(\varphi)$, *if $\varphi \in \mathbf{Sen}(\Sigma)$.*

The first three conditions express that the signature translation functor can somehow be extended to pre-signatures (even if we only get something roughly behaving like a functor there), while the fourth condition expresses modularity: we can translate the symbols of Σ_1 and those added in Σ_2 separately. The fifth condition is a uniformity requirement for the sentence translations: they need to be combinable into a global sentence translation.

[2] Note that this is not the same as a functor **Set** $\to$ **Set**, since pre-signature morphisms are not equipped with codomains, and domains also differ from their standard meaning.

Proposition 12. *If $\rho : \mathcal{I} \to \mathcal{I}'$ is modular, then for any signatures Σ_1, Σ_2 in $\mathcal{I}$ such that $\Sigma_1 \cup \Sigma_2$ is well-formed,*

$$|\rho^{Sign}(\Sigma_1 \cup \Sigma_2)| = |\rho^{Sign}(\Sigma_1)| \cup |\rho^{Sign}(\Sigma_2)|$$

Indeed, many institutions described in the literature, ranging from propositional over equational, first-order, modal and temporal logics to higher-order logic, can be formalized as institutions with pre-signatures, and many (co)morphisms can be made modular.

4 Heterogeneous Logical Environments

Given the two possible ways to link institutions with each other, a notion of a *heterogeneous logical environment* may be formalized as a collection of institutions linked by institution morphisms and comorphisms.

Definition 13. *A* modular heterogeneous logical environment $\mathcal{HLE}$ *is a collection of institutions with pre-signatures and of modular institution morphisms and comorphisms between them, that is, a pair of diagrams $\langle \mathcal{HLE}^\mu : \mathcal{G}^\mu \to \mathcal{INS}, \mathcal{HLE}^\rho : \mathcal{G}^\rho \to co\mathcal{INS}\rangle$[3] in the category $\mathcal{INS}$ of institutions and their morphisms and $co\mathcal{INS}$ of institutions and their comorphisms, respectively, such that the two underlying graphs have no common edges and diagrams coincide on common nodes, i.e., for all nodes $n \in |\mathcal{G}^\mu| \cap |\mathcal{G}^\rho|$, $\mathcal{HLE}^\mu(n) = \mathcal{HLE}^\rho(n)$.*

We write $\mathcal{G}$ for the union of $\mathcal{G}^\mu$ and $\mathcal{G}^\rho$, and w.l.o.g. assume that all the nodes of the underlying graphs are common, $|\mathcal{G}| = |\mathcal{G}^\mu| = |\mathcal{G}^\rho|$.

For simplicity, we assume that each institution morphisms in $\mathcal{HLE}$ is induced by some institution comorphism in $\mathcal{HLE}$ via some natural transformation (see Def. 3) which is a pointwise inclusion. Most practical examples obey this additional assumption.

Definition 14. *Consider institutions $\mathcal{I}$ and $\mathcal{I}'$ and signatures $\Sigma \in |\mathbf{Sign}|$ and $\Sigma' \in |\mathbf{Sign}'|$.*

A heterogeneous signature morphism *is a pair $\langle \mu, \sigma \rangle : \Sigma \to \Sigma'$ that consists of an institution morphism $\mu : \mathcal{I}' \to \mathcal{I}$ and a signature morphism $\sigma : \Sigma \to \mu^{Sign}(\Sigma')$ in* **Sign**. *It induces the* heterogeneous reduct $\_|_{\langle \mu, \sigma \rangle} : \mathbf{Mod}'(\Sigma') \to \mathbf{Mod}(\Sigma)$ *defined as the composition $\mathbf{Mod}(\sigma) \circ \mu^{Mod}_{\Sigma'}$, i.e., $M'|_{\langle \mu, \sigma \rangle} = \mu^{Mod}_{\Sigma'}(M')|_\sigma$, for all $M' \in \mathbf{Mod}'(\Sigma')$.*

A heterogeneous pre-signature morphism *is a pair $\langle \mu, \Delta \rangle$ that consists of an institution morphism $\mu : \mathcal{I}' \to \mathcal{I}$ and a pre-signature Δ. It is* well-formed *wrt. a source signature Σ and target signature Σ' if there is some heterogeneous signature morphism $\langle \mu, \sigma \rangle : \Sigma \to \Sigma'$ such that $|\sigma|$ is an inclusion and $\rho^{Sign}(\Sigma') \setminus \Sigma = \Delta$. In this case, $\langle \mu, \sigma \rangle$ is called the heterogeneous signature morphism from Σ to Σ' induced by $\langle \mu, \Delta \rangle$.*

---

[3] We assume that $\mathcal{G}^\mu$ is a graph that gives the shape of the diagram; its nodes $n \in |\mathcal{G}^\mu|$ carry institutions $\mathcal{HLE}^\mu(n)$ linked by institution morphisms $\mathcal{HLE}^\mu(e) : \mathcal{HLE}^\mu(n) \to \mathcal{HLE}^\mu(m)$ for each edge $e : n \to m$ in $\mathcal{G}$. Similar notation is used for diagrams in other categories.

A heterogeneous signature comorphism *is a pair* $\langle\rho,\sigma'\rangle\colon \Sigma \to \Sigma'$ *that consists of an institution comorphism* $\rho{:}\mathcal{I} \to \mathcal{I}'$ *and a signature morphism* $\sigma'{:}\rho^{Sign}(\Sigma) \to \Sigma'$ *in* $\mathbf{Sign}'$. *It induces the* heterogeneous reduct $\_|_{\langle\rho,\sigma'\rangle}\colon \mathbf{Mod}'(\Sigma') \to \mathbf{Mod}(\Sigma)$ *defined as the composition* $\rho^{Mod}_{\Sigma} \circ \mathbf{Mod}'(\sigma')$, *i.e.,* $M'|_{\langle\rho,\sigma'\rangle} = \rho^{Mod}_{\Sigma}(M'|_{\sigma'})$, *for all* $M' \in \mathbf{Mod}'(\Sigma')$.

A heterogeneous pre-signature comorphism *is a pair* $\langle\rho,\bar\sigma\rangle$ *that consists of an institution comorphism* $\rho\colon \mathcal{I} \to \mathcal{I}'$ *and a pre-signature morphism* $\bar\sigma$. *It is* well-formed *if there is some heterogeneous signature comorphism* $\langle\rho,\sigma\rangle\colon \Sigma \to \Sigma'$ *such that* σ *is the signature morphism (in* $\mathcal{I}'$*) from* $\rho^{Sign}(\Sigma)$ *to* Σ' *induced by* $\bar\sigma$. *In this case,* $\langle\rho,\sigma\rangle$ *is called the heterogeneous signature comorphism from* Σ *to* Σ' *induced by* $\langle\rho,\bar\sigma\rangle$.

Definition 15. *Given institutions* $\mathcal{I},\mathcal{I}'$ *and an* $\mathcal{I}$*-signature* Σ. *Two heterogeneous pre-signature comorphisms* $\langle\rho_1,\bar\sigma_1\rangle$ *and* $\langle\rho_2,\bar\sigma_2\rangle$ *with* $\rho_1,\rho_2 : \mathcal{I} \to \mathcal{I}'$ *are* equivalent on Σ, *written* $\langle\rho_1,\bar\sigma_1\rangle \equiv_\Sigma \langle\rho_2,\bar\sigma_2\rangle$, *if* $\rho_1 = \rho_2$ *and* $fun_{\rho_1^{PreSign}(\Sigma)}(\bar\sigma_1) = fun_{\rho_1^{PreSign}(\Sigma)}(\bar\sigma_2)$.

Proposition 16. *Two heterogeneous pre-signature comorphisms* $\langle\rho_1,\bar\sigma_1\rangle$ *and* $\langle\rho_2,\bar\sigma_2\rangle$ *are equivalent on* Σ *if and only if* $\rho_1 = \rho_2$ *and* $\bar\sigma_1(x) = \bar\sigma_2(x)$ *for any* $x \in \rho_1^{PreSign}(\Sigma)$.

Definition 17. *Let* $\langle\rho,\sigma\rangle : \Sigma \to \Sigma'$ *be a heterogeneous signature comorphism. It induces the heterogeneous pre-signature comorphism* $\langle\rho,\bar\sigma\rangle$ *where* $\bar\sigma$ *is the pre-signature morphisms induced by the signature morphism* $\sigma : \rho^{PreSign}(\Sigma) \to \Sigma'$.

Proposition 18. *The heterogeneous pre-signature comorphism induced by a heterogeneous signature co-morphism* $\langle\rho,\sigma\rangle : \Sigma \to \Sigma'$ *is well-formed and induces the same signature co-morphism* $\langle\rho,\sigma\rangle$ *between* Σ *and* Σ'.

Given two heterogeneous signature comorphisms $\langle\rho_1,\sigma_1\rangle\colon \Sigma_1 \to \Sigma_2$ and $\langle\rho_2,\sigma_2\rangle\colon \Sigma_2 \to \Sigma_3$, their *composition* is defined as

$$\langle\rho_2,\sigma_2\rangle \circ \langle\rho_1,\sigma_1\rangle := \langle\rho_2 \circ \rho_1, \sigma_2 \circ \rho_2^{Sign}(\sigma_1)\rangle\colon \Sigma_1 \to \Sigma_3.$$

The problem of composing heterogeneous signature morphisms with heterogeneous signature comorphisms is solved by ε-inducibility:

Definition 19. *Given a heterogeneous signature morphism* $\langle\mu,\sigma\rangle\colon \Sigma \to \Sigma'$ *such that* μ *is* ε*-induced by the institution comorphism* ρ *(see Def. 3), the* ε-translation of $\langle\mu,\sigma\rangle$ *is the heterogeneous signature comorphism* $\langle\rho, \varepsilon_{\Sigma'} \circ \rho^{Sign}(\sigma)\rangle\colon \Sigma \to \Sigma'$.

Now compositions involving heterogeneous signature morphisms are computed by first moving to their ε-translations, and then performing composition of heterogeneous signature comorphisms. Note that the resulting heterogeneous signature comorphism in general cannot be translated back to a heterogeneous signature morphism; however, in the light of the following proposition, we do not care about this.

Proposition 20. *Sentence translation and model reduction for a heterogeneous signature morphism coincide with those of its ε-translation.*

Given two heterogeneous pre-signature comorphisms $\langle\rho_1,\bar{\sigma}_1\rangle$ and $\langle\rho_2,\bar{\sigma}_2\rangle$ their *composition* is defined as

$$\langle\rho_2,\bar{\sigma}_2\rangle \circ \langle\rho_1,\bar{\sigma}_1\rangle := \langle\rho_2 \circ \rho_1, \bar{\sigma}_2 \circ \rho_2^{PreSign}(\bar{\sigma}_1)\rangle.$$

Theorem 21 (Compatibility of Compositions). *Given heterogeneous pre-signature comorphisms $\langle\rho_1,\bar{\sigma}_1\rangle$ and $\langle\rho_2,\bar{\sigma}_2\rangle$, such that there are heterogeneous signature comorphisms $\langle\rho_1,\sigma_1\rangle\colon \Sigma_1 \to \Sigma_2$ and $\langle\rho_2,\sigma_2\rangle\colon \Sigma_2 \to \Sigma_3$ induced by $\langle\rho_1,\bar{\sigma}_1\rangle$ and $\langle\rho_2,\bar{\sigma}_2\rangle$, respectively, then*

$$\langle\rho_2,\sigma_2\rangle \circ \langle\rho_1,\sigma_1\rangle\colon \Sigma_1 \to \Sigma_3 \textit{ is induced by } \langle\rho_2,\bar{\sigma}_2\rangle \circ \langle\rho_1,\bar{\sigma}_1\rangle$$

Proof. Assume $|\sigma_1| = fun_{|\rho_1(\Sigma_1)|}(\bar{\sigma}_1)$ and $|\sigma_2| = fun_{|\rho_2(\Sigma_2)|}(\bar{\sigma}_2)$. We need to show $|\sigma_2 \circ \rho_2(\sigma_1)| = fun_{|\rho_2(\rho_1(\Sigma_1))|}(\bar{\sigma}_2 \circ \rho_2^{PreSign}(\bar{\sigma}_1))$. Now

$$\begin{aligned}
|\sigma_2 \circ \rho_2(\sigma_1)| &= |\sigma_2| \circ |\rho_2(\sigma_1)| \\
&= |\sigma_2| \circ \rho_2^{PreSign}(|\sigma_1|) \\
&= fun_{|\rho_2(\Sigma_2)|}(\bar{\sigma}_2) \circ \rho_2^{PreSign}(fun_{|\rho_1(\Sigma_1)|}(\bar{\sigma}_1)) \\
&= fun_{|\rho_2(\Sigma_2)|}(\bar{\sigma}_2) \circ fun_{|\rho_2(\rho_1(\Sigma_1))|}(\rho_2^{PreSign}(\bar{\sigma}_1)) \\
&= fun_{|\rho_2(\rho_1(\Sigma_1))|}(\bar{\sigma}_2 \circ \rho_2^{PreSign}(\bar{\sigma}_1)).
\end{aligned}$$

The last equation follows from Prop. 6 by noticing that $codef(fun_{|\rho_2(\rho_1(\Sigma_1))|}(\rho_2^{PreSign}(\bar{\sigma}_1))) \subseteq |\rho_2(\Sigma_2)|$ because $\rho_2(\sigma_1)\colon \rho_2(\rho_1(\Sigma_1)) \to \rho_2(\Sigma_2)$. □

Definition 22. *Given a heterogeneous pre-signature morphism $\langle\mu,\Delta\rangle$ such that μ is ε-induced by the institution comorphism ρ (see Def. 3), the* ε-translation *of $\langle\mu,\Delta\rangle$ is the heterogeneous pre-signature comorphism $\langle\rho,\emptyset\rangle$. The latter will induce a heterogeneous signature comorphism with a signature morphism component being an inclusion. Note that this is general enough because both ε and hiding wrt. Δ give inclusion signature morphisms.*

Again, compositions involving heterogeneous pre-signature morphisms are computed by first moving to their ε-translations, and then performing composition of heterogeneous pre-signature comorphisms.

5 Heterogeneous Development Graphs

We now define development graphs over modular heterogeneous logical environments. In the definition we carefully make explicit how the signature of a theory is built from the pre-signatures of imported nodes. Furthermore, we make explicit how the set of axioms of a theory is obtained from the imported set of axioms, where we also allow for the import of axioms via hiding links if they do not contain hidden symbols.

Definition 23. *Let $\mathcal{HLE}$ be a modular heterogeneous logical environment. A* heterogeneous development graph *over $\mathcal{HLE}$is an acyclic, directed graph $\mathcal{S} = \langle \mathcal{N}, \mathcal{L} \rangle$.*

$\mathcal{N}$ is a set of nodes. Each node $N \in \mathcal{N}$ is a tuple $(\mathcal{I}^N, \Sigma^N, \Gamma^N)$ such that $\mathcal{I}^N$ is an institution from $\mathcal{HLE}$, Σ^N is a $\mathcal{I}^N$-pre-signature called the **local signature** *of N, and Γ^N a set of $\mathcal{I}$-sentences called the* **local axioms** *of N.*

$\mathcal{L}$ is a set of directed links, so-called **definition links**, *between elements of $\mathcal{N}$. Global definition links import the whole subgraph below a node, while local definition links import only its local signature and local axioms. Hiding definition links are like global definition links, with the possibility to hide some symbols of the signature. Free definition links are like global definition links with the possibility to declare which symbols are freely generated in the target node. Formally, each definition link from a node M to a node N is either*

- **global** *(denoted $M \xRightarrow{\langle \rho, \bar{\sigma} \rangle} N$), annotated with a heterogeneous pre-signature comorphism $\langle \rho, \bar{\sigma} \rangle$ such that ρ is a comorphism from $\mathcal{I}^M$ to $\mathcal{I}^N$, or*
- **local** *(denoted $M \xrightarrow{\langle \rho, \bar{\sigma} \rangle} N$), again annotated with a heterogeneous pre-signature comorphism $\langle \rho, \bar{\sigma} \rangle$ such that ρ is a comorphism from $\mathcal{I}^M$ to $\mathcal{I}^N$, or*
- **hiding** *(denoted $M \xRightarrow[hide]{\langle \mu, \Delta \rangle} N$), annotated with a heterogeneous pre-signature morphism $\langle \mu, \Delta \rangle$ where Δ is a $\mathcal{I}^M$-pre-signature of symbols to hide, or*
- **free** *(denoted $M \xRightarrow[free]{\Sigma_F} N$), annotated with a pre-signature of symbols over which N is freely generated.*

The global pre-signature $Sig_{\mathcal{S}}(N)$ of some node N wrt. $\mathcal{S}$ *is defined inductively over the definition links:*

$$
\begin{aligned}
Sig_{\mathcal{S}}(N) = \Sigma^N \cup & \bigcup_{M \xRightarrow{\langle \rho, \bar{\sigma} \rangle} N \in \mathcal{S}} \bar{\sigma}(\rho^{PreSign}(Sig_{\mathcal{S}}(M))) \\
\cup & \bigcup_{M \xrightarrow{\langle \rho, \bar{\sigma} \rangle} N \in \mathcal{S}} \bar{\sigma}(\rho^{PreSign}(\Sigma^M \cup sym(\Gamma^M))) \\
\cup & \bigcup_{M \xRightarrow[hide]{\langle \mu, \Delta \rangle} N \in \mathcal{S}} \mu^{PreSign}(Sig_{\mathcal{S}}(M)) \setminus \Delta \\
\cup & \bigcup_{M \xRightarrow[free]{\Sigma_F} N \in \mathcal{S}} Sig_{\mathcal{S}}(M)
\end{aligned}
$$

A node N has a well-formed signature iff $Sig_{\mathcal{S}}(N)$ is a valid $\mathcal{I}^N$-signature. A development graph has a well-formed signature iff all its nodes have well-formed signatures.

Let M be a node with well-founded signature: we call the signature $Sig^{loc}_{\mathcal{S}}(M) := \langle \Sigma^M \cup sym(\Gamma^M) \rangle_{Sig_{\mathcal{S}}(M)}$ *the* local signature *of M.*

Given two nodes M and N with well-formed signatures, then

- $M \overset{\langle\rho,\bar{\sigma}\rangle}{\Longrightarrow} N$ *induces a heterogeneous signature comorphism* $\langle\rho,\sigma\rangle$ *from* $Sig_{\mathcal{S}}(M) \to Sig_{\mathcal{S}}(N)$*;*
- $M \overset{\langle\rho,\bar{\sigma}\rangle}{\longrightarrow} N$ *induces a heterogeneous signature comorphism* $\langle\rho,\sigma\rangle$ *from* $Sig^{loc}_{\mathcal{S}}(M) \to Sig_{\mathcal{S}}(N)$*;*
- $M \underset{hide}{\overset{\langle\mu,\Delta\rangle}{\Longrightarrow}} N$ *induces a heterogeneous signature morphism* $\langle\mu,\iota\rangle$ *where* $\iota : Sig_{\mathcal{S}}(N) \to \mu^{PreSign}(Sig_{\mathcal{S}}(M))$ *is the identity inclusion;*
- $M \underset{free}{\overset{\Sigma_F}{\Longrightarrow}} N$ *induces the trivial heterogeneous signature morphism* $\langle Id,\iota\rangle$.

We agree to use the above relation between heterogeneous pre-signature comorphisms and morphisms on links as notation throughout the rest of this paper.

The set of **global axioms** *of some N with well-formed signature is also defined inductively over the definition link structure:*

$$
\begin{aligned}
Ax_{\mathcal{S}}(N) = \Gamma^N \cup & \bigcup_{M \overset{\langle\rho,\bar{\sigma}\rangle}{\Longrightarrow} N \in \mathcal{S}} \sigma(\rho^{PreSen}(Ax_{\mathcal{S}}(M))) \\
\cup & \bigcup_{M \overset{\langle\rho,\bar{\sigma}\rangle}{\longrightarrow} N \in \mathcal{S}} \sigma(\rho^{PreSen}(\Gamma^M)) \\
\cup & \bigcup_{M \underset{hide}{\overset{\langle\mu,\Delta\rangle}{\Longrightarrow}} N \in \mathcal{S}} \{\varphi \in \mu^{PreSen}(Ax_{\mathcal{S}}(M)) | sym(\varphi) \cap \Delta = \emptyset\} \\
\cup & \bigcup_{M \underset{free}{\overset{\Sigma_F}{\Longrightarrow}} N \in \mathcal{S}} Ax_{\mathcal{S}}(M)
\end{aligned}
$$

A node N is well-formed iff it has a well-formed signature $Sig_{\mathcal{S}}(N)$ and $Ax_{\mathcal{S}}(N) \subseteq \mathbf{Sen}_{\mathcal{I}^N}(Sig_{\mathcal{S}}(N))$. A development graph is well-formed, if all its nodes are well-formed.

To simplify matters, we write $M \overset{\sigma}{\Longrightarrow} N \in \mathcal{S}$ instead of $M \overset{\sigma}{\Longrightarrow} N \in \mathcal{L}$ when $\mathcal{L}$ are the links of $\mathcal{S}$.

Since development graphs are acyclic, we can use induction principles in definitions and proofs concerning development graphs.

The next definition captures the existence of a path of local and global definition links between two nodes. Notice that such a path must not contain any hiding links.

Definition 24. *Let $\mathcal{S}$ be a development graph. The notion of* global reachability *is defined inductively: a node N is globally reachable from a node M via a heterogeneous pre-signature comorphism $\langle\rho,\bar{\sigma}\rangle$, $M \overset{\langle\rho,\bar{\sigma}\rangle}{\rightarrowtail\!\!\!\Rightarrow} N$ for short, iff*

- *either $M = N$ and $\rho = id$, $\bar{\sigma} = id$, or*
- *$M \overset{\langle\rho',\bar{\sigma}'\rangle}{\Longrightarrow} K \in \mathcal{S}$, and $K \overset{\langle\rho'',\bar{\sigma}''\rangle}{\rightarrowtail\!\!\!\Rightarrow} N$, with $\langle\rho,\bar{\sigma}\rangle = \langle\rho'',\bar{\sigma}''\rangle \circ \langle\rho',\bar{\sigma}'\rangle$.*

A node N is **locally reachable** *from a node M via a heterogeneous pre-signature comorphism $\langle\rho,\bar{\sigma}\rangle$, $M \overset{\langle\rho,\bar{\sigma}\rangle}{\rightarrowtail} N$ for short, iff $M \overset{\langle\rho,\bar{\sigma}\rangle}{\rightarrowtail\!\!\!\Rightarrow} N$ or there is a node K with $M \overset{\langle\rho',\bar{\sigma}'\rangle}{\longrightarrow} K \in \mathcal{S}$ and $K \overset{\langle\rho'',\bar{\sigma}''\rangle}{\rightarrowtail\!\!\!\Rightarrow} N$, such that $\langle\rho,\bar{\sigma}\rangle = \langle\rho'',\bar{\sigma}''\rangle \circ \langle\rho',\bar{\sigma}'\rangle$.*

Obviously global reachability implies local reachability.

Definition 25. *Let $\mathcal{S} = \langle\mathcal{N},\mathcal{L}\rangle$ be a development graph. A node $N \in \mathcal{N}$ is* flattenable *iff for all nodes $M \in \mathcal{N}$ with incoming hiding or free definition links, it holds that N is not globally reachable from M.*

The models of flattenable nodes do not depend on existing hiding or free links. For flattenable nodes N, $Ax_{\mathcal{S}}(N)$ captures N completely. However, this is not the case for nodes that are not flattenable. Therefore, we cannot define a theory semantics of development graphs and use a model-theoretic semantics, which is compatible with the theory semantics (see Prop. 28 below).

Definition 26. *Given a node $N \in \mathcal{N}$ with well-formed signature, its associated class $\mathbf{Mod}^{\mathcal{S}}(N)$ of models (or N-models for short) consists of those $Sig_{\mathcal{S}}(N)$-models n for which*

(i) n satisfies the local axioms Γ^N,

(ii) for each $K \overset{\langle\rho,\bar{\sigma}\rangle}{\Longrightarrow} N \in \mathcal{S}$, $n|_{\langle\rho,\sigma\rangle}$ is a K-model,

(iii) for each $K \overset{\langle\rho,\bar{\sigma}\rangle}{\longrightarrow} N \in \mathcal{S}$, $n|_{\langle\rho,\sigma\rangle}$ is a $Sig^{loc}_{\mathcal{S}}(K)$-model which satisfies the local axioms Γ^K, and

(iv) for each $K \overset{\langle\mu,\Delta\rangle}{\underset{hide}{\Longrightarrow}} N \in \mathcal{S}$ with $\iota : \mu^{PreSign}(Sig_{\mathcal{S}}(K)) \setminus \Delta \rightarrow Sig_{\mathcal{S}}(N)$ the corresponding inclusion mapping, $n|_{\langle id,\iota\rangle}$ has a $\langle\mu,\theta\rangle$-expansion k (i.e. $k|_{\langle\mu,\theta\rangle} = n|_{\langle id,\iota\rangle}$) that is a K-model where $\langle\mu,\theta\rangle$ is the heterogeneous signature morphism from $\mu^{PreSign}(Sig_{\mathcal{S}}(K)) \setminus \Delta$ to $Sig_{\mathcal{S}}(K)$ induced by $\langle\mu,\Delta\rangle$;

(v) for each $K \overset{\langle Id,\Sigma_F\rangle}{\underset{free}{\Longrightarrow}} N \in \mathcal{S}$, n is a K-model which is free (in the class of K-models) over its own ι-reduct, where ι: $\langle\Sigma_F\rangle_{Sig_{\mathcal{S}}(K)} \rightarrow Sig_{\mathcal{S}}(K)$ is the inclusion.

This definition of model classes nicely interacts with reachability:

Proposition 27. *Let $\mathcal{S}$ be a heterogeneous development graph. Then:*

1. *if $M \overset{\langle\rho,\bar{\sigma}\rangle}{\rightarrowtail\!\Rightarrow} N$ and $n \in \mathbf{Mod}^{\mathcal{S}}(N)$, then $n|_{\langle\rho,\sigma\rangle} \in \mathbf{Mod}^{\mathcal{S}}(M)$ where $\langle\rho,\sigma\rangle : Sig_{\mathcal{S}}(M) \to Sig_{\mathcal{S}}(N)$ is induced by $\langle\rho,\bar{\sigma}\rangle$.*
2. *if $M \overset{\langle\rho,\bar{\sigma}\rangle}{\rightarrowtail} N$ and $n \in \mathbf{Mod}^{\mathcal{S}}(N)$, then $n|_{\langle\rho,\sigma\rangle} \models \Gamma^M$ where $\langle\rho,\sigma\rangle : Sig^{loc}_{\mathcal{S}}(M) \to Sig_{\mathcal{S}}(N)$ is induced by $\langle\rho,\bar{\sigma}\rangle$.*

Proof. We prove (1) by easy induction over the definition of global reachability, and (2) by (1) and Definition 26. □

In the following we denote the class of Σ-models that fulfill the Σ-sentences Ψ by $\mathbf{Mod}_\Sigma(\Psi)$.

Proposition 28. *(1) $\mathbf{Mod}^{\mathcal{S}}(N) \subseteq \mathbf{Mod}_{Sig_{\mathcal{S}}(N)}(Axs(N))$.*
(2) If N is flattenable, then $\mathbf{Mod}^{\mathcal{S}}(N) = \mathbf{Mod}_{Sig_{\mathcal{S}}(N)}(Axs(N))$.

Proof. Let the height of some node N be the longest sequence of definition links $N_1 \to N_2 \ldots N_k \to N$ such that each transition $N_i \to N_{i+1}$ corresponds to some global, hiding, or free definition link and the first one $N_1 \to N_2$ may also be a local definition link.

(1) We proceed by induction over the height of N and assume $n \in \mathbf{Mod}^{\mathcal{S}}(N)$ and let $\varphi \in Axs(N)$. We consider the cases of the definition of $Axs(\_)$:
   - $\varphi \in \Gamma^N$: From Def. 26(i) it follows $n \models \varphi$.
   - $\varphi \in \langle\rho,\sigma\rangle(Axs(K))$ for some $K \overset{\langle\rho,\bar{\sigma}\rangle}{\Longrightarrow} N$: by Def. 26(iii) $n|_{\langle\rho,\sigma\rangle}$ is in $\mathbf{Mod}^{\mathcal{S}}(K)$ and by induction hypothesis $n|_{\langle\rho,\sigma\rangle} \models Axs(K)$; it follows $n \models \langle\rho,\sigma\rangle(Axs(K))$ by the satisfaction condition and hence $n \models \varphi$.
   - $\varphi \in \langle\rho,\sigma\rangle(\Gamma^K)$ for some $K \overset{\langle\rho,\bar{\sigma}\rangle}{\longrightarrow} N$: by Def. 26(ii) $n|_{\langle\rho,\sigma\rangle}$ is a $Sig^{loc}_{\mathcal{S}}$-model of Γ^K, i.e. $n \in \mathbf{Mod}_{Sig^{loc}_{\mathcal{S}}}(\Gamma^K)$; it follows $n \models \langle\rho,\sigma\rangle(\Gamma^K)$ by the satisfaction condition and hence $n \models \varphi$.
   - $\varphi \in \mu^{PreSen}(Axs(K)), sym(\varphi) \cap \Delta = \emptyset$ for some $K \underset{hide}{\overset{\langle\mu,\Delta\rangle}{\Longrightarrow}} N$: let $\iota : \mu^{PreSign}(Sig_{\mathcal{S}}(K)) \setminus \Delta \to Sig_{\mathcal{S}}(N)$, be the inclusion, then by Def. 26(iv) $n|_{\langle id,\iota\rangle}$ has $\langle\mu,\theta\rangle$-expansion k such that $k \in \mathbf{Mod}^{\mathcal{S}}(K)$. By induction hypothesis $k \models Axs(K)$ and hence $k|_{\langle\mu,\theta\rangle} \models \{\psi \in \mu^{Sen}(Axs(K)) | sym(\psi) \cap \Delta = \emptyset\}$; Since $n|_{\langle id,\iota\rangle} = k|_{\langle\mu,\theta\rangle}$ (see Def. 26(iv)), it follows that $n|_{\langle id,\iota\rangle} \models \varphi$ and thus by satisfaction condition and $\iota(\varphi) = \varphi$ it follows $n \models \varphi$.
   - $\varphi \in \langle id,\iota\rangle(Axs(K))$ for some $K \underset{free}{\overset{\langle\rho,\Sigma_F\rangle}{\Longrightarrow}} N$: by Def. 26(v) $n \in \mathbf{Mod}^{\mathcal{S}}(K)$ and by induction hypothesis $n \models Axs(K)$ and thus $n \models \varphi$.

(2) By (1), it suffices to prove the "$\supseteq$" direction. We proceed again by induction of the height of N and assume n is an $Axs(N)$-model. Since N is flattenable, we only have to show the clauses (i) to (iii) of Definition 26:

(i) since $\Gamma^N \subseteq Ax_{\mathcal{S}}(N)$ it holds that $n \models \Gamma^N$.

(ii) let $K \overset{\langle\rho,\bar{\sigma}\rangle}{\Longrightarrow} N$: since $\langle\rho,\sigma\rangle(Ax_{\mathcal{S}}(K)) \subseteq Ax_{\mathcal{S}}(N)$, it holds $n \models \langle\rho,\sigma\rangle(Ax_{\mathcal{S}}(K))$. By satisfaction condition it follows $n|_{\langle\rho,\sigma\rangle} \models Ax_{\mathcal{S}}(K)$ and thus $n \in \mathbf{Mod}^{\mathcal{S}}(K)$ by induction hypothesis.

(iii) let $K \overset{\langle\rho,\bar{\sigma}\rangle}{\longrightarrow} N$: since $\langle\rho,\sigma\rangle(\Gamma^K) \subseteq Ax_{\mathcal{S}}(N)$, it holds $n \models \langle\rho,\sigma\rangle(\Gamma^K)$, where $\langle\rho,\sigma\rangle : Sig^{loc}_{\mathcal{S}}(K) \to Sig_{\mathcal{S}}(N)$. By the satisfaction condition $n|_{\langle\rho,\sigma\rangle} \models \Gamma^K$ and is a $Sig^{loc}_{\mathcal{S}}(K)$-model. □

Complementary to definition links, which *define* the theories of related nodes, we introduce the notion of a *theorem link* with the help of which we are able to *postulate* relations between different theories. Theorem links are the central data structure to represent proof obligations arising in formal developments. Again we distinguish between local and global theorem links (denoted by $N \overset{\langle\rho,\bar{\sigma}\rangle}{= = \Rightarrow} M$ and $N \overset{\langle\rho,\bar{\sigma}\rangle}{- - \rightarrow} M$ respectively). Moreover, we introduce *local implications* of form $N \Rightarrow \Gamma$, where Γ is a set of $Sig_{\mathcal{S}}(N)$-sentences. $N \Rightarrow \{\varphi\}$ also is written $N \Rightarrow \varphi$. Finally, we also need theorem links $N \underset{hide\ \langle\mu,\Delta\rangle}{\overset{\langle\rho,\sigma\rangle}{= = \Rightarrow}} M$ (where for $\Sigma_H := \mu^{PreSign}(Sig_{\mathcal{S}}(N)) \setminus \Delta$, $\langle\mu,\Delta\rangle : Sig_{\mathcal{S}}(N) \to \Sigma_H$ and $\langle\rho,\sigma\rangle : \Sigma_H \to Sig_{\mathcal{S}}(M)$) involving hiding, as well as $N \underset{free\ \langle Id,\Sigma_F\rangle}{\overset{\langle\rho,\bar{\sigma}\rangle}{= = \Rightarrow}} M$ involving freeness.

The semantics of theorem links is given by the next definition.

Definition 29. *Let $\mathcal{S}$ be a development graph and N, M nodes in $\mathcal{S}$.*

$\mathcal{S}$ **satisfies** *a global theorem link $N \overset{\langle\rho,\bar{\sigma}\rangle}{= = \Rightarrow} M$ (denoted $\mathcal{S} \models N \overset{\langle\rho,\bar{\sigma}\rangle}{= = \Rightarrow} M$) iff for all $m \in \mathbf{Mod}^{\mathcal{S}}(M)$, $m|_{\langle\rho,\sigma\rangle} \in \mathbf{Mod}^{\mathcal{S}}(N)$ where $\langle\rho,\sigma\rangle$ is the heterogeneous signature comorphism from $Sig_{\mathcal{S}}(N)$ to $Sig_{\mathcal{S}}(M)$ induced by $\langle\rho,\bar{\sigma}\rangle$.*

$\mathcal{S}$ **satisfies** *a local theorem link $N \overset{\langle\rho,\bar{\sigma}\rangle}{- - \rightarrow} M$ (denoted $\mathcal{S} \models N \overset{\langle\rho,\bar{\sigma}\rangle}{- - \rightarrow} M$) iff for all $m \in \mathbf{Mod}^{\mathcal{S}}(M)$, $m|_{\langle\rho,\sigma\rangle} \in \mathbf{Mod}_{Sig^{loc}_{\mathcal{S}}(N)}(\Gamma^N)$ where $\langle\rho,\sigma\rangle$ is the heterogeneous signature comorphism from $Sig^{loc}_{\mathcal{S}}(N)$ to $Sig_{\mathcal{S}}(M)$ induced by $\langle\rho,\bar{\sigma}\rangle$.*

$\mathcal{S}$ **satisfies** *a local implication $N \Rightarrow \Gamma$, written $\mathcal{S} \models N \Rightarrow \Gamma$, if for all $n \in \mathbf{Mod}_{\mathcal{S}}(N)$, $n \models \Gamma$.*

$\mathcal{S}$ **satisfies** *a hiding theorem link $N \underset{hide\ \langle\mu,\Delta\rangle}{\overset{\langle\rho,\bar{\sigma}\rangle}{= = \Rightarrow}} M$ (denoted $\mathcal{S} \models N \underset{hide\ \langle\mu,\Delta\rangle}{\overset{\langle\rho,\bar{\sigma}\rangle}{= = \Rightarrow}} M$) iff for all $m \in \mathbf{Mod}^{\mathcal{S}}(M)$, $m|_{\langle\rho,\sigma\rangle\circ\langle id,\iota\rangle}$ has a $\langle\mu,\theta\rangle$-expansion to some N-model where $\langle\mu,\theta\rangle$ is the heterogeneous signature morphism from $\mu^{PreSign}(Sig_{\mathcal{S}}(N)) \setminus \Delta \to Sig_{\mathcal{S}}(N)$ induced by $\langle\mu,\Delta\rangle$, $\langle id,\iota\rangle : \mu^{PreSign}(Sig_{\mathcal{S}}(N))\Delta \to Sig_{\mathcal{S}}(M)$ is the identity inclusion, and $\langle\rho,\sigma\rangle$ is the heterogeneous signature comorphism from $\mu^{PreSign}(Sig_{\mathcal{S}}(N)) \setminus \Delta \to Sig_{\mathcal{S}}(M)$ induced by $\langle\rho,\bar{\sigma}\rangle$*

$\mathcal{S}$ **satisfies** *a free theorem link $N \underset{free\ \langle Id,\Sigma_F\rangle}{\overset{\langle\rho,\bar{\sigma}\rangle}{= = \Rightarrow}} M$ if for all $m \in \mathbf{Mod}^{\mathcal{S}}(M)$ it holds that $m|_{\langle\rho,\sigma\rangle}$ is an N-model which is free (in the class of N-models) over its* *own ι-reduct, where $\iota\colon \langle \Sigma_F \rangle_{Sig_S(N)} \rightarrow Sig_S(N)$ is the inclusion and $\langle \rho, \sigma \rangle$ is the heterogeneous signature comorphism from $Sig_S(N)$ to $Sig_S(M)$ induced by $\langle \rho, \bar{\sigma} \rangle$.*

Common proof obligations in a formal development can be encoded into properties such that specific global theorem links are implied by the actual development graph.

A global definition link $M \stackrel{\sigma}{\Longrightarrow} N$ in a development graph is a *conservative extension*, if every M-model can be expanded along σ to an N-model. We will allow to annotate a global definition link as $M \underset{cons}{\stackrel{\sigma}{\Longrightarrow}} N$, which shall express that it is a conservative extension. Such annotations can be seen as another kind of proof obligation.

6 Proof Rules for Development Graphs

The development graph calculus consists of eight basic rules: global theorem links can either be decomposed into a set of local theorem links, global theorem links, hiding theorem links and free theorem links following the structure of the source node using **(Global-Decomposition)**. Or else they can be subsumed by existing paths in the graph with an equivalent heterogeneous signature comorphism using **(Global-Subsumption)**. Local theorem links can either be decomposed into local implications by **(Local-Inference)** or, like global theorem links, be subsumed by existing paths with equivalent heterogeneous signature comorphism using **(Local-Subsumption)**. Local implications can be discharged by proving the individual conjectures in a sound calculus of the underlying institution by **(Basic-Inference)**.

In order to get rid of hiding links going into the *source* of a global theorem link, one first applies **(Global-Decomposition)**, ending up with some local and hiding theorem links. The rule **(Hide-Theorem-Shift)** allows to prove the latter, using conservativity of definition links. **(Borrowing)** can be used for shifting a proof goal along a conservative extension; hence, it also exploits conservativity of theorem links. Another rule of the proof system is the rule **(Theorem-Hide-Shift)**. It is used to get rid of hiding definition links going into the *target* of a global theorem link.

Global-Decomposition Rule:

$$\frac{\begin{array}{c} N \stackrel{\langle\rho,\bar{\sigma}\rangle}{- - \rightarrow} K \\ P \stackrel{\langle\rho,\bar{\sigma}\rangle\circ\langle\rho',\bar{\tau}\rangle}{- - \rightarrow} K \text{ for each } P \stackrel{\langle\rho',\bar{\tau}\rangle}{\longrightarrow} N \\ P \stackrel{\langle\rho,\bar{\sigma}\rangle\circ\langle\rho',\bar{\tau}\rangle}{= = \Rightarrow} K \text{ for each } P \stackrel{\langle\rho',\bar{\tau}\rangle}{\Longrightarrow} N \\ P \underset{hide\ \langle\mu,\Delta\rangle}{\stackrel{\langle\rho,\bar{\sigma}\rangle}{= = \Rightarrow}} K \text{ for each } P \underset{hide}{\stackrel{\langle\mu,\Delta\rangle}{\Longrightarrow}} N \\ P \underset{free\ \Sigma_F}{\stackrel{\langle\rho,\bar{\sigma}\rangle}{= = \Rightarrow}} K \text{ for each } P \underset{free}{\stackrel{\Sigma_F}{\Longrightarrow}} N \end{array}}{N \stackrel{\langle\rho,\bar{\sigma}\rangle}{= = \Rightarrow} K}$$

Soundness: assume that

$$\mathcal{S} \models N \overset{\langle \rho, \bar{\sigma} \rangle}{- - \rightarrow} K \tag{1}$$

$$\mathcal{S} \models P \overset{\langle \rho, \bar{\sigma} \rangle \circ \langle \rho', \bar{\tau} \rangle}{- - \rightarrow} K \text{ for each } P \xrightarrow{\langle \rho', \bar{\tau} \rangle} N \tag{2}$$

$$\mathcal{S} \models P \overset{\langle \rho, \bar{\sigma} \rangle \circ \langle \rho', \bar{\tau} \rangle}{= = \Rightarrow} K \text{ for each } P \overset{\langle \rho', \bar{\tau} \rangle}{\Longrightarrow} N \tag{3}$$

$$\mathcal{S} \models P \underset{hide\ \langle \mu, \Delta \rangle}{\overset{\langle \rho, \bar{\sigma} \rangle}{= = \Rightarrow}} K \text{ for each } P \underset{hide}{\overset{\langle \mu, \Delta \rangle}{\Longrightarrow}} N \tag{4}$$

$$\mathcal{S} \models P \underset{free\ \Sigma_F}{\overset{\langle \rho, \bar{\sigma} \rangle}{= = \Rightarrow}} K \text{ for each } P \underset{free}{\overset{\Sigma_F}{\Longrightarrow}} N \tag{5}$$

In order to show $\mathcal{S} \models N \overset{\langle \rho, \bar{\sigma} \rangle}{= = \Rightarrow} K$, let m be a K-model and we show $m|_{\langle \rho, \sigma \rangle}$ is an N-model where $\sigma : \rho^{PreSign}(Sig_{\mathcal{S}}(N)) \to Sig_{\mathcal{S}}(K)$. We then consider the cases (i) to (v) of Definition 26:

1. Γ^N: by (1) we know $m|_{\langle \rho, \sigma' \rangle} \in \mathbf{Mod}_{Sig^{loc}_{\mathcal{S}}(N)}(\Gamma^N)$, where $\sigma' : \rho^{PreSign}(Sig^{loc}_{\mathcal{S}}(N)) \to Sig_{\mathcal{S}}(K)$. Since $Sig^{loc}_{\mathcal{S}}(N) \subseteq Sig_{\mathcal{S}}(N)$ it holds $\sigma' = \sigma \circ \iota$ by Proposition 7 where $\iota : Sig^{loc}_{\mathcal{S}}(N) \to Sig_{\mathcal{S}}(N)$ is the identity inclusion. Hence, it holds

$$\begin{aligned} m|_{\langle \rho, \sigma' \rangle} \in \mathbf{Mod}_{Sig^{loc}_{\mathcal{S}}(N)}(\Gamma^N) &\Rightarrow m|_{\langle \rho, \sigma \circ \iota \rangle} \in \mathbf{Mod}_{Sig^{loc}_{\mathcal{S}}(N)}(\Gamma^N) \\ &\Rightarrow m|_{\langle \rho, \sigma \rangle} \in \mathbf{Mod}_{Sig_{\mathcal{S}}(N)}(\iota(\Gamma^N)) \\ &\Rightarrow m|_{\langle \rho, \sigma \rangle} \in \mathbf{Mod}_{Sig_{\mathcal{S}}(N)}(\Gamma^N). \end{aligned}$$

2. $P \xrightarrow{\langle \rho', \bar{\tau} \rangle} N$ where $\tau : {\rho'}^{PreSign}(Sig^{loc}_{\mathcal{S}}(P)) \to Sig_{\mathcal{S}}(N)$: from (2) and Theorem 21 it follows $(m|_{\langle \rho, \sigma \rangle \circ \langle \rho', \tau \rangle} \in \mathbf{Mod}^{\mathcal{S}}(P)$.
3. $P \overset{\langle \rho', \bar{\tau} \rangle}{\Longrightarrow} N$ where $\tau : {\rho'}^{PreSign}(Sig_{\mathcal{S}}(P)) \to Sig_{\mathcal{S}}(N)$: from (3) and Theorem 21 it follows $(m|_{\langle \rho, \sigma \rangle \circ \langle \rho', \tau \rangle} \in \mathbf{Mod}^{\mathcal{S}}(P)$.
4. $P \underset{hide}{\overset{\langle \mu, \Delta \rangle}{\Longrightarrow}} N$ where $\iota : \mu^{PreSign}(Sig_{\mathcal{S}}(P)) \setminus \Delta \to Sig_{\mathcal{S}}(N)$ is the identity inclusion morphism and $\langle \mu, \theta \rangle : \mu^{PreSign}(Sig_{\mathcal{S}}(P)) \setminus \Delta \to Sig_{\mathcal{S}}(P)$: from (4) and Theorem 21 it follows $m|_{\langle \rho, \sigma \rangle \circ \langle id, \iota \rangle}$ has a $\langle \mu, \theta \rangle$-expansion in $\mathbf{Mod}^{\mathcal{S}}(P)$.
5. $P \underset{free}{\overset{\langle id, \Sigma_F \rangle}{\Longrightarrow}} N$: from (5) and Theorem 21 it follows $m|_{\langle \rho, \sigma \rangle \circ \langle id, \iota \rangle} \in \mathbf{Mod}^{\mathcal{S}}(P)$.

□

Remark 30. Note the use of Theorem 21 in the soundness proof above to lift the composition of heterogeneous pre-signature comorphisms to the induced heterogeneous signature comorphisms. The compatibility of compositions occurs in the soundness proofs of most other proof rules as well and we will make use of it without mentioning it explicitly.

Global-Subsumption Rule:

$$\frac{K \xrightarrow{\langle \rho', \bar{\sigma}' \rangle} N}{K \overset{\langle \rho, \bar{\sigma} \rangle}{\Longrightarrow} N} \text{ if } \langle \rho, \bar{\sigma} \rangle \equiv \langle \rho', \bar{\sigma}' \rangle \text{ wrt. } Sig_{\mathcal{S}}(K)$$

Soundness: Since the heterogeneous pre-signature comorphisms are equivalent wrt. $Sig_{\mathcal{S}}(K)$ the induced heterogeneous signature comorphisms are equal, from which the soundness follows trivially. □

Local-Subsumption Rule:

$$\frac{K \xrightarrow{\langle \rho', \bar{\theta} \rangle} N}{K \overset{\langle \rho, \bar{\sigma} \rangle}{\dashrightarrow} N} \text{ if } \langle \rho, \bar{\sigma} \rangle \equiv \langle \rho', \bar{\theta} \rangle \text{ wrt. } Sig_{\mathcal{S}}^{loc}(K)$$

Soundness: assume that $\mathcal{S} \models K \xrightarrow{\langle \rho', \bar{\theta} \rangle} N$ and $\langle \rho, \bar{\sigma} \rangle \equiv \langle \rho', \bar{\theta} \rangle$ wrt. $Sig_{\mathcal{S}}^{loc}(K)$. Then the respective induced heterogeneous signature comorphisms $\langle \rho, \sigma \rangle$, $\langle \rho', \theta \rangle$: $Sig_{\mathcal{S}}^{loc}(K)$ are equal (*). Let m be an N-model. By Proposition 27, $m|_{\langle \rho', \theta \rangle} \models \Gamma^K$. From (*) follows $m|_{\langle \rho, \sigma \rangle} \models \Gamma^K$, from which follows $\mathcal{S} \models K \overset{\langle \rho, \bar{\sigma} \rangle}{\dashrightarrow} N$. □

Local-Inference Rule:

$$\frac{N \Rightarrow \langle \rho, \bar{\sigma} \rangle(\Gamma^K)}{K \overset{\langle \rho, \bar{\sigma} \rangle}{\dashrightarrow} N}$$

Soundness: assume that $m \models \langle \rho, \bar{\sigma} \rangle(\Gamma^K)$ for each N-model m and let $\langle \rho, \sigma \rangle$: $Sig_{\mathcal{S}}^{loc}(K) \to Sig_{\mathcal{S}}(N)$ be the heterogeneous signature comorphism induced by $\langle \rho, \bar{\sigma} \rangle$. In order to show $\mathcal{S} \models K \overset{\langle \rho, \bar{\sigma} \rangle}{\dashrightarrow} N$, let m be an N-model. By assumption, $m \models \langle \rho, \bar{\sigma} \rangle(\Gamma^K)$. By the satisfaction condition for institutions, $m|_{\langle \rho, \sigma \rangle} \models \Gamma^K$. By definition, it follows that $\mathcal{S} \models K \overset{\langle \rho, \bar{\sigma} \rangle}{\dashrightarrow} N$. □

Basic-Inference Rule:

$$\frac{P : Ax_{\mathcal{S}}(N) \vdash_{\Sigma^N} \varphi \text{ for each } \varphi \in \Psi}{N \Rightarrow \Psi}$$

where $P : Ax_{\mathcal{S}}(N) \vdash_{\Sigma^N} \varphi$ denotes that P is a proof for $Ax_{\mathcal{S}}(N) \vdash_{\Sigma^N} \varphi$.

Soundness: assume that $Ax_{\mathcal{S}}(N) \vdash_{Sig_{\mathcal{S}}(N)} \varphi$ for each $\varphi \in \Psi$. By soundness of $\vdash_{Sig_{\mathcal{S}}(N)}$, we get $Ax_{\mathcal{S}}(N) \models_{Sig_{\mathcal{S}}(N)} \Psi$. In order to show $\mathcal{S} \models N \Rightarrow \Psi$, let m be an N-model. By Proposition 28, $m \models Ax_{\mathcal{S}}(N)$. Since $Ax_{\mathcal{S}}(N) \models_{Sig_{\mathcal{S}}(N)} \Psi$, also $m \models \Psi$. □

Hide-Theorem-Shift Rule:

$$\frac{K \overset{\langle\rho',\bar\sigma'\rangle}{\underset{cons}{\Rightarrow}} N' \quad N \overset{\langle\rho'',\bar\theta\rangle}{\underset{cons}{\Rightarrow}} N'}{N \overset{\langle\rho'',\bar\theta\rangle}{\underset{cons}{\Rightarrow}} N' \quad K \overset{\langle\rho,\bar\sigma\rangle}{\underset{hide\ \langle\mu,\Delta\rangle}{\Longrightarrow}} N}$$

if $\langle\rho' \circ CoM(\mu), \bar\sigma' \circ CoM(\mu)^{PreSign}(\emptyset)\rangle \equiv \langle\rho'' \circ \rho, \bar\theta \circ \rho^{PreSign}(\bar\sigma)\rangle$ wrt. the signature $\mu^{PreSign}(Sig_{\mathcal{S}}(K)) \setminus \Delta$.

The proof rules are written in a concise notation as above. We will spell out in detail what this notation means for the rule **(Hide-Theorem-Shift)**:

$$\frac{\begin{array}{l}\langle\rho' \circ CoM(\mu), \bar\sigma' \circ CoM(\mu)^{PreSign}(\emptyset)\rangle \equiv \langle\rho'' \circ \rho, \bar\theta \circ \rho^{PreSign}(\bar\sigma)\rangle \\ \qquad\qquad \text{wrt. } \mu^{PreSign}(Sig_{\mathcal{S}}(K)) \setminus \Delta \\ N \overset{\langle\rho'',\bar\theta\rangle}{\underset{cons}{\Longrightarrow}} N' \in \mathcal{S} \\ \mathcal{S} \vdash K' \overset{\langle\rho',\bar\sigma'\rangle}{\Longrightarrow} N'\end{array}}{\mathcal{S} \vdash K' \overset{\langle\rho,\bar\sigma\rangle}{\underset{hide\ \langle\mu,\Delta\rangle}{\Longrightarrow}} N}$$

Soundness: assume that $\mathcal{S} \models K' \overset{\sigma'}{\Longrightarrow} N'$ and $N \overset{\theta'}{\underset{cons}{\Longrightarrow}} N'$ is conservative. We have to show that $\mathcal{S} \models K' \overset{\sigma}{\underset{hide\ \theta}{\Longrightarrow}} N$. Let m be an N-model. Since $N \overset{\theta'}{\underset{cons}{\Longrightarrow}} N'$ is conservative, m can be expanded to an N'-model m' with $m'|_{\theta'} = m$. By the assumption, $m'|_{\sigma'}$ is an K'-model. Thus, $m'|_{\sigma' \circ \theta} = m'|_{\theta' \circ \sigma} = m|_\sigma$ has a θ-expansion to an K'-model. □

Theorem-Hide-Shift Rule:

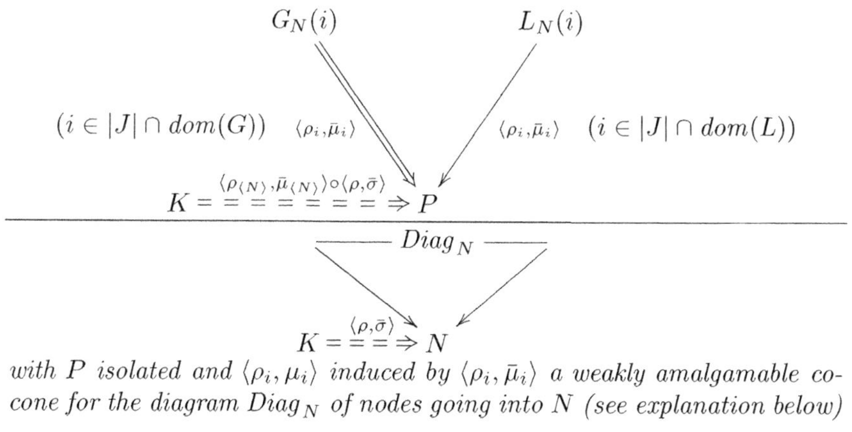

with P isolated and $\langle\rho_i,\mu_i\rangle$ induced by $\langle\rho_i,\bar\mu_i\rangle$ a weakly amalgamable co-cone for the diagram $Diag_N$ of nodes going into N (see explanation below)

Since this rule is quite powerful, we need some preliminary notions. Given a node N in a development graph $\mathcal{S} = \langle \mathcal{N}, \mathcal{L} \rangle$, the idea is that we unfold the subgraph below N into a tree and form a diagram with this tree. More formally, define the *diagram* $\mathit{Diag}_N : J \longrightarrow \mathbf{Sig}$ *associated with* N together with partial maps $G_N : |J| \longrightarrow \mathcal{N}$ and $L_N : |J| \longrightarrow \mathcal{N}$ inductively as follows:

- $\langle N \rangle$ is an object in J, with $\mathit{Diag}_N(\langle N \rangle) = \mathit{Sig}_{\mathcal{S}}(N)$. Let $G_N(\langle N \rangle)$ be just N.
- if $i = \langle\ K \xrightarrow{L_1} \cdots \xrightarrow{L_n} N\ \rangle$ is an object in J with $L_1, \ldots, L_n$ non-local definition links in $\mathcal{L}$, and $L = M \overset{\langle \rho, \bar{\sigma} \rangle}{\Longrightarrow} K$ a global definition link in $\mathcal{L}$, then

$$j = \langle\ M \xrightarrow{L} K \xrightarrow{L_1} \cdots \xrightarrow{L_n} N\ \rangle$$

is an object in J with $\mathit{Diag}_N(j) = \mathit{Sig}_{\mathcal{S}}(M)$, and L is a morphism from j to i in J with $\mathit{Diag}_N(L) = \langle \mu, \sigma \rangle$ where $\langle \mu, \sigma \rangle : \mathit{Sig}_{\mathcal{S}}(M) \to \mathit{Sig}_{\mathcal{S}}(K)$ is the heterogeneous signature comorphism induced by L. If there is no incoming free definition link for M in $\mathcal{S}$, we set $L_N(j) = M$ and otherwise $G_N(j) = M$.
- if $i = \langle\ K \xrightarrow{L_1} \cdots \xrightarrow{L_n} N\ \rangle$ is an object in J with $L_1, \ldots, L_n$ non-local definition links in $\mathcal{L}$, and $L = M \xrightarrow{\langle \rho, \bar{\sigma} \rangle} K$ a local definition link in $\mathcal{L}$, then

$$j = \langle\ M \xrightarrow{L} K \xrightarrow{L_1} \cdots \xrightarrow{L_n} N\ \rangle$$

is an object in J with $\mathit{Diag}_N(j) = \mathit{Sig}_{\mathcal{S}}(M)$, and L is a morphism from j to i in J with $\mathit{Diag}_N(L) = \langle \mu, \sigma \rangle$ where $\langle \mu, \sigma \rangle : \mathit{Sig}^{loc}_{\mathcal{S}}(M) \to \mathit{Sig}_{\mathcal{S}}(K)$ is the heterogeneous signature comorphism induced by L. We set $L_N(j) = M$.
- if $i = \langle\ K \xrightarrow{L_1} \cdots \xrightarrow{L_n} N\ \rangle$ is an object in J with $L_1, \ldots, L_n$ non-local definition links in $\mathcal{L}$, and $L = M \underset{hide}{\overset{\langle \mu, \Delta \rangle}{\Longrightarrow}} K$ a hiding definition link in $\mathcal{L}$, then

$$j = \langle\ M \xrightarrow{L} K \xrightarrow{L_1} \cdots \xrightarrow{L_n} N\ \rangle$$

is an object in J with $\mathit{Diag}_N(j) = \mathit{Sig}_{\mathcal{S}}(M)$, and L is a morphism from i to j in J with $\mathit{Diag}_N(L) = \langle \mu, \theta \rangle$ where $\langle \mu, \theta \rangle : \mathit{Sig}_{\mathcal{S}}(K) \to \mathit{Sig}_{\mathcal{S}}(M)$ is the heterogeneous signature morphism induced by L. If there is no incoming free definition link for M in $\mathcal{S}$, we set $L_N(j) = M$ and otherwise $G_N(j) = M$.

Now in order to apply **(Theorem-Hide-Shift)**, take a weakly amalgamable cocone $(\Sigma, (\langle \rho_i, \mu_i \rangle : \mathit{Diag}_N(i) \longrightarrow \Sigma)_{i \in |J|})$ for Diag_N (in general, we know that such a cocone exists only if the institution is quasi-semi-exact), and let P be a new isolated node with signature Σ and with ingoing global definition links $G_N(i) \overset{\langle \rho_i, \bar{\mu}_i \rangle}{\Longrightarrow} P$ for $i \in |J| \cap \mathit{dom}(G)$ where $\langle \rho_i, \bar{\mu}_i \rangle$ are the heterogeneous presignature comorphisms induced by $\langle \rho_i, \mu_i \rangle$ and with ingoing local definition links $G_N(i) \xrightarrow{\langle \rho_i, \bar{\mu}_i \rangle} P$ for $i \in |J| \cap \mathit{dom}(L)$. Here, an isolated node is one with no local axioms and no ingoing definition links other than those shown in the rule.

Soundness: assume that $\mathcal{S} \models K \overset{\langle\rho_{\langle N\rangle},\bar{\mu}_{\langle N\rangle}\rangle\circ\langle\rho,\bar{\sigma}\rangle}{=\!=\!\Rightarrow} P$. Let m be an N-model. We have to show $m|_{\langle\rho_{\langle N\rangle},\mu_{\langle N\rangle}\rangle\circ\langle\rho,\sigma\rangle}$ to be a K-model in order to establish the holding of $K \overset{\langle\rho_{\langle N\rangle},\bar{\mu}_{\langle N\rangle}\rangle\circ\langle\rho,\bar{\sigma}\rangle}{=\!=\!\Rightarrow} N$. We inductively define a family $(m_i)_{i\in|J|}$ of models $m_i \in \mathbf{Mod}(G_N(i))$ if $i \in dom(G_N)$ or $m_i \in \mathbf{Mod}^{\mathcal{S}}(L_N(i))$ if $i \in dom(L_N)$ by putting

- $m_{\langle N\rangle} = m$;
- $m_{\langle M \xrightarrow{L} Q \xrightarrow{L_1} \cdots \xrightarrow{L_n} N\rangle} = m'|_{\langle\rho,\sigma\rangle}$, where $L = M \overset{\langle\rho,\bar{\sigma}\rangle}{\Longrightarrow} Q$ (note: $\langle\rho,\sigma\rangle : Sig_{\mathcal{S}}(M) \to Sig_{\mathcal{S}}(Q))$ and $m' = m_{\langle Q \xrightarrow{L_1} \cdots \xrightarrow{L_n} N\rangle}$;
- $m_{\langle M \xrightarrow{L} Q \xrightarrow{L_1} \cdots \xrightarrow{L_n} N\rangle} = m'|_{\langle\rho,\sigma\rangle}$, where $L = M \xrightarrow{\langle\rho,\bar{\sigma}\rangle} Q$ (note: $\langle\rho,\sigma\rangle : Sig^{loc}_{\mathcal{S}}(M) \to Sig_{\mathcal{S}}(Q))$ and $m' = m_{\langle Q \xrightarrow{L_1} \cdots \xrightarrow{L_n} N\rangle}$; and
- $m_{\langle M \xrightarrow{L} Q \xrightarrow{L_1} \cdots \xrightarrow{L_n} N\rangle}$ is a $\langle\mu,\theta\rangle$-expansion of $m'|_{\langle Id,\iota\rangle}$ to an M-model (existing since m' is a Q-model), where $L = M \underset{hide}{\overset{\langle\mu,\Delta\rangle}{\Longrightarrow}} Q$, $\langle Id,\iota\rangle : \mu^{PreSign}(Sig_{\mathcal{S}}(M)) \setminus \Delta \to Sig_{\mathcal{S}}(Q)$ the heterogeneous signature identity inclusion comorphism, and $m' = m_{\langle Q \xrightarrow{L_1} \cdots \xrightarrow{L_n} N\rangle}$.

It is easy to show that this family is consistent with $Diag_N$. Since by the side condition of the rule, $(\Sigma, (\langle\rho_i,\mu_i\rangle \colon Diag_N(i) \longrightarrow \Sigma)_{i\in|J|})$ is a weakly amalgamable cocone, there is a Σ^P-model m_P with $m_P|_{\langle\rho_i,\mu_i\rangle} = m_i$, $i \in |J|$. The latter implies that m_P is a P-model. By the assumption, $m_P|_{\langle\rho_{\langle N\rangle},\mu_{\langle N\rangle}\rangle\circ\langle\rho,\sigma\rangle} = m_{\langle N\rangle}|_\sigma = m|_\sigma$ is a K-model.

It remains to show that it is safe to annotate the new definition links in the graph with the induced heterogeneous pre-signature comorphisms $\langle\rho_i,\bar{\mu}_i\rangle$ rather than with the heterogeneous signature comorphisms $\langle\rho_i,\mu_i\rangle$. This is ensured by the fact that the induced heterogeneous pre-signature comorphism induces the same heterogeneous signature comorphism between the same source and target signatures (Proposition 18). □

Borrowing Rule:

$$\frac{\begin{array}{ccc} K & & N \\ \langle\rho,\bar{\theta}\rangle \Downarrow & & \langle\rho',\bar{\theta}'\rangle \Downarrow cons \\ K' & \underset{\langle\rho_{\bar{\sigma}'},\bar{\sigma}'\rangle}{=\!=\!\Rightarrow} & N' \end{array}}{\begin{array}{ccc} K & \underset{\langle\rho_{\bar{\sigma}},\bar{\sigma}\rangle}{=\!=\!\Rightarrow} & N \\ \langle\rho,\bar{\theta}\rangle \Downarrow & & \langle\rho',\bar{\theta}'\rangle \Downarrow cons \\ K' & & N' \end{array}} \quad \begin{array}{l} \text{if } \langle\rho_{\bar{\sigma}'},\bar{\sigma}'\rangle \circ \langle\rho,\bar{\theta}\rangle \equiv \langle\rho',\bar{\theta}'\rangle \circ \langle\rho_{\bar{\sigma}},\bar{\sigma}\rangle \\ \text{wrt. } Sig_{\mathcal{S}}(K) \end{array}$$

Soundness: Assume that (1) $\mathcal{S} \models K \stackrel{\langle \rho, \bar{\theta} \rangle}{\Longrightarrow} K'$, (2) $\mathcal{S} \models N \underset{cons}{\stackrel{\langle \rho', \bar{\theta}' \rangle}{\Longrightarrow}} N'$, and that (3) $\mathcal{S} \models K' \stackrel{\langle \rho_{\bar{\sigma}'}, \bar{\sigma}' \rangle}{\Longrightarrow} N'$. Let m be an N-model. By (2), m has an $\langle \rho', \theta' \rangle$-expansion to an N'-model m' with $m'|_{\langle \rho', \theta' \rangle} = m$. By (3), $m'|_{\langle \rho_{\bar{\sigma}'}, \sigma' \rangle}$ is an K'-model, and hence, by (1) and Proposition 16 $m'|_{\langle \rho_{\bar{\sigma}'}, \sigma' \rangle \circ \langle \rho, \theta \rangle} = m'|_{\langle \rho', \theta' \rangle \circ \langle \rho_{\bar{\sigma}}, \sigma \rangle} = m|_{\langle \rho_{\bar{\sigma}}, \sigma \rangle}$ is a K-model. □

Theorem 31. *The proof rules are sound. The rules are incomplete, but complete if the underlying institutions have complete calculi and relative to a given oracle deciding conservativity and freeness of global definition links.*

Proof. For each rule a soundness proof has been given. For incompleteness, see the counter-example published in [15]. For the relative completeness results see [14]. □

7 Change Impact Analysis

In this section we are concerned with the question of transferring proof work done in one particular development graph to another graph that differs from the first one only in some locally constricted areas such that we are able to relate most of the nodes and (definition) links of the first to nodes and links of the latter. Given this mapping we are interested in the problem of mapping the proof work encoded in theorem links, their decompositions, and proofs of theorems to the new development graph. Proof work is done by applying the development graph rules presented in Section 6 to the actual development graph.

The transfer of proof work from the original development graph to the changed one can be easily done by reapplying the "proof scripts", i.e. the rules used in the first are reused to verify theorem links at corresponding positions in the latter. However, in general the application of the development graph rules has a high price because it involves, for instance, the use of theorem proving or the calculation of compositions of (co-)morphisms. Hence, a major design goal is to define the scope of the rules (in terms of the affected subgraph) as small as possible in order to minimize the test for applicability to a limited area within the development graph but also to keep the rules as generic as possible. As a consequence we may be able to transfer a proof (script) from the original development graph to the new one although the semantics of the represented proof obligation has changed.

We introduced the notions of pre-signatures and local axioms to specify the signature and sentences of a theory in an incremental way. While a node (as the root of its subgraph) represents semantically a (full-fledged) theory, its syntactical representation is restricted to those bits that are not imported from other theories via some incoming definition link. From this point of view, a node considered in its own right denotes a function that maps its imported theories to the theory represented by the subgraph of the node. Several development graph rules (e.g. the global decomposition rule) exploit the constructive nature of these functions rather than inspecting the individual theory represented by the node. In this sense, the rules are rather generic with respect to the semantics of the imported theories. This is important for change management since we are interested in a smart replay of the development graph proofs in a changed environment. The same development graph rules may still be applicable although the semantics of the involved nodes have been significantly affected by a change of the specification. Smart replay means that we want to anticipate the result of applying a rule in a changed setting by adaptation of the result of application in the original setting. Doing this we will know the differences between the two rule applications allowing us to transfer also proof steps incorporating the results of original rule applications to the new setting. In the following we will analyze each individual development graph rule according to how changes in the area in which the rule is applied will affect the result of the rule application. Therefore, we distinguish between the *domain,* which is the subgraph of that graph with all elements that contribute to the semantics of the involved entities, and the *pre-domain* of a proof rule that consists only of those parts that actually (syntactically) matter for the rule application.

Global-Decomposition Rule: Applied on $N \overset{\langle \rho, \bar{\sigma} \rangle}{=\!=\!\Rightarrow} K$ the pre-domain consists exclusively of $\langle \rho, \bar{\sigma} \rangle$, the node N and all direct incoming definition links (local, global, hiding, free) along with their heterogeneous pre-signature morphisms and comorphisms and their source nodes. The domain contains the theorem link and the subgraphs imported into N and K including all signature elements and axioms.

Impact analysis: if some definition link from the pre-domain is deleted, the corresponding (local/global) theorem link needs to be deleted as well. If some definition link has been added to the pre-domain, a new (local/global) theorem link needs to be added. If $\langle \rho, \bar{\sigma} \rangle$ has changed, the heterogeneous pre-signature comorphisms and heterogeneous pre-signature morphisms of the introduced theorem links are affected and must be recomputed. Analogously, if the heterogeneous pre-signature comorphism of some incoming definition link has been changed, the heterogenous pre-signature comorphism of the corresponding theorem link is affected and must be recomputed. If the heterogenous pre-signature morphism of some incoming hiding definition link has been changed, the heterogenous pre-signature morphism of the corresponding hiding theorem link is affected and must be recomputed.

Global-Subsumption Rule: Applied on $K \overset{\langle \rho, \bar{\sigma} \rangle}{=\!=\!\Rightarrow} N$ to subsume it by the path computed by $K \overset{\langle \rho', \bar{\sigma}' \rangle}{\rightarrowtail\!\!\Rightarrow} N$ the pre-domain comprises K, N, $\langle \rho, \bar{\sigma} \rangle$, and all nodes, links and their respective heterogeneous pre-signature comorphisms on the path $K \overset{\langle \rho', \bar{\sigma}' \rangle}{\rightarrowtail\!\!\Rightarrow} N$. The domain includes in addition the transitive closure of incoming definition links, nodes, local signatures and local axioms for K, N and all nodes on the path.

Impact analysis: If some node or link on the path is deleted, the rule is invalid. Otherwise, if $\langle \rho, \bar{\sigma} \rangle$ or some of the heterogeneous pre-signature comorphisms on the path has been changed then the rule must check again if they are still equal wrt. the (new) global signature of K.

Local-Inference Rule: For this proof rule applied on $K \overset{\langle\rho,\bar{\sigma}\rangle}{- - \rightarrow} N$ the pre-domain and the domain coincide and are exclusively the node K, its local signature $Sig_S^{loc}(N)$ and the local axioms Γ^K as well as the heterogeneous pre-signature comorphism. Any changes outside of these are irrelevant for the proof rule application.

Impact analysis: any change in the local signature $Sig_S^{loc}(K)$ has no effect on the proof rule as long as the heterogeneous pre-signature comorphism $\langle\rho,\bar{\sigma}\rangle$ is unchanged. If $\langle\rho,\bar{\sigma}\rangle$ changed, it must be checked whether the mappings of the local axioms from Γ^K are still the same. If a local axiom has been deleted from Γ^K, then the corresponding conjecture in the local implication is superfluous and can be removed. If a local axiom has been added, then a corresponding conjecture has to be added to the local implication.

Local-Subsumption Rule: Applied on $K \overset{\langle\rho,\bar{\sigma}\rangle}{- - \rightarrow} N$ to subsume it by the path computed by $K \overset{\langle\rho',\bar{\sigma}'\rangle}{\rightarrowtail} N$ the pre-domain comprises P and its local signature and axioms N, $\langle\rho,\bar{\sigma}\rangle$, and all nodes, links and their respective heterogeneous pre-signature comorphisms on the path $K \overset{\langle\rho',\bar{\sigma}'\rangle}{\rightarrowtail} N$. The domain includes in addition K and its local signature and local axioms, as well as the transitive closure of incoming definition links, nodes, local signatures and local axioms of N and all nodes on the path.

Impact analysis: If some node or link on the path is deleted, the rule is invalid. Otherwise, any change of $\langle\rho,\bar{\sigma}\rangle$ or some of the heterogeneous pre-signature comorphisms on the path requires to check again if they are still equal wrt. the (new) local signature of K.

Basic-Inference Rule: Applied to reduce $N \Rightarrow \varphi_1 \ldots \varphi_n$ to $P_1 : Axs_S(N) \vdash_{\Sigma^N} \varphi_1 \ldots P_n : Axs_S(N) \vdash_{\Sigma^N} \varphi_n$ the domain consist of the φ_i and the subgraph imported into N including all the axioms and signature elements. The pre-domain, though, only consists of the φ_i and the global set of axioms of N determined by $Axs_S(N)$.

Impact analysis: If some φ_i is deleted, then the rule application is still sound, but over-complete and the superfluous premise $P_i : Axs_S(N) \vdash_{\Sigma^N} \varphi_i$ must be deleted. If there is an additional φ, then the rule application is incomplete and the respective additional premise must be added. If some axiom has been deleted from $Axs_S(N)$, which was used in the proof P_i of some φ_i, then that proof is affected and needs to be redone. If some axiom has been added to $Axs_S(N)$, nothing is affected.

Hide-Theorem-Shift Rule: Applied to prove the hiding theorem link in $K \underset{hide\ \langle\mu,\Delta\rangle}{\overset{\langle\rho,\bar{\sigma}\rangle}{= = \Rightarrow}} N \underset{cons}{\overset{\langle\rho'',\bar{\theta}\rangle}{\Longrightarrow}} N'$ the domain comprises the two links with their heterogeneous pre-signature morphisms and comorphisms, the subgraph imported in the source node K including all signature elements and axioms, as well as the subgraph imported in N' also including all signature elements and axioms. The pre-domain, however, are only the two links with $\langle \rho, \bar{\sigma} \rangle$, $\langle \mu, \Delta \rangle$, and $\langle \rho'', \bar{\theta} \rangle$, as well as the nodes K, N, and N'.

Impact analysis: If $\langle \rho, \bar{\sigma} \rangle$, $\langle \rho'', \bar{\theta} \rangle$ or μ change, then the heterogeneous pre-signature comorphism $\langle \rho', \bar{\sigma}' \rangle$ is also affected and must be recomputed. If the global signature $Sig_S(K)$ or Δ change, the equivalence condition needs to be rechecked. Finally, if the conservativity status of the definition link changes, the rule is incorrect and must be deleted.

Theorem-Hide-Shift Rule: Applying the rule to the global theorem link in

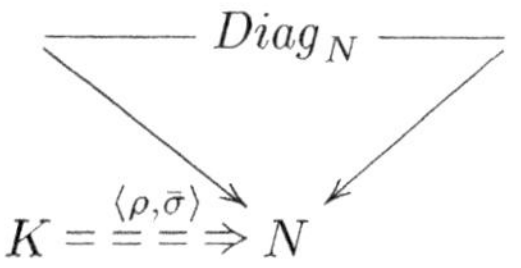

the domain and pre-domain coincide and consist of K, the theorem link with $\langle \rho, \bar{\sigma} \rangle$, as well as N and the whole subgraph imported in N including all signature elements and axioms.

Impact analysis: Any change in the diagram affecting the signatures of the nodes and the heterogeneous pre-signature comorphisms requires to recompute the (heterogeneous) colimit, as there is no means to analyze the impact of changes here to the content of P. To optimize this and extend the impact analysis to the colimit computation would require to transfer the colimit computation from heterogeneous signature comorphisms to heterogeneous pre-signature comorphisms, which is an open task.

Borrowing Rule: For application of the rule to shift the theorem link between K and N in

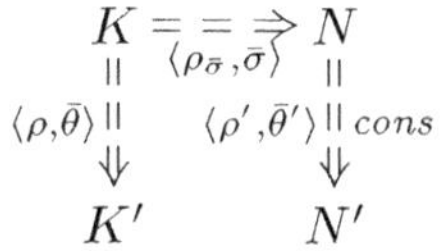

to a theorem link between K' and N', the domain comprises the imported subgraphs with all signature elements and axioms of K, N, K' and N', as well as all three theorem links with heterogeneous pre-signature comorphisms. The pre-domain, however, only consists of these three theorem links and the global signature of K.

Impact analysis: if one of the involved heterogeneous pre-signature comorphisms is affected, the heterogeneous pre-signature comorphism of the new theorem link between K' and N' needs to be recomputed and the side condition rechecked. If the global signature of K has changed, then the side-condition needs to be rechecked.

Remark 32. Note the benefits for change impact analysis of using pre-signature morphisms: first, pre-signature morphisms change less frequently in general than full signature morphisms, which are affected by each change in the global signature of the source node. Thus, changes occur less often using that representation. Second, whether a new heterogeneous pre-signature comorphism maps a given axiom differently than the precedent heterogeneous pre-signature comorphism can be checked locally and without computing the full heterogeneous signature comorphism: take the symbols of an axiom and compare the intersection with the domain of the old and the new heterogeneous pre-signature comorphism: if the intersection is equal and the heterogeneous pre-signature comorphisms are equivalent on this intersection, then the axiom is mapped in the same way and in the rule **(Local-Inference)** the old conjectures in the local implication can remain in place.

Realization. The change impact analysis has been realized for the HETS-tool which is an implementation of heterogeneous development graphs, but with signatures and signature morphisms rather than pre-signatures and pre-signature morphisms. Adapting HETS would have been a major enterprise and we thus implemented it in the *GMoc*-tool for generic change impact analysis [3], which will also allow us to combine change impact analysis for development graphs with change impact analysis of other documents occurring in a software development process, such as source code, requirements documents and general documentation. *GMoc* performs the impact analysis as described above based on a serialized representation of heterogeneous development graphs and provides the results of the analysis in form of impact annotations to the serialized representation. In addition to the information about affected theorem links it also provides information about those development graph nodes and links for which the signature and respectively the signature morphisms need to be recomputed by HETS. The change impact analysis in *GMoc* works on typed graphs obtained from the serialized representation and the impact analysis is formalized as a set of graph rewriting rules (see [3] for details).

8 Conclusion

In this paper we provided a thorough definition of heterogeneous development graphs that allow for an efficient management of change. We introduced pre-signatures and pre-signature morphisms as elementary building blocks to specify complex signatures and signature morphisms, which allows us to specify theories in a completely modular way. The proof rules make use of this modularity in order to restrict the focus of testing the applicability of rules to some few nodes and their relations in the development graph. The locality of rule applications supports the reuse of proofs in case of changing the development graph. We use a smart replay mechanism which anticipates the result of applying a rule in a changed setting by adapting the result of its application in the previous setting.

The idea of development graphs turned out to be very fruitful in the past and various research groups adopted this approach. The proof semantics of CASL [17], the theory structuring mechanisms in OMDoc [10], the recent module system for Twelf [18] and also locales in Isabelle [4] were influenced by the notion of development graphs. The presented approach allows for an efficient support of specification and verification with the help of heterogeneous development graphs. The next step will be to extend the framework of change management to the use of generalized theoroidal institution comorphisms (cf. [5]) generalizing the way how signatures of a source logic can be translated to entire theories of the target one and broadening the class of logic encodings that can be formalized as comorphisms. We already have defined the notion of modular comorphism in a way that anticipates this extension.

References

1. Autexier, S., Hutter, D.: Maintenance of formal software developments by stratified verification. In: Baaz, M., Voronkov, A. (eds.) LPAR 2002. LNCS (LNAI), vol. 2514. Springer, Heidelberg (2002)
2. Autexier, S., Hutter, D.: Mind the gap - maintaining formal developments in MAYA. In: Hutter, D., Stephan, W. (eds.) Mechanizing Mathematical Reasoning. LNCS (LNAI), vol. 2605. Springer, Heidelberg (2005)
3. Autexier, S., Müller, N.: Semantics-based change impact analysis for heterogeneous collections of documents. In: Gormish, M., Ingold, R. (eds.) Proceedings of 10th ACM Symposium on Document Engineering (DocEng2010), Manchester, UK (september 2010)
4. Ballarin, C.: Interpretation of locales in isabelle: Theories and proof contexts. In: Borwein, J.M., Farmer, W.M. (eds.) MKM 2006. LNCS (LNAI), vol. 4108, pp. 31–43. Springer, Heidelberg (2006)
5. Codescu, M.: Generalized theoroidal institution comorphisms. In: Parisi-Presicce, F. (ed.) WADT 1997. LNCS, vol. 1376, pp. 88–101. Springer, Heidelberg (1998)
6. Goguen, J., Roşu, G.: Institution morphisms. Formal Aspects of Computing 13, 274–307 (2002) (10.1007/s001650200013)
7. Goguen, J.A., Burstall, R.M.: Institutions: Abstract model theory for specification and programming. Journal of the Association for Computing Machinery 39, 95–146 (1992); Predecessor in: Clarke, E., Kozen, D. (eds.): Logic of Programs 1983. LNCS, vol. 164, pp. 221–256. Springer, Heidelberg (1984)
8. Goguen, J.A., Rosu, G.: Composing hidden information modules over inclusive institutions. In: Owe, O., Krogdahl, S., Lyche, T. (eds.) From Object-Orientation to Formal Methods. LNCS, vol. 2635, pp. 96–123. Springer, Heidelberg (2004)
9. Hutter, D.: Management of change in verification systems. In: Proceedings 15th IEEE International Conference on Automated Software Engineering, ASE 2000, pp. 23–34. IEEE Computer Society Press, Los Alamitos (2000)
10. Kohlhase, M. (ed.): OMDoc – An Open Markup Format for Mathematical Documents [version 1.2]. LNCS (LNAI), vol. 4180. Springer, Heidelberg (2006)
11. Meseguer, J.: General logics. In: Logic Colloquium 87, pp. 275–329. North-Holland, Amsterdam (1989)
12. Mossakowski, T.: Specifications in an arbitrary institution with symbols. In: Bert, D., Choppy, C., Mosses, P.D. (eds.) WADT 1999. LNCS, vol. 1827, pp. 252–270. Springer, Heidelberg (2000)

13. Mossakowski, T.: Heterogeneous development graphs and heterogeneous borrowing. In: Nielsen, M., Engberg, U. (eds.) FOSSACS 2002. LNCS, vol. 2303, pp. 326–341. Springer, Heidelberg (2002)
14. Mossakowski, T.: Heterogeneous specification and the heterogeneous tool set. Habilitation thesis, University of Bremen (2005)
15. Mossakowski, T., Autexier, S., Hutter, D.: Development graphs - proof management for structured specifications. Journal of Logic and Algebraic Programming, special issue on Algebraic Specification and Development Techniques 67(1-2), 114–145 (2006)
16. Mossakowski, T., Diaconescu, R., Tarlecki, A.: What is a logic translation? Logica Universalis 3(1), 95–124 (2009)
17. Mosses, P.D. (ed.): CASL Reference Manual. LNCS, vol. 2960. Springer, Heidelberg (2004)
18. Rabe, F., Schürmann, C.: A practical module system for lf. In: LFMTP 2009: Proceedings of the Fourth International Workshop on Logical Frameworks and Meta-Languages, pp. 40–48. ACM, New York (2009)
19. Sannella, D.T., Tarlecki, A.: Extended ML: an institution-independent framework for formal program development. In: Poigné, A., Pitt, D.H., Rydeheard, D.E., Abramsky, S. (eds.) Workshop on Category Theory and Computer Programming. LNCS, vol. 240, pp. 364–389. Springer, Heidelberg (1986)
20. Tarlecki, A.: Institution representation. Unpublished note, Dept. of Computer Science, University of Edinburgh (1987)
21. Tarlecki, A.: Moving between logical systems. In: Recent Trends in Data Type Specification, pp. 478–502. Springer, Heidelberg (1998)

The VATES-Diamond as a Verifier's Best Friend

Sabine Glesner, Björn Bartels, Thomas Göthel, and Moritz Kleine

Berlin Institute of Technology (TU Berlin)
Department of Software Engineering and Theoretical Computer Science
{glesner,bbartels,tgoethel,mkleine}@cs.tu-berlin.de

Abstract. Within a model-based software engineering process it needs to be ensured that properties of abstract specifications are preserved by transformations down to executable code. This is even more important in the area of safety-critical real-time systems where additionally non-functional properties are crucial. In the VATES[1] project, we develop formal methods for the construction and verification of embedded systems. We follow a novel approach that allows us to formally relate abstract process algebraic specifications to their implementation in a compiler intermediate representation. The idea is to extract a low-level process algebraic description from the intermediate code and to formally relate it to previously developed abstract specifications. We apply this approach to a case study from the area of real-time operating systems and show that this approach has the potential to seamlessly integrate modeling, implementation, transformation and verification stages of embedded system development.

1 Introduction

The correctness of software in embedded safety-critical real-time systems is a necessary precondition for the correct mode of operation of such systems. Correctness is especially important if a failure entails high costs or even the loss of human lives. Satellites or embedded systems in the medical domain are examples for safety-critical systems. Bugs in these systems are particularly critical since one does not know when they will show up and what consequences they might have. Testing as a validation method cannot find all bugs completely. If one wants to guarantee system correctness, one needs to formally prove the correctness of the employed software with respect to a suitable specification.

In the VATES[1] project, we develop and combine foundations and methods for the construction and verification of embedded reactive concurrent real-time software systems. It is our goal to verify such systems for the entire development chain, starting from a declarative specification, to the source code, to the executable machine code that has been generated by compilers.

In our research, we start with the hypothesis that reactive software systems in embedded systems exhibit certain structures which are characterized by their

[1] VATES = Verification and Transformation of Embedded Systems, funded by the German Science Foundation (DFG).

S. Siegler and N. Wasser (Eds.): Walther Festschrift, LNAI 6463, pp. 81–101, 2010.

processes and their communication patterns. When translating embedded software to executable machine code, these structures should be retained. We investigate such embedded control structures and communication patterns by taking the BOSS operating system [24] as a case study. BOSS is an appropriate case study since it has been used in various embedded systems successfully (for example in a satellite, in medical systems and electronic lottery systems) and has been designed right from the beginning with the goal to verify it later on.

In many embedded systems and especially in those controlled by the BOSS operating system, the number of processes is statically fixed. No new processes are created during run-time of the system. Such systems can be modeled by specifications formulated in the CSP (Communicating Sequential Processes) calculus [14], which is also the calculus that we have chosen as modeling formalism in our research within the VATES project. More precisely, we take the process calculus Timed CSP [26] as mathematical basis for formal proofs. Timed CSP is a formal modeling language that allows for the convenient specification and verification of reactive, concurrent real-time systems. We formalize our specifications and correctness proofs in the Isabelle/HOL theorem prover [25] where proofs are mechanized and (at least partly) automated.

A direct translation from Timed CSP to a programming language such as C++, the actual implementation language of the BOSS operating system, is hard to verify due to the semantic complexity of typical programming languages. Most programming languages offer a rich type system and many language constructs that allow the programmer to write understandable programs. Nevertheless, the semantics of such languages gets complex, and each language feature adds disproportionately more complexity to the semantic description. To avoid the semantic complexity of programming languages in our verification setting, we stepwise transform Timed CSP specifications into a compiler intermediate representation (IR), namely into the Low Level Virtual Machine (LLVM) [21] IR language. From there, LLVM programs can be compiled further to executable assembler or machine code. To verify the correctness of this transformation step from Timed CSP into LLVM code, we re-translate the LLVM code automatically into a structurally simpler Timed CSP model and prove that it is a refinement of the original Timed CSP model. In doing so we avoid the complex semantic descriptions of typical programming languages such as C++, which is a huge advantage of our approach.

In this paper, we present the current state of our approach and apply it to the verification of the BOSS scheduler to show its principal applicability to the verification of embedded systems. As the treatment of timing properties in its entirety is still work in progress, we partly restrict ourselves to variants of untimed CSP in this paper. The rest of this paper is organized as follows: In Section 2, we introduce our VATES diamond approach together with the formalisms and languages that we are using in the VATES project. In Section 3, we present the verification steps that are necessary in our proof framework for relating high-level Timed CSP specifications to executable code in the LLVM intermediate representation. In Section 4, we informally describe the BOSS scheduler, develop a formal

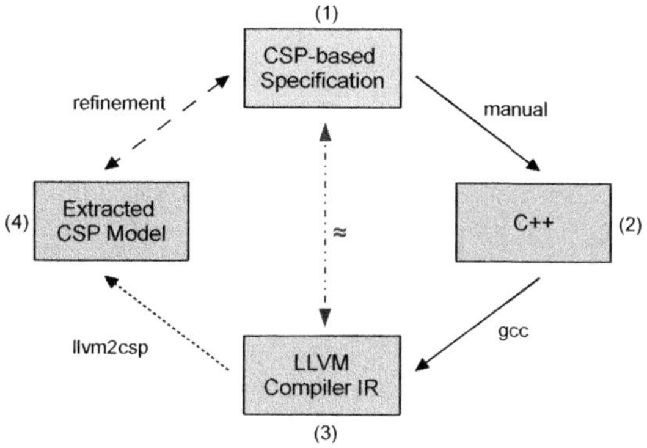

Fig. 1. The VATES Diamond-like Proof Framework

high-level model of it in CSP-OZ [9] and prove crucial properties to be correct. A generated low-level model of the scheduler is given in Section 5. Furthermore, we formally relate the low-level and the high-level model of the scheduler. Related work is discussed in Section 6. Finally, in Section 7, we conclude this paper and discuss ideas for future work.

2 The VATES Diamond Approach

The context of our approach is the VATES project [1]. Its aim is to develop concepts for verifying the correctness of embedded software. In this section we summarize our approach, which is described in more detail in [4].

The goal of the VATES project is to support the verification of crucial properties on all abstraction levels of embedded software, from the abstract specification down to executable code. The general (diamond-like) structure of our approach is given in Figure 1. We start with a high-level CSP-based specification where crucial properties are verified (1). Then, a software developer implements a program, conforming to the specification, in a high-level programming language such as C++ (2). By further employing an LLVM-based compiler we get to an LLVM representation of the C++ code (3). Now, the idea is to formally prove that the LLVM code conforms to the abstract specification. This property is established in two steps: 1. A low-level CSP based model (4) is automatically extracted from the LLVM code. 2. This low-level CSP model is shown to be a formal refinement of the abstract specification using existing verification tools such as the FDR2 refinement checker.

This section briefly introduces the formalisms, languages and tools that we are using within the VATES project.

2.1 Brief Introduction to CSP, Timed CSP and CSP-OZ

CSP (Communicating Sequential Processes) is a process calculus developed in the early 1980s [14]. It is capable of specifying and verifying reactive and concurrent systems, where the modeling of communication plays a key role. CSP is equipped with a rich set of process operators for defining possibly infinite transition systems by, for example, prefixing ($a \rightarrow P$), sequential composition ($P_1; P_2$), external ($\Box$) and internal ($\sqcap$) choice, hiding ($P \backslash A$) and parallel composition ($P_1 [|A|] P_2$). STOP is a process which cannot do anything, SKIP cannot do anything except terminating indicated by the communication of the special event $\surd$, $a \rightarrow P$ first communicates a and then behaves like process P.

There are several semantic models of CSP. The most popular semantics for CSP are trace semantics, failure semantics and failure-divergence semantics [26]. In the trace semantics of CSP, a process is represented by the set of all its possible communication sequences. By contrast, the failure semantics also records the refusals of a process, i.e. the events a process can refuse after a particular communication sequence. Both these semantics are unable to recognize processes with infinite internal behavior. The failure-divergence semantics fills exactly this gap.

Timed CSP shares most of the operators with (untimed) CSP. It extends the CSP calculus with the timed primitives $P \overset{d}{\triangleright} Q$ (*Timeout*) and $P \triangle_d Q$ (*Timed Interrupt*). Intuitively, the meaning of a *Timeout* is that the process P can be triggered by some (external) event within d time units. If this happens, the *Timeout* is resolved in favor of P. If the time expires without P being triggered, process Q handles this situation, i.e., the *Timeout* is resolved in favor of Q. The *Timed Interrupt* construction has a similar meaning. Here, P can (successfully) *terminate* within d time units, otherwise Q is started. The syntax of (Timed) CSP is given by the following grammar:

$$\begin{aligned} P := & \; STOP \mid SKIP \mid a \rightarrow P \mid a : A \rightarrow P_a \mid P ; P \mid P \Box P \\ & \mid P \sqcap P \mid P \underset{A}{\parallel} P \mid P \backslash A \mid P \triangle P \mid P \overset{d}{\triangleright} P \mid P \triangle_d P \mid X \end{aligned}$$

There are two main types of semantics which are typically used in the context of Timed CSP: The denotational Timed Failures semantics and the operational semantics which interprets Timed CSP as labeled transition system.

CSP-OZ [9] is a combination of CSP and Object-Z [28]. With CSP alone, modeling explicit states is rather complex and in practical situations not feasible. CSP-OZ blends the strong state space modeling capabilities provided by Object-Z and the process description facilities offered by CSP. This leads to a formalism that allows well-structured specifications focusing simultaneously on the state variables and process characteristics of a system in a modular fashion.

In addition to the Object-Z parts, CSP-OZ classes consist of (typed) channel and method declarations that define the interface of the specified class. These can be used for communication with the environment, i.e. other CSP-OZ classes and their methods. Channels from the CSP part may have supporting operations defined in the Object-Z part that are divided into two schemas: the enabling schema specifying conditions that have to be satisfied to execute an operation and the effect schema describing the effect of the operation on the state of the class.

Furthermore, the class contains a CSP part that describes the behavior of the class and its operations from a process-oriented point of view. The CSP part consists of CSP terms and must provide a *main* process that determines the dynamic behavior of the class, i.e. the order of applying operations. The channel names used in the CSP part must be a subset of the channels defined in the interface of the class.

The semantics of CSP-OZ can be given in terms of the CSP semantics [10]. The Object-Z part of a class is translated into a CSP process P_{OZ} and glued together with the CSP part *main* of the respective class by parallel composition.

The idea is to offer the operations of the class through an external choice in P_{OZ}. This process is synchronized with the CSP part of the class. This means that the synchronization set A comprises all events representing operations of the Object-Z part that are also present in the *main* process. The composition is formally given by $P_{OZ}|[A]|main$.

Tool Support. All three mentioned semantics of CSP are supported by the FDR2 [11] refinement checker. FDR2 is well-suited for refinement checking of specifications based on the denotational semantics of CSP. Another CSP tool is ProB [22] which is well-suited for the verification of temporal properties based on the transition semantics of CSP.

For Timed CSP, no comprehensive tool support exists yet. Therefore, we have formalized Timed CSP in the Isabelle/HOL theorem prover [12] and provide a theory for the verification of parameterized systems [13] based on network invariants [20]. This is briefly explained in Section 2.

As documented in [10] and [16], it is possible to transform Object-Z and CSP-OZ specifications into CSP_M, which is the input language of the FDR2 refinement checker. The transformation is based on the semantical idea of CSP-OZ as described above. It is realized by an operator in the functional language provided by CSP_M. Therefore, FDR2 can be used to also verify CSP-OZ models.

2.2 LLVM

The LLVM compiler infrastructure provides a modular framework that can be easily extended by user-defined compilation passes. It offers a diverse set of predefined analyses and several optimizations that can be used out of the box. LLVM is tailored for the development of source code transformation and analysis tools. Its intermediate representation (IR) is the heart of the compiler infrastructure project. It is a typed assembler-like language [21], which is used internally as the basis for compiler optimizations. The LLVM framework provides gcc-based frontends for a variety of programming languages, including C++. The existence of the gcc-based frontend enables us to adapt our approach, which currently focuses on C++, to other programming languages with little effort because it is source-language-independent and relies on the LLVM IR only.

2.3 Isabelle/HOL

Isabelle is a generic interactive proof assistant. It enables the formalization of mathematical models and provides tools for proving theorems that are mechanically checked. Isabelle can be instantiated with different so-called object logics. Isabelle/HOL [25] is one particular instantiation of it, which is based on Higher Order Logic. The main advantage of HOL is its high expressiveness. Theorem provers based on HOL require a high level of expertise but allow for reasoning about models whose state space is too large (or even infinite) to be automatically checked by, say, a model checker. Unlike model checking, proving theorems in a theorem prover like Isabelle/HOL is highly interactive. Specifications have to be designed carefully to enable concise proofs about their properties.

3 Verification Steps in the VATES Proof Framework

In the VATES project, we verify implementations by automatically extracting a process-algebraic model out of them and by proving that this extracted model is a refinement of a specification that is supposed to be fulfilled by the implementation. The general diamond-like proof structure of our approach is given in Figure 1 and has been introduced in the previous section. In this section, we discuss the individual proof steps in more detail.

3.1 A Mechanized Theory of Parameterized Systems for Timed CSP

To support machine assisted verification on the level of the abstract specifications, we provide a mechanized theory of Timed CSP in Isabelle/HOL [12]. We especially consider parameterized systems, i.e. systems with arbitrarily many homogeneous components. This is especially helpful when dealing with complex systems that can be divided into a control component and an arbitrary number of homogeneous subcomponents, for example a system that consists of a scheduler and an arbitrary number of threads. Many complex systems can be viewed as exhibiting this structure. The theory of Timed CSP is thus further extended with a framework that supports modeling and analysis of parameterized systems [13]. Additionally, we enrich this framework with capabilities to verify parts of the proof obligations fully automatically by employing the FDR2 refinement checker and the UPPAAL model checker [6].

3.2 Annotations during Compilation to Guide the Verification

After crucial properties have shown to be valid on the abstract level, a software developer implements the abstract models in a high-level programming language like C++. This satisfies the needs of the final system in terms of modularization, performance, code-style and documentation. In the development of embedded systems, advanced code optimizations are often necessary due to performance reasons or restricted resources, for example. Hence, we do not aim to transform the abstract models to source code fully automatically. The implementation of an abstract specification is not a straightforward task, so we are investigating a prototyping approach [17]. The idea is to construct a prototype out of a CSP specification by binding program code to certain CSP events. This prototype can then be simulated using a specialized CSP runtime environment. Optimized implementations can then be manually derived from this prototype. To establish conformance of the implementation to the specification, the programmer annotates the code to support subsequent verification steps when developing the actual C++ implementation. By using annotations on the level of the implementation language and transforming them to the LLVM IR level we are able to use the programmers knowledge in order to achieve a high degree of automatization for our verification tasks. The programmer might for example annotate how a certain feature from the high-level specification is implemented within the code or provide invariants for loops etc. using annotations. The purpose of the previously generated prototype is to help the programmer find the right annotations. Furthermore, the annotations can include assumptions about the timing behavior of the program. This annotated high-level implementation is then compiled with an LLVM-based compiler. To this end, we are using llvm-gcc, a version of gcc that internally uses the LLVM compiler infrastructure and IR. We chose to implement the annotation language using ghost-functions and ghost-variables which are functions and variables that are present for verification purposes only and do not alter the behavior of the original program.

3.3 Model Extraction and Refinement

We have chosen to relate the abstract Timed CSP model and the corresponding intermediate LLVM representation by automatically extracting a low-level CSP based model from it. To this end, we have implemented our llvm2csp tool [18] to perform this task using the annotations of the code. To show the refinement relation between the low-level and the high-level CSP models, the refinement checker FDR2 [11] is used. In [18] we also explained that the low-level models are divided into platform-, domain-, and application-specific parts, as depicted in Figure 2. The platform-specifc part models hardware abstractions. Domain-specific details depend on the application domain. For example, in the case of verification of basic BOSS-applications, this comprises scheduling and context switching. In the long term, platform- and domain-specific models are to be chosen from a library. The two parts are mostly manually modeled but are parameterized so that they can be reused by all applications of the domain they have been designed for. The application-specific part is generated from the LLVM-IR. Parameters (such as types and channels) for the predefined parts are automatically generated from the LLVM IR of the program. In the present case of verifying the BOSS-scheduler, the domain-specific part models calls to

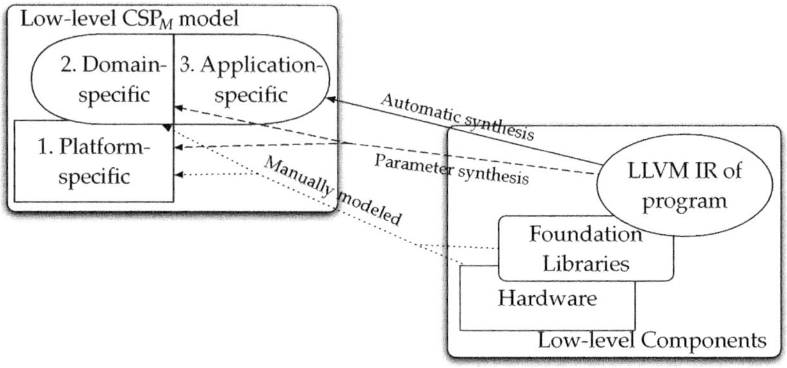

Fig. 2. The three Parts of the Low-Level CSP Model

the scheduler's methods and the application-specific part is generated from the implementations of these methods.

3.4 Verification of Model Extractions and Abstractions

A crucial part in our approach is to show that the extraction algorithm of llvm2csp preserves the semantics of LLVM. We have to ensure that the CSP models emitted by llvm2csp (the dashed arrow between (3) and (4) in Figure 1) correctly reflect the semantics of corresponding LLVM programs. To this end, we developed an operational semantics of LLVM in [3]. Due to the simplicity of intermediate languages, this is less complex than defining a comprehensive formal semantics for a language like C++. We then extend the transition system defined by the operational semantics to a labeled transition system. Information about the behavior of an LLVM program, for example about a variable being written, is attached to the transitions between states. Here, states are identified with the configurations of the operational semantics, i.e. the memory and registers and their values. For CSP the standard operational semantics also defines a labeled transition system where states are identified with the progress of the CSP process. Using the notion of weak bisimulation, we can identify the states of the transition systems and thereby establish the desired relationship between the two. We are also working on formalizing a hoare style proof calculus for the LLVM IR that can be used to prove annotations that abstract over code regions in the implementation and are used by llvm2csp to construct the CSP models of the implementation are indeed correct abstractions.

Altogether, we are able to formally relate the high-level CSP-based specification and its corresponding implementation in LLVM. Note that following the overall approach, we do not have to formalize the semantics of a high-level programming language like C++ which is known to be rather complex. This becomes even more complicated by the introduction of concurrency. Since we want to verify the whole development chain, the formalization of some intermediate representation is inevitable in each case. Furthermore, not considering a high-level language like C++ supports the language-independence of our approach because LLVM-based compilers exist for many different high-level programming languages.

4 The BOSS Scheduler and Its Formalization in CSP-OZ

In the following, we informally introduce the real-time operating system BOSS and present a CSP-OZ model of its scheduler. The implementation of the scheduler is verified with respect to this model in Section 5.

4.1 The BOSS Operating System and Its Scheduler

BOSS was designed and implemented to meet the needs of embedded real-time systems [24]. Its developers followed the basic principle that the overall design and all components should be as simple as possible. This principle, together with the assumption that no hostile application will ever be deployed on it, justify the decision not to separate address spaces in BOSS. Thus, its multitasking implementation is multithreading, which allows for fast context switching and simple communication between applications.

In this paper, we consider the C++ class of the scheduler along with its method implementations for verification. This implies that we do not need to include any information about the threads other than their control data, which are known to the scheduler. The threads' concrete behaviors and the platform-specific implementation of context switching affect neither the scheduler's internal state nor its behavior. The number of threads that can be deployed on a BOSS installation is fixed. This is, however, a technical limitation of BOSS. We are in principal interested in the verification for arbitrary numbers of threads by employing verification techniques for parameterized systems. Nevertheless, in this paper we only consider various finite instantiations of the scheduler because our theory for the verification of parameterized systems is still work in progress. Another design decision of BOSS was that threads can neither be dynamically created nor destroyed. The possible states of a thread are running, sleeping and waiting. The distinction between sleeping and waiting is that a waiting thread is ready to run, while a sleeping thread is not. A sleeping thread is not considered during scheduling until it becomes a waiting one.

The control data of a thread consists of its priority, time stamp and waiting-until time value. The priority of a thread is an unsigned integer. The time stamp of the thread is used to record the time whenever the thread is activated. More precisely, it is updated each time the processor is assigned to that particular thread. The waiting-until value can be interpreted as a readiness flag that controls whether or not a thread considers itself ready to do anything useful (for example process data). If the time value of waiting-until is in the past, the thread is ready to run (and thus waiting or running), otherwise it is sleeping. There is only one predefined thread, the *idle* thread, which has the lowest possible priority and is never sleeping. When running, it only initiates dispatch operations so that other threads get the control.

In addition to the readiness of a thread, both its priority and its time stamp are taken into account when the scheduler is looking for the next thread to run. The scheduler performs the following search:

1. Pick all threads that are ready to run.
2. Of those, pick all threads that have the highest priority.
3. Of those, pick the one with the longest waiting time.

The existence of the idle thread ensures that the search method described above always succeeds. Given the total ordering of the threads' time stamps, the result of the search is unique. During the initilisation of the system each thread is given a unique time stamp so that a total ordering of the time stamps is always ensured. Stack and context are used to track the progress of the state and to save and restore its current state while the thread is not running. The scheduler itself simply records the pointer to the currently running thread.

The scheduling-relevant methods of BOSS are accessible via the *Thread* interface by calling one of the methods *yield*, *resume* or *suspend* of a thread. These methods alter the thread's readiness flag (or explicitly set the waiting-until time value of the thread) and immediately trigger the scheduler. There are two differences between *suspend* and *yield*. The method *suspend* either takes a time value as parameter or suspends a thread until it is manually resumed. The call of *yield* initiates a dispatch. This means that a ready thread of the same priority and with the longest waiting time is given control. In the case that there are no other ready threads with the same priority, the calling thread simply regains control immediately.

4.2 Modeling the Scheduler in CSP-OZ

This section presents the abstract CSP-OZ model of the BOSS scheduler (corresponding to (1) in Figure 1). We choose CSP-OZ as a formalism for the abstract model because it allows object-oriented specifications that are structured in a fashion similar to object-oriented programming languages like C++, and can be refined to serve as a basis for the actual implementation. The model presented in this section considers the scheduler exclusively and abstracts from any details of the threads that it schedules except for their method calls to the scheduler (*resume*, *suspend*) and their scheduler-internal representation. The call of *yield* in BOSS is abstracted away and captured in the model by communicating the *suspend* operation and the possibility to wakeup before dispatching another thread. We assume that the priority of a thread is immutable during runtime and that the waiting-until value of the threads will never be directly written by any component apart from the scheduler itself. Waiting-until is abstracted away in the model by introducing a readiness-flag of threads and an artificial *wakeup* operation that is invoked nondeterministically to simulate timeouts of waiting-until timers. The time stamp recording the thread's waiting time is abstracted away

```
Scheduler
method resume, suspend : [n? : Names \ {Idle}]
method dispatch : [n! : Names]
method findNextThread, wakeup
main = findNextThread → (DispatchIdle □ DispatchOther)
DispatchIdle = dispatch.Idle → main
DispatchOther = □ x : Names • dispatch.x → (main ⊓ ThreadOp)
ThreadOp = ⊓ op : {resume, suspend} • op?n → main

rNow, rNext : Names
Threads : seq (Names × (ℕ × 𝔹))
-----
#Names = #Threads
∀ x : Names • #(Threads ↾ {find(Threads, x)}) = 1
        [Every thread name uniquely defines a thread and there are no other threads in the list]
isSortedByPriority(Threads)
let idleT == head(Threads ↾ {find(Threads, Idle)}) • isReady(idleT) ∧ getPrio(idleT) = 0
        [Idle is always ready and has priority 0]
getName(last(Threads)) = Idle

INIT
        [Any state satisfying the invariant is a valid initial state]

effect_resume
Δ(Threads)
n? : Names \ {Idle}
-----
Threads' = setStatus(Threads, n?, true)

enable_resume
rNow ≠ Idle

effect_suspend
Δ(Threads)
n? : Names \ {Idle}
-----
Threads' = setStatus(Threads, n?, false)

enable_suspend
rNow ≠ Idle

effect_dispatch
Δ(Threads)
n! : Names
-----
rNow' = rNext
Threads' = updateThreadList(Threads, rNext)
n! = rNow'

effect_findNextThread
Δ(rNext)
-----
rNext' = getName(head(getReadyList(Threads)))

effect_wakeup
Δ(Threads)
n : Names        [n is an arbitrary sleeping thread]
-----
¬ isReady(head(Threads ↾ {find(Threads, n)}))
Threads' = setStatus(Threads, n, true)

enable_wakeup
#getReadyList(Threads) < #Threads
```

Fig. 3. CSP-OZ Model of the Scheduler

by organizing the threads in a sorted list such that threads with longer waiting times have higher indexes compared to threads with shorter waiting times. Within the scheduler, threads are represented as triples consisting of name, priority and readiness flag. As shown in Figure 3, this control data is maintained in the *Threads* list, which is sorted by priority and implicitly by waiting time. To handle the manipulations of the *Threads* list in the CSP-OZ model, we defined various utility functions. The function *updateThreadList(list,(n,p,r))* is used to update a given *list* so that the triple representing the thread identified by *(n,p,r)* is moved to the appropriate place with respect to the order of the list. It is put in after the last thread with the same priority to keep track of the order of waiting times of the threads. The rest of the utility functions have the intuitive meaning given by their names.

The invariants of the scheduler in Figure 3 constrain the state space: The number of available threads does not change. The idle thread has a special role. It is always enabled. Furthermore it has the lowest priority of all threads which is ensured by the assertion that it is always the last element of the *Threads* list. If another thread had priority 0, this thread and the idle thread could switch places. The name of a thread is a unique identifier, so it can only occur once in the list.

The actual scheduling method is represented in the *Scheduler* CSP-OZ class by the combination of the operation schemas *findNextThread* and *dispatch*. Since the *Threads* list is always ordered by priority and waiting time, the scheduling decision within the *dispatch* operation is reduced to taking the name of the first element of the list of ready threads (i.e. the thread with the highest priority and the longest waiting time). When dispatching, its new place in the *Threads* list is behind all other threads that have the same priority.

In the BOSS implementation, dispatching is triggered directly by a timer interrupt or by a thread that either chooses to resume or suspend another thread or to give up control. This behavior is modeled by the `main` process of the *Scheduler* class. After a thread has been given control by the scheduler's *dispatch* operation, there are two possibilities: either a *resume* or *suspend* event may occur before dispatching a new thread or the scheduler may choose another thread directly by communicating the *findNextThread* and *dispatch* events modeling the occurrence of a timer interrupt.

The *suspend* operation modifies the *Threads* list by taking a name as input and setting the readiness flag of the respective thread to false, while the *resume* operation sets the readiness flag of the respective thread to true.

The operation *wakeup* is enabled whenever at least one thread does not have the readiness flag set. Although the *wakeup* event does not appear in the `main` process, it can still be communicated whenever enabled. This follows from the semantics of CSP-OZ.

4.3 Analyzing the CSP-OZ Model

As described in Section 2.1, CSP-OZ can be transformed into CSP_M. We have used FDR2 to show that this model is deadlock and livelock (divergence) free. These properties are shown w.r.t. all legal thread lists up to a fixed maximal length.

Furthermore, we have analyzed the temporal behavior of the model using the LTL model checking capabilities of ProB for several concrete lists of threads. Due to some bugs in ProB, we have not been able to consider the verification w.r.t. all intitial states of the corresponding CSP-OZ class of the scheduler. Instantiating the scheduler with concrete lists can be done by providing the process `System(list) = Scheduler(list^<(Idle,0, true)>)` with a list of process description triples and a set consisting of the process names. The triple representing the idle process is always appended to the list of processes. Model checking is performed using a script that produces the relevant LTL formulas for the respective settings, i.e. the number of threads is a parameter of the script. One

```
SysT2T1 = System(<(T2,2,true),(T1,1, true)>)

1. not(([dispatch.T1]) U [dispatch.T2])
2. GF[dispatch.T2] => G([suspend.T2]
                   => ((not [dispatch.T2]) U ([resume.T2] or [wakeup])))
```

Fig. 4. LTL Assertions about the CSP-OZ Model

example is given in Figure 4. First, we instantiate the system with two threads (named T1 and T2) that have increasing priority. Since thread T2 has the highest priority, it must have the exclusive right to consume CPU time until it gives up control itself. This is reflected by the first LTL formula in Figure 4. When a thread (T2 in this example) is suspended, the scheduler only transfers control to the thread after it has been resumed. The second property indicates that the scheduler transfers control to the suspended thread number two only after it has been resumed or woken up.

So far, we have presented a model in CSP-OZ that captures the most important properties of the BOSS scheduler. In the next section, we demonstrate how this model can be used to verify the implementation of the scheduler.

5 Case Study: Verifying the Implementation of the BOSS Scheduler

In this section, we present the low-level model of the BOSS scheduler that corresponds to its LLVM implementation. Parts of the low-level CSP_M model have been automatically extracted from the LLVM intermediate representation of the original BOSS implementation in C++ (see (2) to (4) in Figure 1). We start by presenting the domain- and platform-specific parts of the low-level model. Then, we present a manually simplified version of the automatically extracted application-specific parts of the low-level model. Finally, we formally relate the high-level model and the low-level model of the BOSS scheduler. Note that even using the optimized CSP_M models presented in [19], the low-level model generated by our llvm2csp tool contains too many states for verification with FDR2. Thus, for the purposes of the case study in this paper, we manually simplified the generated model and plan to further automate abstractions to generate more abstract models for subsequent analysis with FDR2.

5.1 Modeling the Domain- and Platform-Specific Parts of the Low-Level Model

As described in Section 3, a CSP model can be synthesized from the LLVM IR of a program. An LLVM-method is translated into a function that takes an integer and a state description and returns a sequential process modeling a non-empty sequence of LLVM instructions and its possible effect on the current state of the system.

```
LLSys(0,1) = CALL(Dispatch_ID,1,1)
LLSys(1,1) = []x:{Resume_ID, Suspend_ID}@
     not isNameMatch(getRunner(1),Idle) & CALL(x,1,1)
       [] CONTINUE(0,1)
LowLevelModel(1) = LLSys(0,1)
```

Fig. 5. Model of the `LLSys` Process Glueing together the Methods of the Scheduler

The final low-level model is then made up of such sequential processes modeling the functions of the system (the application-specific part) that are synthesized from the implementation. These processes maintain a list that models registers and the global memory. This list is modified by functions modeling basic operations such as integer arithmetics, store and load operations and so forth.

The state that may be modified by an operation is modeled as an n-tuple (fixed-size list). This n-tuple represents the memory used by the program and contains global variables as well as typed registers that can be shared among the methods. Since BOSS does not support dynamic memory management, the parameter n can be statically computed during compilation. Furthermore, LLVM provides typing information that is used to construct the n-tuple. The state contains the stack of a method, which is modeled as a list of pairs, each holding the identifier of the method's process definition and its current program counter in that method.

The resulting application-specific processes are glued together with processes that may model library calls or other components whose implementation details are unknown. Verifying the scheduler of an operating system is different from verifying applications running atop an operating system. The reason is that in the latter case, the implementation of operating system components is commonly abstracted away. Verifying the scheduler requires modeling aspects such as timer interrupts that invoke the scheduler, for example. In our case, the domain-specific part cannot yet be chosen from a library but is manually modeled here. This is done in the process `LLSys` shown in Fig. 5.

Initially this process behaves like the `CALL` process, modeling a call to the *dispatch* method of the scheduler. When the call returns, it will continue at position 1 of the `LLSys` process. At position 1, either one of the operations resume and suspend is chosen and invoked, or the process continues at position 0, which means that it starts over again. This process has been manually developed and models the abstract behavior of threads and the timer interrupt that is commonly used to invoke the scheduler in a predefined time interval. The `LLSys` process is the entry to a nonterminating sequential process, which carries the scheduler's state including the list of threads, the currently running thread and its own stack as it evolves. For the sake of convenience, we define the process `LowLevelModel`, which is the `LLSys` process starting at position 0 with a given initial state. This process is the one we use for verification purposes.

The definitions of the processes `CONTINUE`, `CALL` and `RETURN` are given in Fig. 6. They also belong to the domain-specific part of the low-level model. They show

```
CONTINUE(pc,state) =
    if null(getStack(state)) then e_stack_underflow -> STOP else
        elemAt(procDefs,getID(state))(pc,state)
    [] isSleeping(getThreads(state)) & []x:getNames(state)@wakeup.x ->
        CONTINUE(pc,setThreads(state,setReady2(getThreads(state),x,true)))
CALL(defId, pc, state) = let stack = getStack(state) within
    if #stack > max_call_depth then e_stack_overflow -> STOP else
        CONTINUE(0,setStack(state,<(pc,defId)>^stack))
RETURN(state) = let stack = getStack(state)
        nstate = setStack(state,tail(stack)) within
    if null(getStack(nstate)) then e_stack_underflow -> STOP else
    elemAt(procDefs,getID(nstate))(getPC(state),nstate)
```

Fig. 6. Processes Modeling Function Call, Returns and Continuations

how the stack is used to store program counter and process definition id to handle function calls, returns or continuations. Stack overflow and stack underflow is detected by emitting a special event (error code). As stated above, the awakening of threads that have been suspended for some time has to be modeled. This is done within the definition of `CONTINUE`: whenever there is any sleeping thread, a nondeterministically chosen thread's ready flag can be toggled. This can be repeated until all threads are ready again before the process continues. Observe that these three processes ultimately use the `elemAt` function to obtain a process identified by the return value of `getID(state)` from the `procDefs` list, which contains the functions that return application-specific processes and the `LLSys` process itself.

5.2 The Application-Specific Part of the Scheduler's Low-level Model

The application-specific part of the scheduler's low-level model is generated from the implementations of the methods *resume*, *suspend*, *findNextThreadToRun* and *dispatch*. The `procDefs` list created for this case study:

```
procDefs = <LLSys, Resume, Suspend, FindNextThreadToRun, Dispatch>
```

Thus, `elemAt(procDefs, 4)` returns the function `Dispatch`, which in turn, given the program counter n and the current state, yields the process modeling the n-th sequence of instructions of the *Scheduler::dispatch* method.

An excerpt from the implementation of the *Scheduler::dispatch* is given in Fig. 7. These lines show that a candidate for the next thread to run is chosen. The current time is used to determine whether a thread is ready to run or if it is still sleeping. The method *Scheduler::findNextThreadToRun* considers the waiting times and priorities of the threads in order to determine the candidate. In the next line, the case that all threads are sleeping is handled by assigning the address of the idle thread to the candidate variable. Line 4 of Fig. 7 shows that a call to the scheduling method does not necessarily lead to a context switch.

```
1 nextRunner = Scheduler::findNextThreadToRun(now);
2 if(nextRunner == NULL) nextRunner = &idleThread;
3
4 if(runningNow->priority <= nextRunner->priority){
5   nextRunner->lastTimeActivated = now;
6   oldRunner  = (Thread *)runningNow;
7   runningNow = nextRunner;
8   transfer(&(oldRunner->context),
9              nextRunner->context);
10 }
11 llvm2csp_annotate(``dispatch.'',runningNow);
```

Fig. 7. Excerpt from the BOSS Scheduler Implementation

Since the currently running thread is not a member of the global list holding the waiting and sleeping threads, the candidate may have a lower priority than the currently running thread and switching must be avoided. If the candidate has at least the same priority as the currently running thread, its time stamp is updated, the currently running thread is updated and control is passed to the new runner (lines 5 - 8). Line 11 makes use of CSP annotations to define arbitrary observation points in the LLVM IR by using the ghost function *llvm2csp_annotate*. The LLVM IR of this method consists of 118 instructions in the unoptimized version. Accordingly its representation in CSP is also not small enough to be presented here. A simplified version is shown in Fig. 8. At position 0, the process `Dispatch` begins by calling the `FindNextThreadToRun` process. This process computes and modifies an entry of the n-tuple modeling the global state which is accessible by `getNewRunner` and `setNewRunner`. This entry is only used to hold the return value of *Scheduler::findNextThreadToRun*. Note that the new runner may be equal to the current runner. At position 1, the new runner is removed from the list of threads, and at position 2 it is inserted into the list again. This models the update of the thread's *lateTimeActivated* time stamp. At position 3, the new runner is assigned to the entry of the n-tuple modeling the *runningNow* pointer. At position 4, the CSP annotation comes into play and the name of the current runner is communicated over the `dispatch` channel for verification purposes. This is necessary to make the outcome of the *Scheduler::dispatch* method observable, which is the possible modification of the *runningNow* pointer, and thus the internal state of the scheduler.

As explained in Section 5.1, a function in LLVM-IR is translated into a CSP_M function that takes an integer denoting the position within the function and a list l which is the current state of the system. This is shown in Figure 8. Each of these processes culminates in a process modeling the next instruction of the modeled method. In most cases, this is the `CONTINUE` process, which immediately evolves to the subprocess modeling the next instruction. This process also provides a way to model branching. The instructions *call* and *return* do not culminate in the `CONTINUE` process but in `CALL` or `RETURN`, respectively.

```
Dispatch(0,l) = CALL(FindNextThreadToRun_ID, 1, l)
Dispatch(1,l) =
    CONTINUE(2,setThreads(l,deleteFrom(getThreads(l),getNewRunner(l))))
Dispatch(2,l) =
    CONTINUE(3,setThreads(l,insert(getThreads(l),getNewRunner(l))))
Dispatch(3,l) = CONTINUE(4,setRunner(l,getNewRunner(l)))
Dispatch(4,l) = dispatch.getName(getRunner(l)) -> RETURN(l)
```

Fig. 8. Simplified Version of the Process Modeling the Scheduler's Dispatch Operation

From the LLVM IR, we obtain processes describing the behavior of the scheduler's operations. These processes deal with the data types that are present in the LLVM IR and have to be manually modified in some cases. As explained in Section 4.1, the control data of a thread consist of a waiting-until time value, a time stamp and a priority. The waiting-until field is modeled by a boolean readiness flag because we use model-checking and refinement-checking tools to investigate our models and must therefore do some rigorous abstractions to keep the models small enough. The semantics of the waiting-until field is preserved by this abstraction. To obtain a complete proof of the schedulers implementation this needs to be shown formally, of course. We are working on a hoare style proof calculus for the LLVM IR to show that annotations that abstract over code regions and are used for the model construction indeed reflect the code behavior . The second field that records a time value is the time stamp `lastTimeActivated`, which we abstract away by introducing a sorted list that holds the threads and in which the order of its elements represents the time stamp of the threads. Thus, to keep the model in shape for subsequent model-checking, we use abstractions regarding the waiting-until field and the thread's last activation time stamp similar to the ones used in the scheduler's CSP-OZ model.

Threads are represented as triples of name, priority and readiness flag. The actual values can be extracted from the triple using pattern matching. For the sake of convenience, we have defined three selectors: `getName`, `getPrio` and `getReady`. The priority of threads needs less abstraction: it suffices to reduce its range to the number of available threads so that each thread can have its own priority. Scheduling considers priorities first and waiting time as a secondary search criterion. Thus, we organize the list of threads as a sorted list with priority as the primary and waiting time as the secondary order criterion. Whenever a thread is activated, it is deleted from the sorted list of threads and then inserted into it again.

5.3 Relating the Models of the Scheduler

In the preceding sections, we have presented two models of the BOSS scheduler. We not only used different formalisms but also developed the system from different perspectives. In the CSP-OZ-based model, we focused on the object-oriented implementation and modeled state, functionality and behavior of the relevant classes, whereas in the CSP_M encoding of the scheduler's implementation the system is regarded as a single sequential process.

The behaviors of the two models can be compared after translating the CSP-OZ model to CSP_M. Following this approach, we can do refinement proofs using FDR2. To show that the low-level model is an implementation that respects the CSP-OZ specification, we proved that it is a failure-divergence refinement of the CSP-OZ model. This implies that the low-level model is also deadlock and livelock free because it was already shown on the level of the abstract specification. Note that the events modeling special error codes for stack overflow, stack underflow or violations of abstractions are not hidden and thus do not occur in the low-level model. Given the fact that failures refinement preserves satisfaction of LTL formulas [23], the properties proved in Sect. 4.3 also hold on the corresponding instances of the low-level model. The CSP_M script containing the CSP_M version of the high-level model, the low-level model presented here, and the assertions relating the two models, is available at `http://user.cs.tu-berlin.de/~mkleine/scheduler.csp`.

Altogether, this case study demonstrates the feasibility of our approach as it allows us to work with implementations given in real-life programming languages (C++ and LLVM) while at the same time relating these implementations to abstract models. These abstract models are formulated in process-algebraic terms and are used to verify the correctness of the implementations via refinement proofs.

6 Related Work

The verification of low-level software systems and embedded operating systems has attracted several research projects.

Spec# [2] and VCC [7] are verification methodologies that translate high-level languages like C# and C to the intermediate language BoogiePL. Necessary verification information is annotated to the source code. To discharge the resulting verification conditions, the automatic theorem prover Z3 is used. In contrast to our approach, BoogiePL is not a compiler-intermediate representation but a language tailored for verification purposes. Furthermore, we focus on refinement and transformation of a high-level specification to executable code rather than direct source-code verification.

The AVACS [5] project deals with the verification of complex (real-time) systems. Verification is carried out at the specification level. Transformations to and the verification of executable code are not considered within that project.

There are two further projects concerned with the verification of a real-time operating system kernel. In the VFiasco project [15], verification is carried out at source code level by defining the denotational semantics for a subset of C++. One of its results is the verification of Duff's Device but the techniques were not applied to existing operating system components. The L4.verified project [8] uses a refinement approach that proves different layers of abstraction to be consistent. The lowest level of abstraction is given by C code, which is shown to be a refinement of a more abstract design. Neither of these two approaches, L4.verified and VFiasco, covers concurrency. Furthermore, the transformation to intermediate and executable code is not considered.

Closely related to our work is the verification of a real-time operating system controlling a space satellite using Timed-CSP-Z [27]. Timed-CSP-Z models are translated into a petri-net-based formalism and the resulting petri-nets are analyzed. The approach focuses on deadlock detection. Neither refinement proofs nor transformations to code are within the focus of this work.

7 Conclusion and Future Work

In this paper we have described the VATES approach to embedded systems verification. After a short introduction to the VATES diamond approach and the most important formalisms, tools and languages used in VATES, namely (Timed) CSP, CSP-OZ, Isabelle/HOL and LLVM, we have outlined the general approach taken in the VATES project in more detail.

We have demonstrated the feasibility of our approach by verifying the scheduler component of the BOSS operating system. We have started from a high-level specification in CSP-OZ for which we have analyzed crucial properties and semi-automatically extracted a CSP model from the LLVM IR representation of the schedulers implementation in C++. Subsequently, we have been able to show that the LLVM implementation, i.e. the extracted model, is a refinement of the abstract specification w.r.t. the failure divergence semantics of CSP. This implies that the implementation fulfills the same properties as the abstract specification.

Moreover, we have also given some pointers to ongoing and future work that completes our approach. In our case study, we have used CSP-OZ and the model checker FDR2 to specify and verify crucial system properties. Since the nature of model checking imposes a limit on the kinds of systems we can handle with this approach we are combining model checking and theorem proving techniques to enable the semi-automatic verification of potentially infinite state systems using the theory of parameterized systems tailored for Timed CSP specifications. As the model extraction algorithm is a crucial part of our approach, we are currently working on its verification. As a formal framework, we are developing a formalization of the LLVM IR in Isabelle/HOL that enables us to formally relate the LLVM IR programs to Timed CSP specifications via a bisimulation relation. This relation can then be mechanically verified and used to verify the correctness of the extraction algorithm in an inductive manner. Using the defined operational semantics we are currently constructing a proof calculus that is used to prove correct annotations, for example abstractions over the LLVM code. We are also currently working on the integration of timing behavior into our framework. Timing analyses are already possible on the most abstract layer using our formalization of Timed CSP. As a next step, we need to extend the llvm2csp tool to generate Timed CSP models. To realize this, we plan to augment the LLVM syntax and semantics with information about timing behavior. This includes accounting for processor-specific features like pipelining and cache management.

Our results obtained so far are very promising. In future work, we will apply our verification approach to more complex systems, starting with the integration of further system components into the verification of the BOSS operating system.

We are convinced that our approach has the potential to enable a methodology that seamlessly integrates the modeling, implementation, transformation and verification stages of embedded real-time system development.

References

1. VATES project website, `https://group.swt.tu-berlin.de/vates`
2. Barnett, M., Leino, K.R.M., Schulte, W.: The Spec# Programming System: An Overview. In: Barthe, G., Burdy, L., Huisman, M., Lanet, J.-L., Muntean, T. (eds.) CASSIS 2004. LNCS, vol. 3362, pp. 49–69. Springer, Heidelberg (2005)
3. Bartels, B., Glesner, S.: Formal Modeling and Verification of Low-Level Software Programs. In: 10th International Conference on Qualtiy Software (QSIC 2010), IEEE Computer Society, Los Alamitos (2010)
4. Bartels, B., Glesner, S., Göthel, T.: Model Transformations to Mitigate the Semantic Gap in Embedded Systems Verification. In: International Colloquium on Graph and Model Transformation – on the occasion of the 65th birthday of Hartmut Ehrig (2010) (accepted for publication)
5. Becker, B., Damm, W., Fränzle, M., Olderog, E., Podelski, A., Wilhelm, R.: SFB/TR 14 AVACS – Automatic Verification and Analysis of Complex Systems. It – Information Technology 49(2), 118–126 (2007)
6. Bengtsson, J., Yi, W.: Timed Automata: Semantics, Algorithms and Tools. Lectures on Concurrency and Preti Nets, pp. 87–124. Springer, Heidelberg (2004)
7. Cohen, E., Dahlweid, M., Hillebrand, M., Leinenbach, D., Moskal, M., Santen, T., Schulte, W., Tobies, S.: VCC: A Practical System for Verifying Concurrent C. In: Berghofer, S., Nipkow, T., Urban, C., Wenzel, M. (eds.) TPHOLS 2009. LNCS, vol. 5674, pp. 23–42. Springer, Heidelberg (2009)
8. Elphinstone, K., Klein, G., Derrin, P., Roscoe, T., Heiser, G.: Towards a Practical, Verified Kernel. In: HOTOS 2007 Proceedings of the 11th USENIX workshop on Hot topics in operating systems, Berkeley, CA, USA, pp. 1–6 (2007)
9. Fischer, C.: CSP-OZ: a combination of object-Z and CSP. In: FMOODS 1997 Proceedings of the IFIP TC6 WG6.1 international workshop on Formal methods for open object-based distributed systems, pp. 423–438. Chapman & Hall, Ltd., London (1997)
10. Fischer, C., Wehrheim, H.: Model-Checking CSP-OZ Specifications with FDR. In: IFM, pp. 315–334 (1999)
11. Goldsmith, M., Roscoe, B., Armstrong, P.: Failures-Divergence Refinement - FDR2 User Manual (2005)
12. Göthel, T., Glesner, S.: An Approach for Machine-Assisted Verification of Timed CSP Specifications. Innovations in Systems and Software Engineering - A NASA Journal 7 (2010) (to appear)
13. Göthel, T., Glesner, S.: Towards the Semi-Automatic Verification of Parameterized Real-Time Systems using Network Invariants. In: Proceedings of the 8th IEEE International Conference on Software Engineering and Formal Method (2010) (accepted for publication)
14. Hoare, C.A.R.: Communicating Sequential Processes. Prentice Hall International, London (1985)

15. Hohmuth, M., Tews, H.: The VFiasco Approach for a Verified Operating System. In: Proc. 2nd ECOOP Workshop on Programming Languages and Operating Systems (2005)
16. Kassel, G., Smith, G.: Model Checking Object-Z Classes: Some Experiments with FDR. In: APSEC, pp. 445–452 (2001)
17. Kleine, M., Bartels, B.: On Using CSP for the Construction of Concurrent Programs. In: International Conference on Software Engineering Theory and Practice (SETP 2010), Orlando, Florida, USA (2010)
18. Kleine, M., Helke, S.: Low Level Code Verification Based on CSP Models. In: Oliveira, M., Woodcock, J. (eds.) SBMF 2009. LNCS, vol. 5902, pp. 266–281. Springer, Heidelberg (2009)
19. Kleine, M.: Using CSP for Software Verification. In: Mousavi, Sekerinski (eds.) Proceedings of Formal Methods 2009 Doctoral Symposium, Eindhoven University of Technology, pp. 8–13 (2009)
20. Kurshan, R.P., McMillan, K.L.: A structural induction theorem for processes. Inf. Comput. 117(1), 1–11 (1995)
21. Lattner, C., Adve, V.: LLVM: A Compilation Framework for Lifelong Program Analysis & Transformation. In: Proceedings of the 2004 International Symposium on Code Generation and Optimization (CGO 2004), Palo Alto, California (2004)
22. Leuschel, M., Fontaine, M.: Probing the Depths of CSP-M: A new FDR-compliant Validation Tool. In: Liu, S., Maibaum, T., Araki, K. (eds.) ICFEM 2008. LNCS, vol. 5256, pp. 278–297. Springer, Heidelberg (2008)
23. Leuschel, M., Massart, T., Currie, A.: How to make FDR Spin: LTL model checking of CSP using Refinement. In: Oliveira, J.N., Zave, P. (eds.) FME 2001. LNCS, vol. 2021, p. 99. Springer, Heidelberg (2001)
24. Montenegro, S., Briess, K., Kayal, H.: Dependable Software (BOSS) for the BEESAT Pico Satellite. In: Data System. Aerospace - DASIA 2006, Berlin (2006)
25. Nipkow, T., Paulson, L.C., Wenzel, M.: Isabelle/HOL— A Proof Assistant for Higher-Order Logic. LNCS, vol. 2283. Springer, Heidelberg (2002)
26. Schneider, S.: Concurrent and Real Time Systems: The CSP Approach. John Wiley & Sons, Inc., New York (1999)
27. Sherif, A.M., Sampaio, A., Cavalcante, S.: Specification and Validation of the SACI-1 On-Board Computer Using Timed-CSP-Z and Petri Nets. In: van der Aalst, W.M.P., Best, E. (eds.) ICATPN 2003. LNCS, vol. 2679, pp. 161–180. Springer, Heidelberg (2003)
28. Smith, G.: The Object-Z specification language. Kluwer Academic Publishers, Norwell (2000)

Dynamic Rippling, Middle-Out Reasoning and Lemma Discovery

Moa Johansson[1], Lucas Dixon[2], and Alan Bundy[2]

[1] Dipartimento di Informatica, Università degli Studi di Verona*
[2] School of Informatics, University of Edinburgh
moakristin.johansson@univr.it, {l.dixon,a.bundy}@ed.ac.uk

Abstract. We present a succinct account of *dynamic rippling*, a technique used to guide the automation of inductive proofs. This simplifies termination proofs for rippling and hence facilitates extending the technique in ways that preserve termination. We illustrate this by extending rippling with a terminating version of *middle-out reasoning* for lemma speculation. This supports automatic speculation of schematic lemmas which are incrementally instantiated by unification as the rippling proof progresses. Middle-out reasoning and lemma speculation have been implemented in higher-order logic and evaluated on typical libraries of formalised mathematics. This reveals that, when applied, the technique often finds the needed lemmas to complete the proof, but it is not as frequently applicable as initially expected. In comparison, we show that theory formation methods, combined with simpler proof methods, offer an effective alternative.

1 Introduction

Inductive proof techniques are required for reasoning about repetition. Examples include recursively defined data structures, such as natural numbers, lists and trees. A significant strand of research in automated inductive theorem proving revolves around a technique called *rippling*, which is primarily used to guide rewriting of the step-case [23,11,6]. The guidance provided by rippling is based on observing and annotating syntactic differences between the step-case subgoal and the induction hypothesis. Rippling ensures termination without requiring rewrite rules to be oriented in advance, which makes it easy to configure, and allows it to solve some problems that are otherwise difficult with traditional approaches to rewriting. Recent work has focused on *dynamic rippling* which computes the differences between the goal and the induction hypothesis after each step [23,11]. In the rest of this paper, we refer to dynamic rippling simply as rippling.

Automating inductive proofs gives rise to several challenging problems, including the discovery of lemmas [5]. It has generally been assumed that lemma

* This research was funded by EPSRC grants EPE/005713/1 and EP/P501407/1, and by grant 2007-9E5KM8 of the Ministero dell'Istruzione Università e Ricerca. We would also like to thank Andrew Ireland for many helpful discussions.

S. Siegler and N. Wasser (Eds.): Walther Festschrift, LNAI 6463, pp. 102–116, 2010.

discovery requires user intervention. Interactive theorem provers, such as Isabelle [21], have large libraries of previously proved theorems and carefully configured proof tools that use them. However, for new theory developments, users often spend considerable time identifying and proving the required background lemmas.

Lemma speculation is a heuristic technique for automatically constructing a missing lemma using information from a failed inductive proof attempt. It has long been considered a promising technique to improve rippling based proofs [6,5,15], and a similar approach has also been proposed in [18]. Lemma speculation constructs a schematic lemma which preserves parts of the goal that are similar to the inductive hypothesis and introduces meta-variables to stand for unknown term-structure. The meta-variables are then incrementally instantiated by rewriting steps. This approach, of gradually instantiating the meta-variables in each step, is called *middle-out reasoning*, and has been proposed to tackle a wide variety of problems [8,15,19,7].

The main novel contributions in this paper are as follows:

- A logical account of *dynamic-rippling*. This separates the issues of annotation, guidance, and termination. In particular, it describes how these issues fit together. The result is a succinct formal description which is easy to extend and experiment with. Furthermore, it results in much simpler termination proofs than that of Basin and Walsh [3].
- An illustration of how our formalism for rippling can be extended by describing lemma speculation with middle-out reasoning. This improves on earlier work as it applies to higher-order domains, ensures the termination of middle-out reasoning and enjoys the property that every middle-out rippling proof corresponds to a traditional rippling proof with the speculated lemma.
- An implementation and evaluation of rippling with lemma speculation in IsaPlanner [11]. The implementation builds on the LCF-design methodology of the Isabelle system [21]; all proofs are compositions of a small set of basic trusted inference rules in Isabelle. Our evaluation considers a variety of common theories, including lists, natural numbers, trees and inequalities.

Although our evaluation is positive for our middle-out reasoning, and generally positive for the effectiveness of lemma speculation, it highlights an important and interesting negative result for the applicability of lemma speculation. We remark that this is necessarily an empirical result: there are infinitely many problems which lemma speculation works for, and infinitely many for which it fails. Our empirical evaluation is based on a study of typical theories in interactive proof assistants.

Another approach to lemma discovery is to attempt to automate the synthesis of a richer background theory, given the initial definitions of datatypes and functions, as implemented in the IsaCoSy system [17]. IsaCoSy synthesises progressively larger conjectures using the available theory and avoids the generation of any reducible terms. We compare IsaPlanner's performance using lemma speculation against using a background theory generated by IsaCoSy along with a simpler technique called *lemma calculation*. This shows that more theorems are proved in the latter case. Theory formation offers an effective alternative to the more complex lemma speculation technique.

Notation. We use the symbol @ for the list append function, # for cons, [] for nil, as well as the usual notation where [1, 2, 3] is the list 1#2#3#[]. Variables which are allowed to be instantiated by unification are written $?F$, following the Isabelle convention. These are referred to as *meta-variables.* A *schematic* goal (or lemma) is a goal containing meta-variables. We use the equals symbol (=) for object level equality and the symbol ($\equiv$) to denote that two terms are syntactically identical. We use := for definitions. Finally, we write $t\sigma$, for a term, t, under substitution σ.

2 Proof-Planning and Rippling

Proof-planning is a technique used to guide search in automated theorem proving by exploiting the fact that there are families of proofs with a similar structure [9]. One such family is proof by induction. The development of proof-planning was motivated by the observation that human mathematicians often have a high level plan for how to go about solving a proof and then fill in the exact details. Rippling is a proof plan commonly used to guide rewriting of the step-case in inductive proofs [6]. It works by identifying and annotating differences and similarities between two terms, typically referred to as the *skeleton* and the *goal*. In an inductive proof, the skeleton is the inductive hypothesis of the step-case, and the inductive conclusion of the step case is the goal. Rippling guides rewriting to reduce the differences between the goal and the skeleton, with the aim of arriving at a situation where the goal can be justified by the skeleton. This justification is called *strong fertilisation.*

A term can be annotated, with respect to a given skeleton, by identifying the *wave-fronts*, *wave-holes*, and *sinks*. The wave-fronts are the parts of a term that differ between the goal and the skeleton. In constructor-based inductive proofs, these are initially the constructors introduced in the step-case goal. Wave-holes are sub-terms inside a wave-front that are part of the skeleton. Sinks are the positions corresponding to universally quantified variables in the skeleton, which can be instantiated during fertilisation. Wave-fronts have directions: *outward* wave-fronts intend to move the differences to the top-of the term tree, while *inward* wave-fronts intend to move them to a sink.

A typical example of an annotated goal is the step-case in the inductive proof of the commutativity of addition:

$$\begin{array}{ll} \textbf{Skeleton} \text{ (inductive hypothesis):} & \forall b'.\ a + b' = b' + a \\ \textbf{Goal} \text{ (step-case goal):} & \boxed{Suc\ \boxed{a}}^{\uparrow} + \lfloor b \rfloor = \lfloor b \rfloor + \boxed{Suc\ \boxed{a}}^{\uparrow} \end{array} \qquad (2.1)$$

The position of the universally quantified variable b' becomes a sink in the goal, annotated as $\lfloor b \rfloor$. Wave-fronts are visualised by shaded boxes with an arrow indicating outward or inward direction. For our purposes, annotations can be viewed as function symbols on the term. Wave-fronts are annotated by the function $wf : (\alpha \Rightarrow \alpha) \Rightarrow \alpha \Rightarrow \alpha$, where the first argument is the term inside the wave-front, and the second argument is the wave-hole. Sinks are annotated by the function $sink : \alpha \Rightarrow \alpha$. For the term in the example above this becomes: $(wf\ Suc\ a) + (sink\ b) = (sink\ b) + (wf\ Suc\ a)$. For a more detailed account of annotated terms see [12,11].

During proof search, each application of a rule moves the wave-fronts towards the top of the term tree. As we shall see in Example 1, this decreases the *ripple-measure* (see Def. 4) which guides the proof search. In the final step, the goal is an instance of the skeleton and no wave-fronts remain. The inductive hypothesis is then applied to conclude the proof by strong fertilisation.

Example 1: Rippling and Strong Fertilisation. As an example of a rippling proof we return to the step-case of the inductive proof of the commutativity of addition (from equation 2.1). The rippling proof of the step case is given below. Note that this should be read bottom up to see how the proof was discovered:

$$
\begin{array}{lll}
\hline & \text{Strong Fertilisation} & \\
a + \lfloor b \rfloor = \lfloor b \rfloor + a & \text{Measure: } 0 & \\
\hline & \text{ripple-step, using: } ((Suc\ x) = (Suc\ y)) = (x = y) & (2.2) \\
\boxed{Suc(\underline{a + \lfloor b \rfloor})}^{\uparrow} = \boxed{Suc(\underline{\lfloor b \rfloor + a})}^{\uparrow} & \text{Measure: } 2 & \\
\hline & \text{ripple-step, using: } x + (Suc\ y) = Suc(x + y) & (2.3) \\
\boxed{Suc(\underline{a + \lfloor b \rfloor})}^{\uparrow} = \lfloor b \rfloor + \boxed{Suc(\underline{a})}^{\uparrow} & \text{Measure: } 3 & \\
\hline & \text{ripple-step, using: } (Suc\ x) + y = Suc(x + y) & (2.4) \\
\boxed{Suc(\underline{a})}^{\uparrow} + \lfloor b \rfloor = \lfloor b \rfloor + \boxed{Suc(\underline{a})}^{\uparrow} & \text{Measure: } 4 &
\end{array}
$$

There are two functions of interest for annotated terms, *erasure* which returns the unannotated term, and *skel* which returns the instance of the skeleton that is within the goal.

Definition 1 (Erasure). *The function $erasure(t)$ replaces every wave front symbol (wf), in the term t, by the lambda term $\lambda f\ t.\ f\ t$, and every sink symbol ($sink$) by the identity function.*

Definition 2 (Skel). *The function $skel(t)$ replaces every wave front symbol (wf), in the term t, by the projection lambda term $\lambda f\ t.\ t$, and every sink symbol by the identity function.*

Definition 3 (Annotion set). *The set of annotations for a given term, t, with respect to a skeleton, s, is defined by:*

$$annot(s, t) := \{a \mid erasure(a) \equiv t \wedge \exists \sigma.\ skel(a) \equiv s\sigma\}$$

Annotation algorithms are described in [23,11]. After the initial goal has been annotated, rippling proceeds by applying rules derived from function definitions, axioms and existing theorems and lemmas. These rules are referred to as *wave-rules*. To guide the application of wave-rules so that the differences between the skeleton and the goal are decreased, rippling uses a well-founded measure on annotated terms, called a *ripple-measure*.

Definition 4 (Ripple-Measure). *A ripple measure is a well-founded (strict) partial-order on annotated terms, parametrised by a common skeleton, such that when the skeleton unifies with the annotated term, the measure is minimal. We write $Mes_s(t_1) < Mes_s(t_2)$ when t_1 is less than t_2 with respect to a ripple-measure parametrised by skeleton s.*

We use the *sum of distances* measure, from [11], which sums the distance from outward wave-fronts to the top of the term tree, and from inward wave-fronts to the nearest sink (see Example 1). This results in a natural number. The ripple-measure is the usual less-than ordering on natural numbers.

Theorem 1 (Sum of distances is a ripple-measure). *The sum of distances measure is well-founded and when the goal unifies with the skeleton, it is minimal.*

Proof. The well-foundedness follows directly from the less-than ordering on natural numbers. When a goal term t unifies with a skeleton s, then t contains no unsunk wave-fronts (otherwise t is not an instance). Hence the sum of distances measure for all annotations is 0, the minimal value.

Definition 5 (Dynamic Rippling, Ripple-Step). *Let W be a context containing a set of wave-rules, s be a skeleton, and a_i be an annotated term. A* rippling step *is an inference of the form:*

$$\frac{W,\ s,\ a_2 \vdash g[t_2\sigma]}{W,\ s,\ a_1 \vdash g[t_1\sigma]} \quad \begin{array}{l} ((t_1 = t_2) \in W \vee (t_2 = t_1) \in W) \\ a_1 \in annot(s, g[t_1\sigma]) \\ a_2 \in annot(s, g[t_2\sigma]) \\ Mes_s(a_2) < Mes_s(a_1) \end{array}$$

The first condition identifies an equational wave rule in the context W. The next two conditions ensure that the goals have rippling annotations, and the last condition ensures that the ripple measure decreases. Rippling *is the repeated application of ripple-steps.*

Using the above definition of rippling, the proof of termination follows easily:

Theorem 2 (Termination of Rippling). *Rippling always terminates.*

Our formalism renders this theorem as a trivial consequence of the well-foundedness of the ripple measure; there is no infinite sequence of ripple-steps.

Definition 6 (Blocked). *Rippling is blocked at a goal when the set of ripple-steps is empty. This happens when no measure decreasing wave-rules can be applied.*

Example 2. Returning to example 1, if rule 2.2 was not available, then rippling would be blocked at the subgoal: $\boxed{Suc(a + \lfloor b \rfloor)}^{\uparrow} = \boxed{Suc(\lfloor b \rfloor + a)}^{\uparrow}$. When rippling is blocked, in many cases, including this one, it is still possible to complete the proof by rewriting the goal with the inductive hypothesis. This is called *weak fertilisation.*

Definition 7 (Weak Fertilisation)

$$\frac{W,\ s \vdash g[t_2\sigma]}{W,\ s,\ a \vdash g[t_1\sigma]} \quad \begin{array}{l}(s \equiv (t_1 = t_2) \vee s \equiv (t_2 = t_1)) \\ a \in annot(s, g[t_1\sigma])\end{array}$$

In example 2, the blocked goal can be weak-fertilised to produce the new subgoal $Suc(b + a) = Suc(b + a)$, which is true by reflexivity.

Lemma calculation is a lemma discovery technique that is simpler than lemma speculation. While the latter applies when rippling becomes blocked before fertilisation, lemma calculation proves residual goals as lemmas after fertilisation. Logically, it is justified by the cut-rule. Although simple, variants of this technique are widely used by automatic inductive provers.

Definition 8 (Lemma Calculation)

$$\frac{W,\ s \vdash l \qquad W \cup l, s \vdash g}{W,\ s \vdash g} \quad l \equiv generalise(g)$$

where the generalise function produces a lemma such that $\exists\sigma.\ l\sigma \equiv g$

Example 3: Lemma Calculation. In example 1, note that only rule 2.4 comes from the standard definition of addition in Peano arithmetic. If rippling is only given the definition of '+' with no extra lemmas, then rippling gets blocked even earlier, at the subgoal: $\boxed{Suc(a + \lfloor b \rfloor)}^{\uparrow} = \lfloor b \rfloor + \boxed{Suc(a)}^{\uparrow}$. Weak-fertilisation is then applied to the left-hand side of the blocked goal, resulting in the new subgoal: $Suc(b + a) = b + (Suc\ a)$. However, this goal cannot be solved by simplification. This is when the lemma calculation is applied. In this case, the lemma is simply the remaining subgoal, which is the missing rule 2.3.

In our implementation in IsaPlanner, calculated lemmas are generalised using common sub-term generalisations (replacing equal sub-terms occurring on both sides of an equation with a new variable). The lemma created by calculation is then subjected to an inductive proof attempt. Other generalisation techniques used in lemma calculation have been studied in [1]. The proof-plan for the step-case of our inductive prover is summarised by the functional pseudo-tactic shown in Fig. 1. The interested reader may examine the implementation at: `http://dream.inf.ed.ac.uk/projects/isaplanner`

3 Middle-Out Rippling and Lemma Speculation

If rippling becomes blocked before the inductive hypothesis can be applied, the basic proof-plan using lemma calculation after weak fertilisation fails (Fig. 1,

```
rippling = blocked ORELSE
  (ripple_step THEN rippling);

fertilisation =
  strong_fertilisation ORELSE
    (weak_fertilisation THEN
    (simplification THEN
    (solved ORELSE
      (lemma_calculation THEN
      (inductive_proof AND apply_lemma)))
    ));
```

```
stepcase_lemma_calc =
  rippling THEN fertilisation;

stepcase_lemma_spec =
  rippling THEN
  (fertilisation ORELSE
    (speculate_lemma THEN
     middle_out_rippling THEN
     ((solved ORELSE
         stepcase_lemma_spec)
      AND inductive_proof)));
```

Fig. 1. A tactic-style presentation of the proof-plans for the step-case of an inductive proof. Left: shows rippling and fertilisation with lemma calculation. Right: shows the basic step-case proof plan as well as its extension with lemma speculation. The `solved` tactic succeeds only if the goal was solved; the `THEN`, `ORELSE` have the standard behaviour; the `AND` tactical attempts to solve the first subgoal by the first tactic and if that is successful then attempts the second subgoal with the second tactic; the `inductive_proof` tactic is the top-level inductive prover.

top-right). Lemma speculation solves this difficult class of problems by creating a schematic equational lemma to unblock rippling. Like lemma calculation, the lemma is cut into the proof. However, unlike lemma calculation, the lemma is applied to the goal as a rewrite before the lemma has been proved. This introduces the schematic variables into the subgoal. Subsequent specialised ripple-steps, called middle-out ripples, are then used to rewrite the goal and instantiate the meta-variables (see §3.2). Finally, once the goal has been proved and the lemma is fully instantiated, a proof of the lemma is attempted. The tactic for rippling with lemma speculation is shown at the right of Fig 1, with the corresponding formal definition of a lemma speculation step being:

Definition 9 (Lemma Speculation)

$$\frac{W \cup (l = r),\ s,\ a,\ c \vdash g[r] \qquad W \vdash (l = r)}{W,\ s,\ a[l'] \vdash g[l]} \quad \begin{array}{l} (l = r) \in \mathit{LemmaSpecSet}(a) \\ c \equiv \mathit{Trace}(s, [g[r], g[l]]) \\ \lambda x.\ \mathit{erasure}(a[x]) \equiv \lambda x.\ g[x] \\ a[l'] \in \mathit{annot}(s, g[l]) \end{array}$$

The schematic lemma $(l = r)$ *is said to unblock the subterm* l. *The last two conditions ensure that* $l \equiv \mathit{erasure}(l')$ *and* l *is the subterm corresponding to* l'.

The lemma speculation rule extends the context with a trace (c) which is used to maintain a list of the goals following a lemma speculation step. The trace is used to ensure the termination of middle-out reasoning (see §3.1). The set $\mathit{LemmaSpecSet}(a)$ is all equations of the form $l = r$ where l is the erasure of a subterm, l', of the annotated goal, and l' contains at least one wave front. The right hand, r, is the skeleton of l' with meta-variables inserted into all positions where a wave-front may occur, i.e. above each function symbol and in each sink position.

For example, consider the goal $g[l] \equiv p\ (f\ (h\ x)\ y)$ with the annotated subterm l' as: $f\ (\boxed{h\ \underline{x}}^{\uparrow})\ \lfloor y \rfloor$. A schematic lemma for this term is $f\ (h\ x)\ y = ?F_1\ (f\ x\ (?F_2\ y))$. The new subgoal produced by lemma speculation is then:

$$p\ (\ ?F_1\ (f\ x\ (\lfloor ?F_2\ y \rfloor))\ ) \tag{3.1}$$

The dashed box marks the location of an unsunk meta-variable which is called a *potential wave-front* in [15]; instantiation of the meta-variable may introduce wave-fronts into the goal.

3.1 Measures for Schematic Goals

The key invariant initiated by lemma speculation is that there exists a substitution that will result in the lemma's application being a valid ripple-step. This invariant is then extended to the application of ripple-steps as they instantiate the meta-variables. This is captured by the predicate *MesDecr* which, for the list of goals in the trace ($[g_n, \ldots, g_1]$), is true if there is a substitution that makes $[g_1, \ldots, g_n]$ sequentially measure decreasing with respect to a given skeleton s:

$$\begin{aligned} &\mathit{MesDecr}(\sigma, \mathit{Trace}(s, [g_n, \ldots, g_1])) \equiv \exists a_n \ldots a_1 .\ \mathit{Projection}(\sigma, \mathit{Vars}([g_n, \ldots, g_1])) \\ &\quad \wedge a_n \in \mathit{annot}(s, g_n\sigma) \wedge \cdots \wedge a_1 \in \mathit{annot}(s, g_1\sigma) \\ &\quad \wedge \mathit{Mes}_s(a_n) < \ldots < \mathit{Mes}_s(a_1) \end{aligned} \tag{3.2}$$

where $\mathit{Projection}(\sigma, \mathit{Vars}([g_n, \ldots, g_1]))$ ensures that σ consists of projections for all meta-variables in the goals.

Theorem 3 (Lemma Speculation is Measure Decreasing). *By construction, all lemmas produced by lemma speculation will initially result in a list of measure decreasing subgoals:* $\exists \sigma.\ \mathit{MesDecr}(\sigma, \mathit{Trace}(s, [g[r], g[l]]))$.

Proof. The projection of the meta-variables onto their arguments will result in $g[r]$ removing all wave fronts. This is always measure decreasing for the sum-of-distances measure.

3.2 Middle-Out Rippling

After speculation, the lemma subgoal, $W \vdash (l = r)$, and the main subgoal, $W \cup (l = r),\ s,\ c \vdash g[r]$, contain shared meta-variables. If ordinary rippling were applied to the main subgoal, the presence of these meta-variables would let higher-order unification find unifiers with any rewrite rule, causing the search space to become intractably large. In order to manage the rippling search space and ensure termination of rippling, we use a variant of the ripple-step rule, called *middle-out ripple-step*.

Definition 10 (Middle-Out Ripple-Step)

$$\frac{(\Delta \quad W,\ s,\ c_2 \vdash g[t_2])\sigma_1}{\Delta \quad W,\ s,\ c_1 \vdash g[t_1]} \quad \begin{array}{l} (t_1' = t_2) \in W \vee (t_2 = t_1') \in W \\ \mathit{RestrUnifiers}(t_1, t_1', \sigma_1) \\ c_1 \equiv \mathit{Trace}(s, l) \quad c_2 \equiv \mathit{Trace}(s, (g[t_2]\#l)\sigma_1) \\ \exists \sigma_2.\ \mathit{MesDecr}(\sigma_2, c_2) \end{array}$$

This rule differs from a regular rewrite step in that the substitutions can involve variables in both the rule and the goal. Meta-variables shared with the lemma are also instantiated in all other subgoals (Δ), notably in the lemma subgoal. The relation *RestrUnifiers*, embodies a heuristic that restricts the unifiers (σ_1) so as to avoid trivial ones which can occur with any wave-rule (see §3.3).

The *MesDecr* relation ensures that the new subgoal forms part of a measure decreasing chain. This holds if there exists a grounding substitution σ_2 for the remaining meta-variables, which makes the trace measure decreasing. Note that the definition of *MesDecr* requires σ_2 to be a projection of the uninstantiated variables of the trace (see equation 3.2). This is the key condition that ensures termination of middle-out rippling (see §3.4).

Each middle-out step is followed by an attempt to find projection-instantiations for the remaining meta-variables using either of the following *eager-fertilisation* rules:

Definition 11 (Eager Strong Fertilisation)

$$\frac{\Delta\sigma}{\Delta \quad W,\ s,\ c \vdash g} \quad \begin{array}{l} s\sigma \equiv g\sigma \\ \mathit{MesDecr}(\sigma, c) \end{array}$$

Definition 12 (Eager Weak Fertilisation)

$$\frac{(\Delta \quad W \vdash g[t_2])\sigma}{\Delta \quad W,\ s,\ c \vdash g[t_1]} \quad \begin{array}{l} s \equiv (t_1' = t_2) \vee s \equiv (t_2 = t_1') \\ t_1\sigma \equiv t_1'\sigma \\ \mathit{MesDecr}(\sigma, c) \end{array}$$

As the *MesDecr* condition requires σ to be a projection of all remaining meta-variables, eager fertilisation results in a ground goal. When the goal contains all variables from the speculated lemma, this also results in the speculated lemma having no further meta-variables. Like middle-out steps, the *MesDecr* condition ensures that instantiations result in c being a valid measure-decreasing ripple-trace. When eager fertilisation produces a fully instantiated lemma, a counter-example check is applied before attempting to prove the lemma in order to prune out obviously false lemmas. Our proof machinery does not address subgoals which fail to fully instantiate the lemma.

3.3 Restricted Higher-Order Unification

Rewriting using an equation involves finding a unifier between the equation's left hand side and a sub-term of the goal. However, when the goal contains a meta-variable, there is a trivial higher-order unifier between the subterm with the meta-variable at head-position and every rule's left-hand side[1]. The general characteristic of these trivial unifiers is that all arguments of the meta-variable are ignored. Our restricted form of higher-order unification deliberately sacrifices completeness to avoid such unifiers by ensuring some non-variable argument of the meta-variable is unified with a non-variable subterm of the wave rule's left hand side.

Definition 13 (Restricted Higher-order unification)

$$
\begin{aligned}
&\mathit{RestrUnifiers}(t_1[t'_1], t_2, \sigma_1) \equiv \\
&\quad (\ \ t'_1 \equiv f\ \ldots && (3.3)\\
&\quad \wedge\ t_2 \equiv ?X\ t'_{(2,1)} \ldots t'_{(2,i)} \ldots t'_{(2,n)}) && (3.4)\\
&\quad \wedge\ t'_1\sigma \equiv t'_{(2,i)}\sigma && (3.5)\\
&\quad \wedge\ \sigma_1 \equiv \sigma \cup \{?X \mapsto \lambda x_1 \ldots x_i \ldots x_n.\ t_1[x_i]\}\ \ ) && (3.6)
\end{aligned}
$$

Condition 3.3 ensures that there is a subterm of the first argument which does not contain a head-positioned meta-variable, while condition 3.4 requires that the second argument does contain a meta-variable at head position. To illustrate restricted unification, consider a middle-out ripple on the example from goal 3.1: $p\ (?F_1\ (f\ x\ (?F_2\ y)))$, using the equation $g\ (f\ ?u\ ?v) = f\ ?u\ (g\ ?v)$. Restricted unification will have the arguments:

$$
\begin{aligned}
t_1[t'_1] &:= g[(f\ ?u\ ?v)]\\
t_2 &:= ?F_1\ (f\ x\ (?F_2\ y))\\
\sigma_1 &:= \{?v \mapsto (?F_2\ y), ?u \mapsto x\} \cup \{?F_1 \mapsto (\lambda z.\ g\ z)
\end{aligned}
$$

The result is that the goal is rewritten to $p\ (f\ x\ (g\ (?F_2\ y)))$ and the speculated lemma is instantiated from $f\ (h\ x)\ y = ?F_1\ (f\ x\ (?F_2\ y))$ to $f\ (h\ x)\ y = g\ (f\ x\ (?F_2\ y))$.

3.4 Termination of Middle-Out Rippling

The previous implementation of lemma speculation in the CLAM 3 system did not guarantee termination of middle-out steps [15]. A major improvements of our version is the retention of the termination of rippling, even when extended to schematic goals. As discussed in §3.1, this is achieved by recomputing the ripple-measures for the whole trace of schematic goals.

Theorem 4. *The rule for a middle-out ripple-step may only be applied finitely many times to a schematic goal arising from lemma speculation.*

Proof. Assume we have a trace of schematic goals $[g_n, \ldots g_1]$. By construction, the last goal in the list (g_1) does not contain any meta-variables, and has a fixed ripple measure (by definition 9 and theorem 3). The measure condition (equation 3.2) ensures that there is a substitution such that each step in the

[1] The trivial unifier between a pair of terms t, and $?X\, a_1 \ldots a_n$ is the substitution $?X \mapsto \lambda x_1 \ldots x_n.\ t$.

trace must decrease the measure with respect to the previous step. The fixed initial measure and well-foundedness of the rippling-measure (theorem 1) thus ensures there is no infinite chain of measure decreasing steps from g_1, and hence that middle-out rippling terminates.

4 Evaluation and Limitations of Lemma Speculation

To evaluate our technique, we considered inductive theorems from: the list-library of Isabelle-2009[2] (223 theorems); theories of Peano arithmetic, including Isabelle's natural number library (46 theorems) as well as a large variety of alternative formalisations from [11] (524 theorems); and all previous theorems known to need lemma speculation (the first 7 theorems in Table 1) [15]. We also examined, in a more ad-hoc fashion, theories concerned with inequalities over natural numbers, ordinal arithmetic, additional properties of fold, append, map, and reverse, and problems from the domain of higher-order function synthesis [10].

The important negative result for lemma speculation is that it is rarely applicable. We found only 18 theorems where it can be applied; 7 examples were in the literature, 5 new examples were found by hand, 1 new example was found in Isabelle's list library, and 5 new examples were found in alternative formalisations of Peano arithmetic. The reason for the limited number of examples is that when rippling is blocked, it is rarely the case that the inductive hypothesis cannot be applied. Tables 1 and 2 highlights a representative set of the results[3].

Another limitation of lemma speculation is that when it is applicable and forms the last step required before fertilisation, no middle-out rewriting steps are applied. This results in the speculated lemma being underspecified, as happens for theorems 7-9 in Table 1. Overall, lemma speculation provides fully instantiated lemmas for 11 of the 18 problems.

Our domains consist largely of equational theorems. While lemma speculation was rarely applicable, lemma calculation was frequently so. In non-equational domains, such as inequality proofs, where lemma calculation after weak fertilisation was not applicable, neither was lemma speculation. Proofs in this domain often require more sophisticated reasoning about assumptions, notably something like the extensions to fertilisation described in [2]. This kind of reasoning may allow proofs to get to the point where lemma speculation is applicable. Domains where there is a higher degree of nesting in term-structures and longer chains of rippling may also have more opportunity for lemma speculation. In these problems, the chances for middle-out reasoning to fully instantiate a lemma is also greater. Finding such problem domains and evaluating lemma speculation on them is left as further work.

A positive result for our version of middle-out rippling is that, as well as working in higher-order domains, it supports speculating the same lemmas as the earlier implementation in CLAM 3. This indicates that the power of middle-out rippling has not been adversely affected by ensuring termination.

[2] http://www.cl.cam.ac.uk/research/hvg/Isabelle/dist/library/HOL/List.html

[3] Due to space restrictions, the full results for lemma speculation, including run-times, can be found online:
`http://dream.dai.ed.ac.uk/projects/lemmadiscovery/lemspec_results.php`

Table 1. The sub-columns for lemma speculation indicate when a lemma is found, and when this lemma can be proved automatically. The 'IsaCoSy' column indicates if IsaPlanner can prove the theorem automatically given the background theory produced by IsaCoSy. For Theorems 7-9, lemma speculation fails to fully instantiate the lemma. For theorems 10 - 11, IsaPlanner makes some progress using IsaCoSy's background theory, allowing application of weak fertilisation. The same lemmas as lemma speculation finds can then be produced by the simpler lemma calculation technique.

Theorem		Lemma Speculation		IsaCoSy
		Found Lem	Proved Lem	Proved Thm
1	$x + (Suc\ x) = Suc(x + x)$	yes	yes	yes
2	$even(x + x)$	yes	no	yes
3	$even(len(l\ @\ l))$	yes	no	no
4	$rev((rev\ l)\ @\ m) = (rev\ m)\ @\ l$	yes	yes	yes
5	$rev(rev(l\ @\ m)) = rev(rev\ l)\ @\ rev(rev\ m)$	yes	yes	yes
6	$rev(rev\ l)\ @\ m = rev(rev(l\ @\ m))$	yes	yes	yes
7	$rotate\ (len\ l)\ (l\ @\ m) = m\ @\ l$	fail	-	yes
8	$rev(concat\ l) = concat(map\ rev\ (rev\ l))$	fail	-	yes
9	$len(concat\ (map\ f\ l)) = len(maps\ f\ l)$	fail	-	no
10	$foldl\ (\lambda\ x\ y.\ y + x)\ n\ ((rev\ l)\ @\ m) =$ $foldl\ (\lambda\ x\ y.\ y + x)\ n\ (m\ @\ l)$	yes	no	weak fert.
11	$foldl\ (\lambda\ x.\ y.\ x + (len\ y))\ n\ ((rev\ l)\ @\ m) =$ $foldl\ (\lambda\ x.\ y.\ x + (len\ y))\ n\ (m\ @\ l)$	yes	no	weak fert.
12	$x \leq (y\ +\ x)$	yes	no	yes

4.1 Comparison of Lemma Speculation and Theory Formation

Another approach to automated lemma discovery is to attempt to generate a richer background theory in advance, as done by the IsaCoSy theory formation system [17]. We compared two versions of IsaPlanner's inductive prover: one using lemma speculation and one using just lemma calculation but provided with the lemmas from IsaCoSy's automatically generated background theory. In general, lemma calculation is preferable over speculation, as it has a considerably smaller search space and thus faster run-times. On a 2Ghz, 2GB-RAM desktop PC lemma calculation takes on average less than 1 second while lemma speculation takes up to 137. Automatically generating the background theory uniformly adds all generated theorems as wave rules and may take several hours, but only needs to be done once. Both experiments have the same initial configuration, consisting of only the function definitions; all lemmas had to be discovered automatically. The evaluation set and results are shown in Table 1, with the lemmas shown in Table 2. When given the background theory generated by IsaCoSy, IsaPlanner proves two theorems (7 and 8) that it cannot prove using lemma speculation. Conversely, using the speculated lemmas, theorem 3 can be proved[4]. However, it seems likely that improvements to IsaCoSy will allow generation of lemmas needed to allow lemma calculation to complete the proofs of the theorems 3 and 9, which currently fail.

[4] The lemma was automatically discovered, but had to be proved interactively.

Table 2. Lemmas discovered by lemma speculation compared to those by syntheses, numbered according to Table 1. Recall that the lemmas speculated for theorems 2 and 3 had to be proved interactively. Using the synthesised background theory results in two alternative proofs for theorem 5, either using the first lemma, or both the others.

Thm	Speculated Lemma(s)	Synthesised Lemma(s) Used
1	$Suc\ x + y = Suc(y + x)$	$x + Suc\ y = Suc(x + y)$
2*	$x + (Suc\ x) = Suc(x + x)$	$x + Suc\ y = Suc(x + y)$
3*	$len(l\ @\ (h\#l)) = Suc(len(l\ @\ l))$ **or** $len(l\ @\ (h\#l)) = len(h\#(l\ @\ l))$	-
4	$rev\ (h\#l)\ @\ m = rev\ l\ @\ (h\#m)$	$rev(xs\ @\ ys) = (rev\ ys)\ @\ (rev\ xs)$
5	$rev\ (l\ @\ [h]) = h\#(rev\ l)$	$rev\ (l\ @[h]) = h\#(rev\ l)$ **or** $rev(xs\ @\ ys) = (rev\ ys)\ @\ (rev\ xs)$ **and** $(xs\ @\ ys)\ @\ zs = xs\ @\ (ys\ @\ zs)$
6	$rev\ (l\ @\ [h]) = h\#(rev\ l)$	$rev(l\ @\ [h]) = h\#(rev\ l)$
7	-	$(xs\ @\ ys)\ @\ zs = xs\ @\ (ys\ @\ zs)$
8	-	$rev(xs\ @\ ys) = (rev\ ys)\ @\ (rev\ xs)$ **and** $map\ f\ (rev\ l) = rev(map\ f\ l)$
9	-	-
10	$foldl\ (\lambda\ x\ y.\ y + x)\ n\ (l\ @\ (h\#m)) = foldl\ (\lambda\ x\ y.\ y + x)\ h\ (n\#(l\ @\ m))$	$(xs\ @\ ys)\ @\ zs = xs\ @\ (ys\ @\ zs)$
11	$foldl\ (\lambda\ x\ y.\ x + (len\ y))\ n\ (l\ @\ (h\#m)) = foldl\ (\lambda\ x\ y.\ x + (len\ y))\ n\ (h\#(l\ @\ m))$	$(xs\ @\ ys)\ @\ zs = xs\ @\ (ys\ @\ zs)$
12	$Suc\ z \leq a + (Suc\ z) = z \leq Suc(a + z)$	$x + Suc\ y = Suc(x + y)$ **and** $(x \leq (x\ +\ y)) = True$

For two theorems (10 and 11) the background theory allows lemma calculation to conjecture the same lemmas as lemma speculation.

It is frequently the case that the lemmas constructed by lemma speculation cannot be proved. This happens for 5 out of 9 speculated lemmas. Speculated lemmas tend to be more specialised compared to lemmas produced and proved by IsaCoSy. This makes the latter generally easier to apply and prove (the proofs are easier because the induction hypothesis is stronger). The lemmas produced by IsaCoSy for theorems 2 and 12, and arguably also 4 and 5, are more general than those found by lemma speculation. The wider variety of general lemmas also result in an alternative proof for theorem 5. Finally, we remark that the background theories generated by IsaCoSy are useful for a wider variety of proofs than those to which lemma speculation is applicable. See [17] for a more detailed evaluation of IsaCoSy.

5 Related Work

Middle-out rippling is an instance of narrowing, i.e. rewriting where both the goal and rule may contain variables instantiated by unification. However, it differs from the account of higher-order narrowing in [22], as we allow meta-variables to occur as arguments to each other in schematic lemmas.

By separating the concepts of annotations, measures and rippling-steps, our formalisation becomes significantly more succinct than that of Basin and Walsh [3]. In particular, it makes the termination proof simpler and supports extensions more easily. The main improvement over the previous versions of middle-out reasoning, e.g. [13,15], is that ours ensures termination. Our restricted unification heuristic also efficiently cuts out undesirable unifiers, while previous work had to apply filtering of unwanted results after unification [13], or use heuristics specific to rippling [15].

Lemma speculation sometimes fails to fully instantiate schematic lemmas. Previous work attempted to instantiate such a lemma by during the lemma's proof [15]. However, this heuristic works very few examples, and it was thus not implemented in IsaPlanner. Another approach to finding lemmas is *interactive lemma speculation* [16], which can provide the user with some useful feedback, even when the lemma cannot be fully instantiated. A lemma discovery algorithm similar to speculation has been proposed in [18]. Like lemma speculation, subterms in the goal are equated with the hypothesis, and meta-variables used for unknown term-structure. However, we are not aware of any experimental evaluation of this algorithm. Finally, the MATHsAiD [20] and Theorema [14,4] systems have also been applied to inductive theory formation, although only to natural numbers. The similarity of their results in this domain suggests that if extended to other domains, they would provide similar results to IsaCoSy.

6 Conclusions and Further Work

We have extended techniques for middle-out reasoning and lemma speculation to dynamic rippling and higher-order domains. We also provided a novel, concise and formal account of dynamic rippling, which extends to the middle-out case. The main improvement over previous approaches is the ability to prove termination easily, and extend it naturally to middle-out rippling.

We have implemented middle-out rippling in the IsaPlanner system and performed a practical evaluation in the context of lemma speculation. The lemma speculation technique attempts to construct missing lemmas from failed proof attempts. Contrary to expectations, our results suggest that lemma speculation is not widely applicable. We also showed that, for the otherwise hard problems to which lemma speculation is applicable, theory formation techniques in combination with simpler proof methods offer an effective alternative. Further work includes extending rippling-based proof methods so that other domains can be examined, where lemma speculation may be more applicable, and exploring other applications of middle-out reasoning and theory formation.

References

1. Aderhold, M.: Improvements in formula generalization. In: Pfenning, F. (ed.) CADE 2007. LNCS (LNAI), vol. 4603, pp. 231–246. Springer, Heidelberg (2007)
2. Armando, A., Smaill, A., Green, I.: Automatic synthesis of recursive programs: the proof-planning paradigm. In: ASE 1997, pp. 2–9. IEEE Computer Society Press, Los Alamitos (1997)

3. Basin, D., Walsh, T.: A calculus for and termination of rippling. Journal of Automated Reasoning 16(1-2), 147–180 (1996)
4. Buchberger, B., Craciun, A., Jebelean, T., Kovacs, L., Kutsia, T., Nakagawa, K., Piroi, F., Popov, N., Robu, J., Rosenkrantz, M., Windsteiger, W.: Theorema: Towards computer-aided mathematical theory exploration. Journal of Applied Logic 4(4), 470–504 (2006)
5. Bundy, A.: The automation of proof by mathematical induction. In: Handbook of Automated Reasoning, ch. 13. MIT Press, Cambridge (2001)
6. Bundy, A., Basin, D., Hutter, D., Ireland, A.: Rippling: Meta-level Guidance for Mathematical Reasoning. Cambridge University Press, Cambridge (2005)
7. Bundy, A., Dixon, L., Gow, J., Fleuriot, J.: Constructing induction rules for deductive synthesis proofs. In: CLASE 2005. ENTCS, vol. 153, pp. 3–21 (2006)
8. Bundy, A., Smaill, A., Hesketh, J.: Turning Eureka steps into calculations in automatic program synthesis. In: UK IT 1990, pp. 221–226 (1990)
9. Bundy, A., van Harmelen, F., Hesketh, J., Smaill, A.: Experiments with proof plans for induction. Journal of Automated Reasoning 7(3), 303–324 (1992)
10. Cook, A., Ireland, A., Michaelson, G.: Higher order function synthesis through proof planning. In: ASE-16, pp. 307–310 (2001)
11. Dixon, L.: A Proof Planning Framework for Isabelle. PhD thesis, University of Edinburgh (2005)
12. Dixon, L., Fleuriot, J.: Higher-order rippling in IsaPlanner. In: Slind, K., Bunker, A., Gopalakrishnan, G.C. (eds.) TPHOLs 2004. LNCS, vol. 3223, pp. 83–98. Springer, Heidelberg (2004)
13. Hesketh, J., Bundy, A., Smaill, A.: Using middle-out reasoning to control the synthesis of tail-recursive programs. In: Kapur, D. (ed.) CADE 1992. LNCS, vol. 607, pp. 310–324. Springer, Heidelberg (1992)
14. Hodorog, M., Craciun, A.: Scheme-based systematic exploration of natural numbers. In: Synasc-8, pp. 26–34 (2006)
15. Ireland, A., Bundy, A.: Productive use of failure in inductive proof. Journal of Automated Reasoning 16(1-2), 79–111 (1996)
16. Ireland, A., Jackson, M., Reid, G.: Interactive proof critics. Formal Aspects of Computing 11(3), 302–325 (1999)
17. Johansson, M., Dixon, L., Bundy, A.: Conjecture synthesis for inductive theories. Journal of Automated Reasoning (to appear, 2010)
18. Kapur, D., Subramaniam, M.: Lemma discovery in automating induction. In: McRobbie, M.A., Slaney, J.K. (eds.) CADE 1996. LNCS, vol. 1104, pp. 538–552. Springer, Heidelberg (1996)
19. Kraan, I., Basin, D., Bundy, A.: Middle-out reasoning for synthesis and induction. Journal of Automated Reasoning 16(1-2), 113–145 (1996)
20. McCasland, R., Bundy, A., Autexier, S.: Automated discovery of inductive theorems. Special Issue of Studies in Logic, Grammar and Rhetoric: Festschrift in Honor of A. Trybulec 10(23), 135–149 (2007)
21. Nipkow, T., Paulson, L.C., Wenzel, M.T.: Isabelle/HOL - A proof assistant for higher-order logic. LNCS, vol. 2283. Springer, Heidelberg (2002)
22. Prehofer, C.: Higher-order narrowing. In: LICS-9, pp. 507–516. IEEE Computer Society Press, Los Alamitos (1994)
23. Smaill, A., Green, I.: Higher-order annotated terms for proof search. In: von Wright, J., Grundy, J., Harrison, J. (eds.) TPHOLs 1996. LNCS, vol. 1125, pp. 399–413. Springer, Heidelberg (1996)

Verifying the Modal Logic Cube Is an Easy Task (For Higher-Order Automated Reasoners)

Christoph Benzmüller*

Articulate Software, Angwin, CA, U.S.

Dedicated to Christoph Walther

Abstract. Prominent logics, including quantified multimodal logics, can be elegantly embedded in simple type theory (classical higher-order logic). Furthermore, off-the-shelf reasoning systems for simple type type theory exist that can be uniformly employed for reasoning *within* and *about* embedded logics. In this paper we focus on reasoning *about* modal logics and exploit our framework for the automated verification of inclusion and equivalence relations between them. Related work has applied first-order automated theorem provers for the task. Our solution achieves significant improvements, most notably, with respect to elegance and simplicity of the problem encodings as well as with respect to automation performance.

1 Introduction

Church's simple type theory $\mathcal{STT}$ [15], also known as classical higher-order logic, has many prominent classical logic fragments, including propositional logic, first-order logic, and second-order logic. Interestingly, also well known non-classical logics, including propositional and quantified multimodal logics, can be elegantly embedded in $\mathcal{STT}$ [9,6].

In this paper we exploit our embedding of quantified multimodal logic in $\mathcal{STT}$ [6] for the automated verification of inclusion relations between prominent propositional modal logics, including the logics **K**, **M** (also known as **T**), **D**, **S4**, and **S5**. Concretely, we analyze inclusion and equivalence relations for modal logics that can be defined from normal modal logic **K** by adding (combinations of) the axioms M, B, D, 4, and 5. In our problem encodings we exploit the well known correspondences of these axioms to semantic properties of accessibility relations. These correspondences can itself be elegantly formalized and effectively automated in our approach.

The automation of $\mathcal{STT}$ currently experiences a renaissance that has been fostered by the recent extension of the successful TPTP infrastructure for first-order logic [26] to higher-order logic, called TPTP THF [27,11]. In our verification study we exploit this new infrastructure and work with different TPTP THF

* This work has been supported by the German Research Foundation (DFG) under grant BE 2501/6-1.

S. Siegler and N. Wasser (Eds.): Walther Festschrift, LNAI 6463, pp. 117–128, 2010.

compliant automated higher-order reasoning systems: TPS [1], LEO-II[1] [10], Satallax [5], IsabelleP[2], Refute [28] and Nitpick [13].[3] TPS, LEO-II and IsabelleP are automated theorem provers, and Refute and Nitpick are countermodel generators. Satallax is an automated theorem prover with additional capabilities for finding countermodels.

Related work [23] has applied first-order automated theorem provers for the verification of inclusion relations between modal logics. Our solution achieves significant improvements, most notably, with respect to elegance and simplicity of the problem encodings as well as with respect to automation performance.

In Sect. 2 we outline our embedding of quantified multimodal logics in $\mathcal{STT}$ (this part is reproduced from [6]). In Sect. 3 we describe how reasoning *about* propositional modal logics and their inclusion relations is facilitated in our approach. The results of our experiments are presented in Sect. 4, and Sect. 5 concludes the paper.

2 (Normal) Quantified Multimodal Logics in $\mathcal{STT}$

$\mathcal{STT}$ [15] is based on the simply typed λ-calculus. The set $\mathcal{T}$ of simple types is usually freely generated from a set of basic types $\{o, \iota\}$ (where o is the type of Booleans and ι is the type of individuals) using the right-associative function type constructor $\to$. Instead of $\{o, \iota\}$ we here consider a set of base types $\{o, \iota, \mu\}$, providing an additional base type μ (the type of possible worlds).

The simple type theory language $\mathcal{STT}$ is defined by (where α, β, $o \in \mathcal{T}$):

$$s, t ::= p_\alpha \mid X_\alpha \mid (\lambda X_\alpha. s_\beta)_{\alpha\to\beta} \mid (s_{\alpha\to\beta}\, t_\alpha)_\beta \mid (\neg_{o\to o}\, s_o)_o \mid \\ (s_o \vee_{o\to o\to o} t_o)_o \mid (s_\alpha =_{\alpha\to\alpha\to o} t_\alpha)_o \mid (\Pi_{(\alpha\to o)\to o}\, s_{\alpha\to o})_o$$

p_α denotes typed constants and X_α typed variables (distinct from p_α). Complex typed terms are constructed via abstraction and application. Our logical connectives of choice are $\neg_{o\to o}$, $\vee_{o\to o\to o}$, $=_{\alpha\to\alpha\to o}$ and $\Pi_{(\alpha\to o)\to o}$ (for each type α).[4] From these connectives, other logical connectives can be defined in the usual way (e.g., $\wedge$ and $\Rightarrow$). We often use binder notation $\forall X_\alpha. s$ for $\Pi_{(\alpha\to o)\to o}(\lambda X_\alpha. s_o)$. We assume familiarity with α-conversion, β- and η-reduction, and the existence of β- and $\beta\eta$-normal forms. Moreover, we obey the usual definitions of free variable occurrences and substitutions.

The semantics of $\mathcal{STT}$ is well understood and thoroughly documented in the literature [2,3,7,20]. The semantics of choice for our work is Henkin semantics.

---

1 LEO-II integrates the first-order automated theorem prover E [24].

2 IsabelleP applies a series of Isabelle/HOL [22] proof tactics in batch mode.

3 Refute and Nitpick, which also belong to the Isabelle/HOL proof assistant, are sometimes called IsabelleM and IsabelleN; this is the case, for example, in the SystemOnTPTP tool `http://www.cs.miami.edu/~tptp/cgi-bin/SystemOnTPTP`, where all reasoning systems mentioned here are available online.

4 This choice is not minimal (from $=_{\alpha\to\alpha\to o}$ all other logical constants can already be defined [4]). It useful though in the context of resolution based theorem proving.

Quantified modal logics have been studied by Fitting [16] (further related work is available by Blackburn and Marx [12] and Braüner [14]). In contrast to Fitting we are here not interested only in **S5** structures but in the more general case of **K** from which more constrained structures (such as **S5**) can be easily obtained. First-order quantification can be constant domain or varying domain. Below we only consider the constant domain case, in which every possible world has the same domain. Like Fitting, we keep our definitions simple by not having function or constant symbols. While Fitting [16] studies quantified monomodal logic, we are interested in quantified multimodal logic. Hence, we introduce multiple $\Box_r$ operators for symbols r from an index set S. The grammar for our quantified multimodal logic $\mathcal{QML}$ is

$$s, t ::= P \mid k(X^1, \ldots, X^n) \mid \neg\, s \mid s \vee t \mid \forall X.s \mid \forall P.s \mid \Box_r\, s$$

where $P \in \mathcal{PV}$ denotes propositional variables, $X, X^i \in \mathcal{IV}$ denote first-order (individual) variables, and $k \in \mathcal{SYM}$ denotes predicate symbols of any arity. Further connectives, quantifiers, and modal operators can be defined as usual.

Fitting introduces three different notions of Kripke semantics for $\mathcal{QML}$: $\mathbf{QS5}\pi^-$, $\mathbf{QS5}\pi$, and $\mathbf{QS5}\pi^+$. In our work [8] we study related notions $\mathbf{QK}\pi^-$, $\mathbf{QK}\pi$, and $\mathbf{QK}\pi^+$ for a modal context **K**, and we support multiple modalities.

$\mathcal{STT}$ is an expressive logic and it is thus not surprising that $\mathcal{QML}$ can be elegantly modeled and even automated as a fragment of $\mathcal{STT}$. The idea of the encoding, called $\mathcal{QML}^{STT}$, is simple. Choose type ι to denote the (non-empty) set of individuals and choose the second base type μ to denote the (non-empty) set of possible worlds. As usual, the type o denotes the set of truth values. Certain formulas of type $\mu \to o$ then correspond to multimodal logic expressions. The multimodal connectives $\neg$, $\vee$, and $\Box$, become λ-terms of types $(\mu \to o) \to (\mu \to o)$, $(\mu \to o) \to (\mu \to o) \to (\mu \to o)$, and $(\mu \to \mu \to o) \to (\mu \to o) \to (\mu \to o)$, respectively.

Quantification is handled as in $\mathcal{STT}$ by modeling $\forall X.p$ as $\Pi(\lambda X.p)$ for a suitably chosen connective Π. Here we are interested in defining two particular modal $\boldsymbol{\Pi}$-connectives: $\boldsymbol{\Pi}^\iota$, for quantification over individual variables, and $\boldsymbol{\Pi}^{\mu\to o}$, for quantification over modal propositional variables that depend on worlds. They become terms of type $(\iota \to (\mu \to o)) \to (\mu \to o)$ and $((\mu \to o) \to (\mu \to o)) \to (\mu \to o)$ respectively.

The $\mathcal{QML}^{STT}$ modal operators $\neg, \vee, \Box, \boldsymbol{\Pi}^\iota$, and $\boldsymbol{\Pi}^{\mu\to o}$ are now simply defined as follows:

$$\begin{aligned}
\neg_{(\mu\to o)\to(\mu\to o)} &= \lambda\phi_{\mu\to o}.\lambda W_\mu.\neg\phi\, W \\
\vee_{(\mu\to o)\to(\mu\to o)\to(\mu\to o)} &= \lambda\phi_{\mu\to o}.\lambda\psi_{\mu\to o}.\lambda W_\mu.\phi\, W \vee \psi\, W \\
\Box_{(\mu\to\mu\to o)\to(\mu\to o)\to(\mu\to o)} &= \lambda R_{\mu\to\mu\to o}.\lambda\phi_{\mu\to o}.\lambda W_\mu.\forall V_\mu.\neg R\, W\, V \vee \phi\, V \\
\boldsymbol{\Pi}^\iota_{(\iota\to(\mu\to o))\to(\mu\to o)} &= \lambda\phi_{\iota\to(\mu\to o)}.\lambda W_\mu.\forall X_\iota.\phi\, X\, W \\
\boldsymbol{\Pi}^{\mu\to o}_{((\mu\to o)\to(\mu\to o))\to(\mu\to o)} &= \lambda\phi_{(\mu\to o)\to(\mu\to o)}.\lambda W_\mu.\forall P_{\mu\to o}.\phi\, P\, W
\end{aligned}$$

Note that our encoding actually only employs the second-order fragment of $\mathcal{STT}$ enhanced with lambda-abstraction.

Further operators can be introduced as usual, for example, $\top = \lambda W_{\mu}.\top, \bot = \neg\top$, $\wedge = \lambda\phi,\psi.\neg(\neg\phi \vee \neg\psi)$, $\supset = \lambda\phi,\psi.\neg\phi \vee \psi$, $\Leftrightarrow = \lambda\phi,\psi.(\phi \supset \psi) \wedge (\psi \supset \phi)$, $\Diamond = \lambda R,\phi.\neg(\Box\, R\, (\neg\phi))$, $\boldsymbol{\Sigma}^{\iota} = \lambda\phi.\neg\boldsymbol{\Pi}^{\iota}(\lambda X.\neg\phi X)$, $\boldsymbol{\Sigma}^{\mu\to o} = \lambda\phi.\neg\boldsymbol{\Pi}^{\mu\to o}(\lambda P.\neg\phi P)$.

For defining $\mathcal{QML}^{STT}$-propositions we fix a set $\mathcal{IV}^{STT}$ of individual variables of type ι, a set $\mathcal{PV}^{STT}$ of propositional variables[5] of type $\mu \to o$, and a set $\mathcal{SYM}^{STT}$ of n-ary (curried) predicate symbols of types $\underbrace{\iota \to \ldots \to \iota}_{n} \to (\mu \to o)$. Moreover, we fix a set $\mathcal{S}^{STT}$ of accessibility relation constants of type $\mu \to \mu \to o$. $\mathcal{QML}^{STT}$-propositions are now defined as the smallest set of $\mathcal{STT}$-terms for which the following hold:

- if $P \in \mathcal{PV}^{STT}$, then $P \in \mathcal{QML}^{STT}$
- if $X^j \in \mathcal{IV}^{STT}$ $(j = 1, \ldots, n)$ and $k \in \mathcal{SYM}^{STT}$, then $(k\, X^1 \ldots X^n) \in \mathcal{QML}^{STT}$
- if $\phi, \psi \in \mathcal{QML}^{STT}$, then $\neg\,\phi \in \mathcal{QML}^{STT}$ and $\phi \vee \psi \in \mathcal{QML}^{STT}$
- if $r \in \mathcal{S}^{STT}$ and $\phi \in \mathcal{QML}^{STT}$, then $\Box\, r\, \phi \in \mathcal{QML}^{STT}$
- if $X \in \mathcal{IV}^{STT}$ and $\phi \in \mathcal{QML}^{STT}$, then $\boldsymbol{\Pi}^{\iota}(\lambda X.\phi) \in \mathcal{QML}^{STT}$
- if $P \in \mathcal{PV}^{STT}$ and $\phi \in \mathcal{QML}^{STT}$, then $\boldsymbol{\Pi}^{\mu\to o}(\lambda P.\phi) \in \mathcal{QML}^{STT}$

We write $\Box_r\, \phi$ for $\Box\, r\, \phi$, $\forall X_{\iota}.\phi$ for $\boldsymbol{\Pi}^{\iota}(\lambda X_{\iota}.\phi)$, and $\forall P_{\mu\to o}.\phi$ for $\boldsymbol{\Pi}^{\mu\to o}(\lambda P_{\mu\to o}.\phi)$.

Note that the defining equations for our $\mathcal{QML}$ modal operators are themselves formulas in $\mathcal{STT}$. Hence, we can express $\mathcal{QML}$ formulas in a higher-order reasoner elegantly in the usual syntax. For example, $\Box_r\, \exists P_{\mu\to o}.\, P$ is a $\mathcal{QML}^{STT}$ proposition; it has type $\mu \to o$.

Validity of $\mathcal{QML}^{STT}$ propositions is defined in the obvious way: a $\mathcal{QML}$-proposition $\phi_{\mu\to o}$ is valid if and only if for all possible worlds w_{μ} we have $w \in \phi_{\mu\to o}$, that is, if and only if $\phi_{\mu\to o}\, w_{\mu}$ holds. Hence, the notion of validity is modeled via the following equation (alternatively, validity could be defined simply as $\Pi_{(\mu\to o)\to o}$):

$$\text{valid} = \lambda\phi_{\mu\to o}.\forall W_{\mu}.\phi\, W$$

Now we can formulate proof problems in $\mathcal{QML}^{STT}$, e.g., valid $\Box_r\, \exists P_{\mu\to o}.\, P$. Using rewriting or definition expanding, we can reduce such proof problems to corresponding statements containing only the basic connectives $\neg$, $\vee$, $=$, Π^{ι}, and $\Pi^{\mu\to o}$ of $\mathcal{STT}$. In contrast to the many other approaches no external transformation mechanism is required. For our example formula valid $\Box_r\, \exists P_{\mu\to o}.\, P$ unfolding and $\beta\eta$-reduction leads to $\forall W_{\mu}.\forall Y_{\mu}.\neg r\, W\, Y \vee (\neg\forall X_{\mu\to o}.\neg(X\, Y))$. It is easy to check that this formula is valid in Henkin semantics: put $X = \lambda Y_{\mu}.\top$.

We have proved soundness and completeness for this embedding [8], that is, for $s \in \mathcal{QML}$ and the corresponding $s_{\mu\to o} \in \mathcal{QML}^{STT} \subset \mathcal{STT}$ we have:

Theorem 1. $\models^{\mathcal{STT}}$ *(valid* $s_{\mu\to o}$*) if and only if* $\models^{\mathbf{QK}\pi}$ s.

This result also illustrates the correspondence between $\mathbf{QK}\pi$ models and Henkin models; for more details see [8].

[5] Note that the denotation of propositional variables depends on worlds.

Obviously, the reduction of our embedding to first-order multimodal logics (which only allow quantification over individual variables), to propositional quantified multimodal logics (which only allow quantification over propositional variables) and to propositional multimodal logics (no quantifiers) is sound and complete. Extending our embedding for hybrid logics is straightforward [21]; note in particular that denomination of individual worlds using constant symbols of type μ is easily possible.

In the remainder we will often omit type information. It is sufficient to remember that worlds are of type μ, multimodal propositions of type $\mu \to o$, and accessibility relations of type $\mu \to \mu \to o$. Individuals are of type ι.

3 Reasoning about Modal Logics

3.1 Accessibility Relation Properties and Modal Logic Axioms

There are well known relationships between properties of accessibility relations and corresponding modal logic axioms (or axiom schemata) [18]. Such meta-theoretic insights can be elegantly encoded in our approach. First we encode various accessibility relation properties in $\mathcal{STT}$:

$$\begin{aligned}
\text{reflexive} &= \lambda R_\centerdot \forall S_\centerdot R\, S\, S \\
\text{symmetric} &= \lambda R_\centerdot \forall S, T_\centerdot ((R\, S\, T) \Rightarrow (R\, T\, S)) \\
\text{serial} &= \lambda R_\centerdot \forall S_\centerdot \exists T_\centerdot (R\, S\, T) \\
\text{transitive} &= \lambda R_\centerdot \forall S, T, U_\centerdot ((R\, S\, T) \wedge (R\, T\, U) \Rightarrow (R\, S\, U)) \\
\text{euclidean} &= \lambda R_\centerdot \forall S, T, U_\centerdot ((R\, S\, T) \wedge (R\, S\, U) \Rightarrow (R\, T\, U))
\end{aligned}$$

The corresponding axioms are given next.

$$\begin{aligned}
M(\text{or } T): &\ \forall \phi_\centerdot \Box_r \phi \supset \phi \\
B: &\ \forall \phi_\centerdot \phi \supset \Box_r \Diamond_r \phi \\
D: &\ \forall \phi_\centerdot \Box_r \phi \supset \Diamond_r \phi \\
4: &\ \forall \phi_\centerdot \Box_r \phi \supset \Box_r \Box_r \phi \\
5: &\ \forall \phi_\centerdot \Diamond_r \phi \supset \Box_r \Diamond_r \phi
\end{aligned}$$

Exploiting our embedding $\mathcal{QML}^{STT}$ we can now elegantly formalize well known correspondence theorems in $\mathcal{STT}$:

$$\forall R_\centerdot (\text{reflexive } R) \Leftrightarrow (\text{valid } \forall \phi_\centerdot \Box_R \phi \supset \phi) \tag{1}$$

$$\forall R_\centerdot (\text{symmetric } R) \Leftrightarrow (\text{valid } \forall \phi_\centerdot \phi \supset \Box_R \Diamond_R \phi) \tag{2}$$

$$\forall R_\centerdot (\text{serial } R) \Leftrightarrow (\text{valid } \forall \phi_\centerdot \Box_R \phi \supset \Diamond_R \phi) \tag{3}$$

$$\forall R_\centerdot (\text{transitive } R) \Leftrightarrow (\text{valid } \forall \phi_\centerdot \Box_R \phi \supset \Box_R \Box_R \phi) \tag{4}$$

$$\forall R_\centerdot (\text{euclidean } R) \Leftrightarrow (\text{valid } \forall \phi_\centerdot \Diamond_R \phi \supset \Box_R \Diamond_R \phi) \tag{5}$$

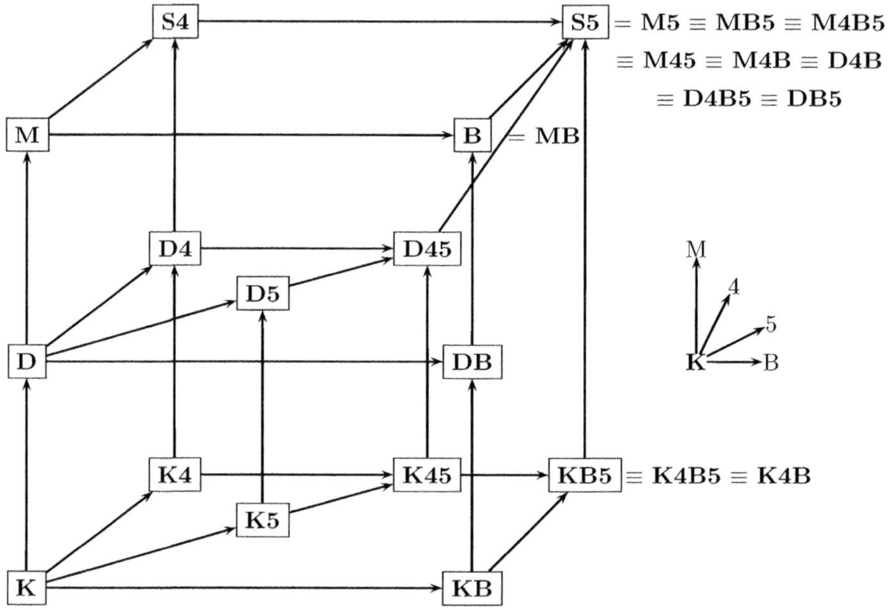

Fig. 1. The Modal Logic Cube; reproduced from [17]

3.2 Alternative Axiomatizations of Modal Logics

The cube in Figure 1 depicts the different modal logics that can be defined from normal modal logic **K** (lower left corner) by adding (combinations of) the axioms M, B, D, 4, and 5. A conjecture implicitly contained in this cube is that there are modal logics that can be axiomatized in alternative ways using these axioms.

For example, for modal logic **S5** we may choose axioms M and 5 as standard axioms. Respectively for logic **KB5** we may choose B and 5. We may then want to investigate the following conjectures about equivalent axiomatizations for **S5**, respectively, for **KB5**:

$$\begin{aligned} \mathbf{S5} = \mathbf{M5} &\Leftrightarrow \mathbf{MB5} \\ &\Leftrightarrow \mathbf{M4B5} \\ &\Leftrightarrow \mathbf{M45} \\ &\Leftrightarrow \mathbf{M4B} \\ &\Leftrightarrow \mathbf{D4B} \\ &\Leftrightarrow \mathbf{D4B5} \\ &\Leftrightarrow \mathbf{DB5} \end{aligned} \qquad \begin{aligned} \mathbf{KB5} &\Leftrightarrow \mathbf{K4B5} \\ &\Leftrightarrow \mathbf{K4B} \end{aligned}$$

Exploiting the correspondence theorems from Sect. 3.1 these problems can be formulated as follows; we give the case for **M5** ⇔ **D4B**:

$$\forall R_\bullet (((\text{reflexive } R) \wedge (\text{euclidean } R)) \Leftrightarrow ((\text{serial } R) \wedge (\text{transitive } R) \wedge (\text{symmetric } R)))$$

3.3 Inclusion Relations between Different Modal Logics

The links in the modal logic cube in Fig. 1 describe unidirectional inclusion relations between modal logics. For example, the link between **D45** and **S5** expresses that modal logic **D45** is included in logic **S5** (we write **D45** $\Subset$ **S5**) but not vice versa. That is, all formulas that are valid in **D45** are also valid in **S5**. On the other hand, there are formulas that are valid in **S5** but not in **D45** (**S5** $\not\Subset$ **D45**).

Exploiting the equivalence (bidirectional inclusion) of **S5** and **D4B5** and monotonicity of entailment the inclusion of **D45** in **S5** is obvious: we simply add axiom B when moving in this direction. These trivial directions of the inclusion links in our modal logic cube are not further addressed in this paper.

The backward directions, however, are more interesting. It are these non-inclusion aspects of the links that we need to verify. The general task in each case is to find a countermodel to the respective inclusion statement. For example, in order to show that logic **M** is not included in logic **D** we may want to find a countermodel to the inclusion statement

$$(\text{valid}\,\forall\phi\centerdot\Box_r\,\phi \supset \Diamond_r\,\phi) \Rightarrow (\text{valid}\,\forall\phi\centerdot\Box_r\,\phi \supset \phi)$$

Again, by exploiting the correspondence theorems from Sect. 3.1 we may instead search for a countermodel to

$$\mathbf{M} \Subset \mathbf{D}: \qquad \forall R\centerdot(\text{serial}\; R) \Rightarrow (\text{reflexive}\; R)$$

The systems that are applicable to these inclusion statements are the countermodel finders Refute, Nitpick, and Satallax.

Alternatively, we may try to find a countermodel to **M** $\Subset$ **D** by tackling the negated inclusion statement with a theorem prover

$$\mathbf{M} \not\Subset \mathbf{D}: \qquad \neg\forall R\centerdot(\text{serial}\; R) \Rightarrow (\text{reflexive}\; R)$$

In the particular case of **M** and **D** the negated statement is clearly not a theorem though: in a model consisting of only one possible world, seriality in fact implies reflexivity. However, since we are in fact interested only in finding a countermodel to the statement **M** $\Subset$ **D** we may simply provide some help to the provers by adding an axiom expressing that there are at least two different worlds:

$$w1 \neq w2$$

When adding such an axiom the statement **M** $\not\Subset$ **D** becomes a theorem (now there is an accessibility relation which is serial but not reflexive: simply choose $\neq$). The systems that are applicable to the negated inclusion statements are the provers TPS, LEO-II, IsabelleP and Satallax.

In the experiment reported below we have actually added axioms stating there are at least three different possible worlds to all negated statements.

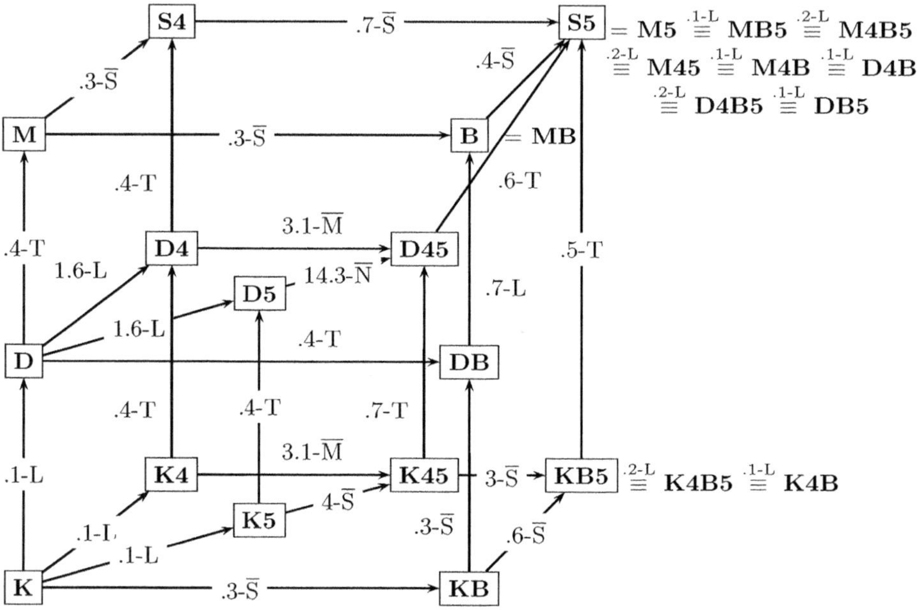

Fig. 2. Verification of the Modal Logic Cube: fastest proofs/countermodels reported

4 Verification Results

In our experiments, we have employed the following system versions: TPS—3.080227G1d, LEO-II—v1.2, Satallax—1.4, IsabelleP—2009-2, IsabelleM—2009-2 (Refute), and IsabelleN—2009-2 (Nitpick). These systems are all available online via the SystemOnTPTP tool [25] and they support the new TPTP THF infrastructure for typed higher-order logic [11]. Exploiting the SystemOnTPTP tool all the experiment runs were done on 2.80GHz computers with 1GB memory and running the Linux operating system, with a 300s CPU limit.

The axiomatizations of $\mathcal{QML}^{STT}$ and $\mathcal{IPL}^{STT}$ are available as LCL013^0.ax and LCL010^0.ax in the TPTP library.[6] The example problems LCL698^1.p and LCL695^1.p ask about the satisfiability of these axiomatizations. Both questions are answered positively by the Satallax model finder in less than a second.

The correspondence theorems (1)–(5) from Sect. 3.1 are trivial: LEO-II solves problems (1),(3), and (4) in .1 seconds each, and it solves problem (2) in .3 seconds. TPS is the fastest prover to solve statement (5), for which it needs .4 seconds.

Figure 2 depicts the further results of our experiments. The timings presented for each link are given in seconds. For each link we present the fastest successful attempt reported by one of our reasoners. Moreover, we indicate with the suffixes

[6] Note that the types μ and ι are unfortunately switched in the encodings available in the TPTP: the former is used for individuals and the latter for worlds. This syntactic switch is completely unproblematic.

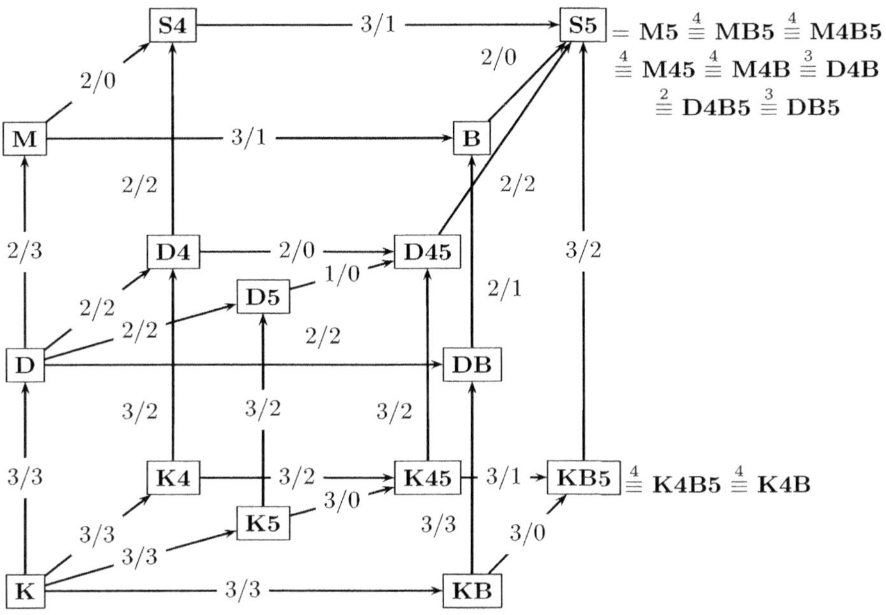

Fig. 3. Verification of the Modal Logic Cube: number of different successful results

-T, -L, -$\overline{\text{N}}$, -$\overline{\text{M}}$, and -$\overline{\text{S}}$ which system contributed this result. T stands for TPS, L for LEO-II, $\overline{\text{N}}$ for Nitpick, $\overline{\text{M}}$ for Refute, and $\overline{\text{S}}$ for Satallax as countermodel finder. IsabelleP and Satallax as prover never contributed a fastest result. As mentioned before, for each link the inclusion statement and the negated inclusion statement as described in Sect. 3.3 were presented to the provers.

Figure 3 presents how many different successful results were reported for each link. For example, the proper subset relation between **K4** and **D4** has been confirmed five times: the link annotation 3/2 says that we received 3 countermodels for **D4** $\Subset$ **K4** and 2 proofs for the negated statement **D4** $\not\Subset$ **K4**. In the equivalence statements the annotations express the number of successful proof attempts, for example, the statement **M5** $\equiv$ **MB5** was confirmed by each of our four provers.

In summary, all links in the modal logic cube can be verified effectively by at least one of the reasoners and most steps take only milliseconds. Furthermore, all equivalence statements in the cube can be solved in a few milliseconds. In all but one case different certificates are provided by the reasoners, raising the level of trust in the results significantly. Summing up all fastest times in our entire experiments results in a sum of less than 40 seconds.

5 Conclusion

The automated analysis and verification of bidirectional and unidirectional inclusions between propositional modal logics has originally been posed as a challenge problem for automated theorem provers by John Halleck and Geoff Sutcliffe. John Halleck was in need for a program as an aid to maintaining his logic systems overview [19].

Subsequently the challenge has been addressed with first-order automated theorem provers [23]. However, the solution presented there employs technically complex and hard to follow problem encodings in first-order logic, and even the fastest automated analysis of a subset relation in this study already requires more than 11 minutes of total reasoning time with state-of-the-art first-order automated theorem provers (if the pre-processing times required in this approach are also taken into account).

In our framework the automated analysis of bidirectional and unidirectional inclusion relations between well known modal logics becomes an easy task for higher-order automated theorem provers. Most notably, our problem encodings are elegant, simple and straightforward and the verification of the entire modal logic cube takes less than 40 seconds.

Future work includes the application of our framework for the exploration of inclusion relations between further modal logics. Note in particular, that our embedding of modal logics in simple type theory is not restricted to propositional logics: it also supports quantifiers and multiple box operators (cf. the Examples 4–6 in [6]). This calls for the development of a workbench for the automated analysis of propositional and quantified multimodal logics based on the approach presented in this paper.

Acknowledgment. I thank Jasmin Blanchette for his valuable input to this paper (he helped in finding a minor issue in the problem encodings which initially prevented his Nitpick system in finding a counterexample to **D45** $\Subset$ **D5**). Thanks to Marvin Schiller for proof reading. Further thanks to the implementors of the higher-order reasoning systems employed in this work. Moreover, I am indebted to Larry Paulson and Geoff Sutcliffe. Larry Paulson, together with the author, initiated the LEO-II project at Cambridge University (EPRSC grant LEO-II EP/D070511/1). Geoff Sutcliffe, in collaboration with the author and supported by several further contributors, developed the new higher-order TPTP THF infrastructure (EU FP7 grant THFTPTP PIIF-GA-2008-219982). Both projects had a significant impact on the work presented in this article.

References

1. Andrews, P.B., Brown, C.: TPS: A Hybrid Automatic-Interactive System for Developing Proofs. Journal of Applied Logic 4(4), 367–395 (2006)
2. Andrews, P.B.: General models and extensionality. Journal of Symbolic Logic 37, 395–397 (1972)
3. Andrews, P.B.: General models, descriptions, and choice in type theory. Journal of Symbolic Logic 37, 385–394 (1972)
4. Andrews, P.B.: An Introduction to Mathematical Logic and Type Theory: To Truth Through Proof, 2nd edn. Kluwer Academic Publishers, Dordrecht (2002)

5. Backes, J., Brown, C.E.: Analytic tableaux for higher-order logic with choice. In: Giesl, J., Hähnle, R. (eds.) Automated Reasoning. LNCS (LNAI), vol. 6173, pp. 76–90. Springer, Heidelberg (2010)
6. Benzmüller, C.: Combining logics in simple type theory. In: The 11th International Workshop on Computational Logic in Multi-Agent Systems, Lisbon, Portugal. Lecture Notes in Artifical Intelligence, Springer, Heidelberg (2010)
7. Benzmüller, C., Brown, C.E., Kohlhase, M.: Higher order semantics and extensionality. Journal of Symbolic Logic 69, 1027–1088 (2004)
8. C. Benzmüller, L.C. Paulson. Quantified Multimodal Logics in Simple Type Theory. SEKI Report SR–2009–02 (ISSN 1437-4447). SEKI Publications, DFKI Bremen GmbH, Safe and Secure Cognitive Systems, Cartesium, Enrique Schmidt Str. 5, D–28359 Bremen, Germany (2009), http://arxiv.org/abs/0905.2435
9. Benzmüller, C., Paulson, L.C.: Multimodal and intuitionistic logics in simple type theory. The Logic Journal of the IGPL (2010)
10. Benzmüller, C., Paulson, L.C., Theiss, F., Fietzke, A.: LEO-II — A Cooperative Automatic Theorem Prover for Higher-Order Logic. In: Baumgartner, P., Armando, A., Gilles, D. (eds.) IJCAR 2008. LNCS (LNAI), vol. 5195, pp. 162–170. Springer, Heidelberg (2008)
11. Benzmüller, C., Rabe, F., Sutcliffe, G.: THF0 — The Core TPTP Language for Classical Higher-Order Logic. In: Baumgartner, P., Armando, A., Gilles, D. (eds.) IJCAR 2008. LNCS (LNAI), vol. 5195, pp. 491–506. Springer, Heidelberg (2008)
12. Blackburn, P., Marx, M.: Tableaux for quantified hybrid logic. In: Egly, U., Fermüller, C.G. (eds.) TABLEAUX 2002. LNCS (LNAI), vol. 2381, pp. 38–52. Springer, Heidelberg (2002)
13. Blanchette, J.C., Nipkow, T.: Nitpick: A counterexample generator for higher-order logic based on a relational model finder. In: Kaufmann, M., Paulson, L.C. (eds.) ITP 2010. LNCS, vol. 6172, pp. 131–146. Springer, Heidelberg (2010)
14. Braüner, T.: Natural deduction for first-order hybrid logic. Journal of Logic, Language and Information 14(2), 173–198 (2005)
15. Church, A.: A formulation of the simple theory of types. Journal of Symbolic Logic 5, 56–68 (1940)
16. Fitting, M.: Interpolation for first order S5. Journal of Symbolic Logic 67(2), 621–634 (2002)
17. Garson, J.: Modal logic. In: Zalta, E.N. (ed.) The Stanford Encyclopedia of Philosophy, Winter 2009 edition (2009)
18. Goldblatt, R.: Logics of Time and Computation, 2nd edn. Lecture Notes, vol. 7. Center for the Study of Language and Information, Stanford (1992)
19. Halleck, J.: John Halleck's Logic Systems, http://www.cc.utah.edu/~nahaj/logic/structures/systems/index.html
20. Henkin, L.: Completeness in the theory of types. Journal of Symbolic Logic 15, 81–91 (1950)
21. Kaminski, M., Smolka, G.: Terminating tableau systems for hybrid logic with difference and converse. Journal of Logic, Language and Information 18(4), 437–464 (2009)
22. Nipkow, T., Paulson, L.C., Wenzel, M.: Isabelle/HOL - A Proof Assistant for Higher-Order Logic. LNCS, vol. 2283. Springer, Heidelberg (2002)
23. Rabe, F., Pudlak, P., Sutcliffe, G., Shen, W.: Solving the $100 Modal Logic Challenge. Journal of Applied Logic (2008) (page to appear)
24. Schulz, S.: E: A Brainiac Theorem Prover. AI Communications 15(2-3), 111–126 (2002)

25. Sutcliffe, G.: TPTP, TSTP, CASC, etc. In: Diekert, V., Volkov, M., Voronkov, A. (eds.) CSR 2007. LNCS, vol. 4649, pp. 7–23. Springer, Heidelberg (2007)
26. Sutcliffe, G.: The TPTP problem library and associated infrastructure. J. Autom. Reasoning 43(4), 337–362 (2009)
27. Sutcliffe, G., Benzmüller, C.: Automated reasoning in higher-order logic using the TPTP THF infrastructure. Journal of Formalized Reasoning 3(1), 1–27 (2010)
28. Weber, T.: SAT-Based Finite Model Generation for Higher-Order Logic. Ph.D. thesis, Dept. of Informatics, T.U. München (2008)

Second-Order Programs with Preconditions

Markus Aderhold

Technische Universität Darmstadt, Germany
aderhold@informatik.tu-darmstadt.de

Abstract. In the implementation of procedures, developers often assume that the input satisfies certain properties; for example, *binary search* assumes the array to be sorted. Such requirements on the input can be formally expressed as preconditions of procedures. If a second-order procedure p (e.g., *map* or *foldl*) is called with a first-order procedure f that has a precondition, the question arises whether p will call f only with arguments that satisfy the precondition of f. In this paper, we propose a method to statically analyze if all procedure calls in a given second-order program satisfy the respective preconditions. In particular, we consider indirect calls of procedures that are passed as an argument to a second-order procedure.

1 Introduction

One key feature of many algorithms is that they solve a given problem for a wide range of input values. For instance, the *quicksort* algorithm is able to sort lists of arbitrary length. Often, however, algorithms are *not* intended to work for completely arbitrary inputs, but expect the input to satisfy certain preconditions. For example, *binary search* requires a *sorted* array, and *division* requires the divisor to be different from zero.

When a program applies an (implementation of an) algorithm to arguments that violate the preconditions of the algorithm, this usually leads to undesirable behavior: The program raises an exception (e.g., division by zero) or produces an unexpected result (e.g., binary search in general fails to find an element in an unsorted array).

As a first step to finding program errors that are due to violated preconditions, it is helpful to write down the preconditions explicitly and formally. Some programming languages such as Eiffel [9] or Spec# [4] offer dedicated constructs to specify so-called *contracts*. For instance, a contract can guarantee that a procedure provides a certain functionality (expressed by a postcondition) provided that the caller supplies appropriate input (expressed by a precondition).

If the preconditions of all procedures in a program are formally specified, one can then try to apply techniques for the static analysis of programs to verify that the preconditions of all procedures are satisfied during any conceivable run of the program. The basic idea is to ensure that for each procedure call $p(t_1, \ldots, t_n)$ in the program, the arguments $t_1, \ldots, t_n$ satisfy the precondition of p. For example, for each occurrence of a procedure call $div(t_1, t_2)$, one needs to show that the divisor t_2 is different from zero.

S. Siegler and N. Wasser (Eds.): Walther Festschrift, LNAI 6463, pp. 129–143, 2010.

In this paper, we consider *second-order* programs with preconditions. A typical example of a second-order procedure is *map*, which takes a function f as well as a list l and returns the list that results from l by applying f to each element of l. Since f may have a precondition, say c_f, a procedure call $map(f, l)$ is only safe (in the sense that executing it will not violate any preconditions) if $c_f[x]$ is satisfied for all elements x of list l:

$$\forall x \in l.\ c_f[x] \tag{1}$$

The technique we propose in this paper automatically generates a formula equivalent to (1) just from the "raw definition" of *map*. In other words, for second-order procedures developers need not specify preconditions that propagate the preconditions of their function parameters (such as precondition (1) for *map*); instead, our technique automatically generates verification conditions to statically analyze if the preconditions of function parameters are respected.

Our technique has been implemented and integrated into √eriFun, a semi-automated verifier for functional programs [17,18]. √eriFun's input language $\mathcal{L}$ [16] for functional programs allows developers to annotate procedures with preconditions [14]. √eriFun generates verification conditions to verify that the precondition of each procedure call in a program is satisfied. Semantically, a procedure with a precondition is considered as an incompletely defined procedure [19] such that the return value is indetermined if the precondition is violated.

The two main contributions of this paper are the following:

- We simplify the semantics of incompletely defined first-order procedures that Walther and Schweitzer proposed in [19]. By treating such procedures as procedures with implicit preconditions, we combine the advantages of [19] and [14] and get a unified view on both concepts.
- We describe a method to statically analyze if preconditions are satisfied in *second-order programs*. For second-order procedures, this method automatically identifies which arguments the function parameter will be applied to and generates the corresponding verification conditions to show that the precondition is satisfied for these calls.

In Sect. 2, we introduce the programming language $\mathcal{L}$ that is used in √eriFun and we present the simplified semantics of first-order polymorphic procedures with preconditions. Sect. 3 extends syntax and semantics to second-order programs. In Sect. 4, we describe our method to statically analyze if the preconditions of all functions that may be called during the evaluation of a given term are satisfied. We point to related work in Sect. 5 and conclude with a discussion of our results in Sect. 6.

2 First-Order Programs

The input language $\mathcal{L}$ of √eriFun that we consider in this section roughly corresponds to the first-order fragment of ML or Haskell with strict evaluation [14,16].

First, we describe the syntax of first-order programs with preconditions (Sect. 2.1). Then we define the semantics of such programs (Sect. 2.2). We show how incompletely defined programs [19] fit into this approach (Sect. 2.3) and compare it with the original definitions described in [14,19] (Sect. 2.4).

In our description of $\mathcal{L}$ we omit some technical details and some syntactical constructions that are not needed in the context of this paper. The interested reader is invited to consult [1,16] for additional information.

2.1 Syntax

$\mathcal{L}$ offers definition principles for freely generated polymorphic data types, for first-order procedures that operate on these data types, and for statements about the data types and procedures. A *base type* is a type variable $@A$ or an expression of the form $str[\tau_1, \ldots, \tau_k]$, where $\tau_1, \ldots, \tau_k$ are base types and str is a k-ary type constructor ($k \geq 0$). *Type constructors* are defined by expressions of the following form:

$$\texttt{structure}\ str[@A_1, \ldots, @A_k] <= \ \ldots,\ cons(sel_1 : \tau_1, \ldots, sel_n : \tau_n),\ \ldots \quad (2)$$

The τ_j are base types, and str may only occur as $str[@A_1, \ldots, @A_k]$ in the τ_j. Each $cons$ is called a *data constructor* and the sel_j are called *selectors.* We write $\mathcal{S}_{cons} := \{sel_1, \ldots, sel_n\}$ for the set of selectors that belong to data constructor $cons$. At least one data constructor of a type constructor definition needs to be *irreflexive*, which means that str does not occur in $\tau_1, \ldots, \tau_n$. An expression $?cons(t)$ checks if t denotes a value of the form $cons(\ldots)$.

Let $\Sigma(P)$ denote the signature of all function symbols defined by an $\mathcal{L}$-program P, including function symbols = for equality and *if* for case analyses. As usual, $\mathcal{T}(\Sigma(P), \mathcal{V})$ denotes the set of all *terms* over $\Sigma(P)$ and a set $\mathcal{V}$ of variables. We write $\mathcal{T}(\Sigma(P))$ instead of $\mathcal{T}(\Sigma(P), \emptyset)$ for the set of all *ground terms* over $\Sigma(P)$. $\Sigma(P)^c \subset \Sigma(P)$ contains all data constructors of P. A *literal* is an *if*-free Boolean term or the negation *if b then false else true* of such a term; e.g., $x \neq y$ abbreviates *if* $x = y$ *then false else true.*

A procedure is defined by an expression of the form

$$\texttt{procedure}\ proc(x_1 : \tau_1, \ldots, x_n : \tau_n) : \tau <= \texttt{assume}\ c_{proc};\ B_{proc} \quad (3)$$

where $c_{proc} \in \mathcal{T}(\Sigma(P), \{x_1, \ldots, x_n\})$ is a Boolean term that specifies the precondition of *proc*, also called the *context requirement* of *proc*. Omitting the context requirement is equivalent to specifying $c_{proc} := true$. The *body* of *proc* is a term $B_{proc} \in \mathcal{T}(\Sigma(P) \cup \{proc\}, \{x_1, \ldots, x_n\})$.

The example program in Fig. 1 defines data types *bool*, $\mathbb{N}$, and $list[@A]$ by enumerating the respective data constructors *true*, *false*, 0, *succ*, ø, and :: as well as the corresponding selectors; e.g., selector *pred* denotes the predecessor function. The context requirements of procedures "/" (for division) and "!!" (for list access by index) express that the divisor must not be zero and that n must be an index within list l, respectively.

$$
\begin{array}{l}
\texttt{structure } bool <= true,\ false\\
\texttt{structure } \mathbb{N} <= 0,\ succ(pred : \mathbb{N})\\
\texttt{structure } list[@A] <= \emptyset,\ ::(hd : @A,\ tl : list[@A])\\[4pt]
\texttt{procedure [infix] } >(x, y : \mathbb{N}) : bool <=\\
\quad if\ x = 0\ then\ false\ else\ if\ y = 0\ then\ true\ else\ pred(x) > pred(y)\\[4pt]
\texttt{procedure [infix] } -(x, y : \mathbb{N}) : \mathbb{N} <=\\
\quad if\ x = 0\ then\ 0\ else\ if\ y = 0\ then\ x\ else\ pred(x) - pred(y)\\[4pt]
\texttt{procedure [infix] } /(x, y : \mathbb{N}) : \mathbb{N} <=\\
\quad \texttt{assume } y \neq 0;\ if\ y > x\ then\ 0\ else\ succ((x - y)/y)\\[4pt]
\texttt{procedure } len(l : list[@A]) : \mathbb{N} <=\\
\quad if\ l = \emptyset\ then\ 0\ else\ succ(len(tl(l)))\\[4pt]
\texttt{procedure [infix] } !!(l : list[@A],\ n : \mathbb{N}) : @A <=\\
\quad \texttt{assume } len(l) > n;\ if\ n = 0\ then\ hd(l)\ else\ tl(l)\ !!\ pred(n)
\end{array}
$$

Fig. 1. A first-order program with preconditions in procedures "/" and "!!"

2.2 Semantics

For a program P and a ground type τ, $\mathbb{V}(P)_\tau$ denotes the *values of type* τ: For each ground base type τ (i.e., $\tau = str[\tau_1, \ldots, \tau_k]$ such that no type variables occur in $\tau_1, \ldots, \tau_k$), $\mathbb{V}(P)_\tau := \mathcal{T}(\Sigma(P)^c)_\tau$. For each ground base type τ there exists at least one value $\omega_\tau \in \mathbb{V}(P)_\tau$. These so-called *witness values* can be obtained by the following definition that simply extends the construction from [15] to polymorphic type constructors:

Definition 1. *For a ground base type τ, the* witness value $\omega_\tau \in \mathbb{V}(P)_\tau$ *is defined by $\omega_\tau := false$ if $\tau = bool$ and by $\omega_\tau := cons(\omega_{\theta(\tau_1)}, \ldots, \omega_{\theta(\tau_n)})$ if $\tau = str[\tau'_1, \ldots, \tau'_k]$ for a type constructor as in (2), where $\theta := \{@A_1/\tau'_1, \ldots, @A_k/\tau'_k\}$ and "cons" is the first data constructor of "str" such that $\mathcal{S}_{cons} = \emptyset$ or—if such a data constructor does not exist—such that "cons" is irreflexive.*

The call-by-value interpreter $\mathsf{eval}_P : \mathcal{T}(\Sigma(P)) \mapsto \mathbb{V}(P)$ defines the operational semantics of $\mathcal{L}$ by mapping ground terms $t \in \mathcal{T}(\Sigma(P))_\tau$ to values $\mathsf{eval}_P(t) \in \mathbb{V}(P)_\tau$. It is a partial function, because some procedures in program P may not terminate. The computation steps of the interpreter eval_P are defined by the so-called *computation calculus*:

Definition 2. *The language of the computation calculus is $\mathcal{T}(\Sigma(P))$. The inference rules of the computation calculus (called* computation rules*) are of the form "$\frac{t}{t'}$, if $\mathsf{cond}[t]$" for a side condition $\mathsf{cond}[t]$ such that $t' \in \mathcal{T}(\Sigma(P))_\tau$ whenever $t \in \mathcal{T}(\Sigma(P))_\tau$ for some ground type τ. We write $t \Rightarrow_P t'$ iff t' results from t by applying some computation rule. $\Rightarrow_P^*$ denotes the reflexive and transitive closure of $\Rightarrow_P$. We write $t \Rightarrow_P^! t'$ iff $t \Rightarrow_P^* t'$ and $t' \not\Rightarrow_P t''$ for all $t'' \in \mathcal{T}(\Sigma(P))$.*

Fig. 2 presents a selection of computation rules (see [1] for an exhaustive list), where *cons* and *cons'* are data constructors and $q_i \in \mathbb{V}(P)$ for all i. To each

$$(1)\ \frac{?cons(cons(q_1,\ldots,q_n))}{true} \qquad (2)\ \frac{?cons'(cons(q_1,\ldots,q_n))}{false}\ ,\ \text{if } cons' \neq cons$$

$$(3)\ \frac{sel_i(cons(q_1,\ldots,q_n))}{q_i}\ ,\ \text{if selector } sel_i \in \mathcal{S}_{cons} \qquad (4)\ \frac{sel'(cons(q_1,\ldots,q_n))}{\omega_\tau}\ ,\ \text{if selector } sel' \notin \mathcal{S}_{cons}$$

$$(5)\ \frac{q_1 = q_2}{true}\ ,\text{if } q_1 = q_2 \qquad (6)\ \frac{q_1 = q_2}{false}\ ,\text{if } q_1 \neq q_2$$

$$(7)\ \frac{proc(q_1,\ldots,q_n)}{(\mathit{if}\ c_{proc}\ \mathit{then}\ B_{proc}\ \mathit{else}\ \omega_\tau)[x_1/q_1,\ldots,x_n/q_n]}$$

Fig. 2. Selected inference rules of the computation calculus

$t \in \mathcal{T}(\Sigma(P))$ at most one computation rule is applicable and $t \Rightarrow^!_P t'$ implies $t' \in \mathbb{V}(P)$ [1]. Thus we define the interpreter by

$$\mathsf{eval}_P(t) := \begin{cases} t' & \text{if } t \Rightarrow^!_P t' \text{ for some } t' \in \mathbb{V}(P) \\ \bot & \text{if } t \not\Rightarrow^!_P t' \text{ for all } t' \in \mathbb{V}(P)\,. \end{cases}$$

A universally quantified formula of the form $\forall x_1 : \tau_1, \ldots, x_n : \tau_n.\ b$, where $b \in \mathcal{T}(\Sigma(P), \mathcal{V})_{bool}$, is *true* iff all procedures in P terminate and $\mathsf{eval}_{P'}(b[q_1,\ldots,q_n]) = true$ for each terminating program $P' \supseteq P$ and all $q_1,\ldots,q_n \in \mathbb{V}(P')$. Program P' may define additional data types and procedures, so this definition of truth ensures monotonicity in the sense that a formula remains true when program P is extended.

Computation rules (1)–(3) and (5)–(6) are straightforward and coincide with the semantics considered in [19]. Computation rule (4) differs from [19], however: If a selector sel' that does not belong to data constructor *cons* is applied to a value $cons(\ldots)$, e.g., $pred(0)$ or $hd(\emptyset)$, Walther and Schweitzer propose to consider the result as an *indetermined* value and do not evaluate such terms further. A so-called *fair completion* [19] resolves the indeterminism by defining a witness term for such "inappropriate" applications of selectors.[1] When reasoning about programs, all such fair completions need to be considered, so neither $pred(0) = 0$ nor $pred(0) \neq 0$ are true formulas, because $pred(0)$ is indetermined. Since subsequent extensions [14] of √eriFun demand that $?cons(t)$ be verified for each selector call $sel(t)$, where *cons* is the constructor that *sel* belongs to, such indetermined values cannot occur anymore. Therefore we simplify the semantics as in computation rule (4), which returns the fixed witness value ω_τ.

Computation rule (7) is also simplified in this spirit. We will discuss this rule further in Sect. 2.4. The idea is that a procedure call is evaluated to the

[1] In addition, a fair completion specifies the result of a procedure if its context requirement is violated. "Fairness" means that the completion does not affect the termination behavior of procedures.

```
procedure [infix] !!(l : list[@A], n : ℕ) : @A <=
if l = ø then ⋆ else if n = 0 then hd(l) else tl(l) !! pred(n)
procedure ∇!!(l : list[@A], n : ℕ) : bool <=
if l = ø then false else if n = 0 then true else ∇!!(tl(l), pred(n))
```

Fig. 3. Alternative implementation of procedure "!!"

witness value of the respective type if the context requirement of the procedure is violated.

2.3 Incompletely Defined Procedures

For some procedures, one needs to implement auxiliary procedures to formulate a suitable context requirement. For instance, procedure "!!" in Fig. 1 uses procedures ">" and "*len*" to express the precondition on its parameters. Instead of formulating the context requirement (including auxiliary procedures) explicitly, one can define procedure "!!" *incompletely* by leaving some cases *underspecified* [6].

Fig. 3 shows an alternative implementation of procedure "!!". Symbol "$\star$" denotes an undefined return value; in other words, this case "should not occur". Walther and Schweitzer [19] show how a *domain procedure* ∇_f can be synthesized for each incompletely defined procedure f. This domain procedure is completely defined and returns *true* if and only if f is determined for the given input. For example, $\nabla_{!!}(l, n)$ returns *true* if and only if n is smaller than the length of list l. Hence one can use $\nabla_{!!}(l, n)$ as an implicit context requirement for procedure "!!" without having to implement procedures ">" and "*len*".

2.4 Discussion

In the previous subsections we described two concepts to implement procedures with preconditions. The first possibility is to specify a context requirement for a procedure explicitly [14]. The second possibility is to define a procedure incompletely by marking certain cases as undefined [19]; this implicitly induces a precondition, namely that the input must not lead to the undefined results.

In √eriFun, support for incompletely defined procedures was added first [19]. The semantics of procedures with context requirements was then defined by reducing them to incompletely defined procedures [14]. Incompletely defined procedures were *not* considered as procedures with (implicit) preconditions, so they could be called without inducing any verification conditions. Only if a precondition was explicitly specified did the verifier generate the verification condition that the context requirement be satisfied for each call of the procedure.

In the previous subsections, we presented a different view on these two concepts. We introduced procedures with context requirements as the basic concept and considered incompletely defined procedure as syntactical sugar that may simplify the definition of procedures by the automated synthesis of domain procedures as implicit preconditions.

```
procedure map(f : @A → @B, l : list[@A]) : list[@B] <=
if l = ∅ then ∅ else f(hd(l)) :: map(f, tl(l))

procedure foldl(f : @A × @B → @A, x : @A, l : list[@B]) : @A <=
if l = ∅ then x else foldl(f, f(x, hd(l)), tl(l))

procedure every(f : @A → bool, l : list[@A]) : bool <=
if l = ∅ then true else if f(hd(l)) then every(f, tl(l)) else false
```

Fig. 4. Second-order procedures

Regarding the theoretical treatment, our view has the benefit that several definitions become considerably simpler. For instance, in [19] the computation rule to execute procedure calls is about three times as long as our computation rule (7), because it needs to take indetermined values into account. Since we will statically enforce that all preconditions (both explicit ones and implicit ones via incomplete definitions) are satisfied in a program, we can simply designate the concrete value ω_τ as the result of a procedure call that violates the precondition c_{proc}. In practice, the advantage of the unified view is that indetermined values may no longer occur in program executions, which eliminates a frequent cause of errors.

3 Second-Order Programs

We define the order $o(\tau)$ of base types τ such as $\mathbb{N}$ or $list[\mathbb{N}]$ as 0; the order of a function type $\tau_1 \times \ldots \times \tau_n \to \tau$ is $1 + \max_i o(\tau_i)$ for a base type τ [3]. A *type* is a base type or an expression of the form $\tau_1 \times \ldots \times \tau_k \to \tau$ for types $\tau_1, \ldots, \tau_k, \tau$.

The procedures in Fig. 1 are *first-order* procedures, because their type has order 1. A *second-order* procedure takes one or more first-order functions as parameters. Fig. 4 shows some common examples of second-order procedures.

The semantics of second-order programs is defined by extending the definitions from Sect. 2.2 in the following way: For each ground type of the form $\tau = \tau_1 \times \ldots \times \tau_k \to \tau_{k+1}$, the set $\mathbb{V}(P)_\tau$ of values of type τ contains all closed λ-expressions of type τ; e.g., $\lambda l : list[\mathbb{N}].\, len(l) \in \mathbb{V}(P)_{list[\mathbb{N}]\to\mathbb{N}}$. The witness value of such a type τ is defined as $\omega_\tau := \lambda x_1 : \tau_1, \ldots, x_k : \tau_k .\, \omega_{\tau_{k+1}}$. The computation calculus is extended by computation rule

$$(8)\quad \frac{(\lambda x_1 : \tau_1, \ldots, x_n : \tau_n .\, t)(q_1, \ldots, q_n)}{t[x_1/q_1, \ldots, x_n/q_n]}\ , \text{if } q_1, \ldots, q_n \in \mathbb{V}(P)$$

to facilitate β-reduction of terms.

We implicitly assume procedure bodies to be in η-long form; e.g., $map(f, tl(l))$ abbreviates $map(\lambda z : @A.\ f(z),\ tl(l))$ in Fig. 4, because $f =_\eta \lambda z : @A.\ f(z)$.

4 Static Analysis of Second-Order Programs

Given a second-order program, we would like to find out if the preconditions of all procedures are satisfied during any conceivable run of the program. For a procedure call t_1/t_2 we obviously need to show $t_2 \neq 0$ according to the context requirement of procedure "/". But what is a suitable verification condition for an indirect call of "/" as in $map(\lambda n : \mathbb{N}.\, c/n,\, l)$, for example? Since *map* will call c/n only for values $n \in l$, it would be sufficient to show "$n \neq 0$ for all $n \in l$". In this verification condition, "$n \neq 0$" comes from the context requirement of procedure "/", while the quantification "for all $n \in l$" comes from our knowledge about the behavior of *map*.

In Sect. 4.1, we describe the concept of *quantification procedures* that were introduced in [2] to synthesize induction axioms for procedures that involve second-order procedures. In Sect. 4.2, we present our method to uniformly generate verification conditions for terms that occur in second-order programs; here we use quantification procedures when procedures are passed as arguments to a second-order procedure in order to capture the behavior of the second-order procedure. We illustrate the benefits of our approach in Sect. 4.3 and give a medium-sized example in Sect. 4.4.

4.1 Quantification Procedures

For each second-order procedure *proc* with a function parameter f, one can uniformly synthesize a quantification procedure *forall.proc* that checks whether some predicate p holds for all arguments that are passed to f by *proc*. The corresponding definition in [2] considered second-order procedures *without* preconditions, so we generalize this definition as follows:

Definition 3. *For each second-order procedure*

$$\texttt{procedure}\ proc(f : \tau_1 \times \ldots \times \tau_m \rightarrow \tau_f,\ x : \tau_x) : \tau_{proc} <=$$
$$\texttt{assume}\ c_{proc};\ B_{proc}$$

the quantification procedure *forall.proc* for *proc is defined by*

$$\texttt{procedure}\ forall.proc(p : \tau_1 \times \ldots \times \tau_m \rightarrow bool,$$
$$f : \tau_1 \times \ldots \times \tau_m \rightarrow \tau_f,\ x : \tau_x) : bool <=$$
$$\mathsf{ALL}_f(c_{proc}) \wedge if\ c_{proc}\ then\ \mathsf{ALL}_f(B_{proc})\ else\ true$$

where

$$\mathsf{ALL}_f(v) := true$$
$$\mathsf{ALL}_f(f(t_1, \ldots, t_m)) := p(t_1, \ldots, t_m) \wedge \mathsf{ALL}_f(t_1) \wedge \ldots \wedge \mathsf{ALL}_f(t_m)$$
$$\mathsf{ALL}_f(g(t_1, \ldots, t_n)) := \mathsf{ALL}_f(t_1) \wedge \ldots \wedge \mathsf{ALL}_f(t_n)$$
$$\mathsf{ALL}_f(h(\lambda \boldsymbol{y}.\, t_0,\, t_1)) := \mathsf{ALL}_f(t_1) \wedge forall.h(\lambda \boldsymbol{y}.\, \mathsf{ALL}_f(t_0),\, \lambda \boldsymbol{y}.\, t_0,\, t_1)$$
$$\mathsf{ALL}_f(if\ t_1\ then\ t_2\ else\ t_3) := \mathsf{ALL}_f(t_1) \wedge if\ t_1\ then\ \mathsf{ALL}_f(t_2)\ else\ \mathsf{ALL}_f(t_3)$$

for any variable v, any first-order function $g \neq if$, $g \neq f$, and any second-order procedure h (including proc). We write $\boldsymbol{y}$ as an abbreviation of $y_1, \ldots, y_k$, and $A \wedge B$ abbreviates "if A then B else false".

Example 1. Procedure $forall.map(p : @A \rightarrow bool,\ f : @A \rightarrow @B,\ k : list[@A]) : bool$ returns *true* if and only if $p(z)$ is satisfied for all elements z of list k, because procedure *map* applies f to all elements z of k. ◇

Example 2. For the second-order procedure *foldl*,

$$\texttt{procedure}\ \mathit{forall.foldl}(p : @A \times @B \to \mathit{bool},\ f : @A \times @B \to @A,\ x : @A,\ k : \mathit{list}[@B]) : \mathit{bool}$$

checks if $p(a, b)$ is satisfied for all pairs (a, b) that f is applied to by *foldl*. ♢

4.2 Generation of Verification Conditions

If a procedure f with a precondition is passed to a second-order procedure *proc*, we can use the quantification procedure *forall.proc* to find out if *proc* calls f only with arguments that satisfy the precondition of f:

Definition 4. *The* verification condition $VC(t) \in \mathcal{T}(\Sigma(P), \mathcal{V})_{bool}$ *for a given term* $t \in \mathcal{T}(\Sigma(P), \mathcal{V})$ *is defined by*

$$\begin{aligned}
&VC(x) := \mathit{true}\\
&VC(f(t_1, \ldots, t_n)) := c_f[t_1, \ldots, t_n] \wedge VC(t_1) \wedge \ldots \wedge VC(t_n)\\
&VC(h(\lambda \boldsymbol{y}.\, t_0,\ t_1)) := c_h[\lambda \boldsymbol{y}.\, t_0,\ t_1] \wedge VC(t_1) \wedge \mathit{forall.h}(\lambda \boldsymbol{y}.\ VC(t_0),\ \lambda \boldsymbol{y}.\, t_0,\ t_1)\\
&VC(\mathit{if}\ t_1\ \mathit{then}\ t_2\ \mathit{else}\ t_3) := VC(t_1) \wedge \mathit{if}\ t_1\ \mathit{then}\ VC(t_2)\ \mathit{else}\ VC(t_3)\\
&VC(\lambda \boldsymbol{y}.\, t_0) := \mathit{true}
\end{aligned}$$

for any variable x*, any first-order function* $f \neq \mathit{if}$ *with context requirement* c_f*, and any second-order procedure* h *with context requirement* c_h*.*

The generation of verification conditions is similar to the synthesis of quantification procedures. However, there are some differences:

- Function f can be any first-order function here, while f refers to a particular parameter of *proc* in Definition 3.
- For calls of second-order procedures h, we need to check whether the context requirement of h is satisfied. Definition 3 does not contain such a check.
- Term t can be a λ-expression, so we have an additional clause for this case.

Example 3. For term $t := t_1/t_2$ we get $VC(t) = t_2 \neq 0 \wedge VC(t_1) \wedge VC(t_2)$. ♢

Example 4. For term $t := \mathit{map}(\lambda n : \mathbb{N}.\, c/n,\ l)$ we get

$$VC(t) = \mathit{forall.map}(\lambda n : \mathbb{N}.\, n \neq 0,\ \lambda n : \mathbb{N}.\, c/n,\ l)\,,$$

which expresses that $n \neq 0$ needs to hold for all values n that *map* calls $\lambda n : \mathbb{N}.\, c/n$ with. This is equivalent to $\forall n \in l.\ n \neq 0$ as desired. ♢

Definition 4 easily generalizes to second-order procedures h with more than two parameters:

Example 5. Suppose that a program contains a procedure

$$\texttt{procedure}\ \mathit{ordered}(l : \mathit{list}[\mathbb{N}]) : \mathit{bool} <= \ldots$$

that returns *true* if and only if list l is ordered and a procedure

```
procedure insert(l : list[ℕ], n : ℕ) : list[ℕ] <=
assume ordered(l); ...
```

that inserts a number n into an ordered list l. Then $foldl(insert, \emptyset, l)$ is an implementation of *insertion sort*. The verification condition for this term is $forall.foldl(\lambda k : list[\mathbb{N}], m : \mathbb{N}.\ ordered(k),\ insert,\ \emptyset,\ l)$, which expresses that all lists k that occur as intermediate results need to be ordered. ◇

4.3 Discussion

When a procedure *proc* calls another procedure f or a function like *pred* or *tl*, it is the responsibility of the calling procedure *proc* to ensure that f is called with arguments that satisfy the precondition of f. For example, it is the responsibility of procedure *len* (cf. Fig. 1) to ensure that $tl(l)$ is only called if $l \neq \emptyset$.

However, if f is not a concrete function, but a function parameter of *proc*, then the precondition of f is unknown to *proc*, because f may be instantiated with quite arbitrary functions. Thus it becomes the responsibility of the *caller* of *proc* to instantiate f in such a way that all f-calls by *proc* meet the precondition of f. For instance, *map* should only be called with a function f and a list l such that f is applicable to all elements of l (cf. Fig. 4).

Using our approach, for each call $proc(f, \ldots)$ of a second-order procedure *proc* a verification condition can be generated that checks whether *proc* calls f only with arguments that satisfy the precondition of f. If one wanted to (or had to) specify this check explicitly as a precondition of *proc*, one could specify $\forall x \in l.\ c_f[x]$ as a precondition of *map*, for example. Even for procedures that are only slightly more complicated than *map*, this would soon become tedious: For instance, procedure *foldl* applies f to tuples (a, b), where $b \in l$ and $a : @A$ is "some intermediate result of $f(\ldots f(f(x, hd(l)), hd(tl(l))), \ldots)$". This is of course too informal to turn the observation into a precondition. Specifying a more general precondition for *foldl* such as $\forall a : @A.\ \forall b \in l.\ c_f[a, b]$ would be an easy way out of this imprecision, but it would be a stronger precondition than what *foldl* actually requires.

In this sense, our approach generates the *weakest* verification condition that ensures that all preconditions of functions are satisfied when a given term is evaluated. Developers only need to specify preconditions that are relevant from the algorithmic point of view (e.g., for procedure "!!" in Fig. 1). Bookkeeping-like preconditions that just propagate the preconditions of function parameters to the respective second-order procedure can be omitted, because our approach analyzes these indirect function calls automatically.

4.4 Example

The program in Fig. 5 uses both of the concepts to implement procedures with preconditions that we described in Sect. 2. Furthermore, it contains both direct

```
structure pair[@A,@B] <= mkpair(fst : @A, snd : @B)
structure variable.symbol <= variable(varID : ℕ)
structure function.symbol <= func(funcID : ℕ)
structure term <=
  var(vsym : variable.symbol),
  apply(fsym : function.symbol, args : list[term])

procedure lookup(key : @A, alist : list[pair[@A,@B]]) : @B <=
if alist = ∅
  then ⋆
  else if key = fst(hd(alist))
         then snd(hd(alist))
         else lookup(key, tl(alist))

procedure sig.known(t : term, arity : list[pair[function.symbol, ℕ]]) : bool <=
if ?var(t)
  then true
  else if ∇_lookup(fsym(t), arity)
         then every(λs : term. sig.known(s, arity), args(t))
         else false

procedure wellformed(t : term, arity : list[pair[function.symbol, ℕ]]) : bool <=
assume sig.known(t, arity);
if ?var(t)
  then true
  else if len(args(t)) = lookup(fsym(t), arity)
         then every(λs : term. wellformed(s, arity), args(t))
         else false
```

Fig. 5. A functional program that checks if a given term is well-formed

and indirect procedure calls that illustrate the generation of the corresponding verification conditions.

Procedure *lookup* returns the second component b of the first pair $mkpair(a, b)$ in list *alist* such that $a = key$. This procedure is incompletely defined, because there might be no such pair in *alist*. The corresponding domain procedure ∇_{lookup} thus returns *true* if and only if *alist* contains a pair $mkpair(a, b)$ with $a = key$. Hence the implicit precondition of *lookup* is given by $\nabla_{lookup}(key, alist)$.

Procedure *sig.known* checks whether the signature of all function symbols occurring in a given term t is known, i.e., whether *arity* defines the arity for each function symbol f in t. This procedure is used in the context requirement of procedure *wellformed*. Given a term t and a list *arity* that defines the arity of each function symbol occurring in t, procedure *wellformed* returns *true* if and only if the number of arguments of each function application in term t is equal to the arity of the leading function symbol.

For the direct call of procedure *lookup* in the body of *wellformed*, we get the verification condition $\nabla_{lookup}(fsym(t), arity)$. Since we may assume that $sig.known(t, arity)$ holds, this verification condition is true. For the indirect call of procedure *wellformed* via the second-order procedure *every*, we get the verification condition

$$\begin{aligned} forall.every(&\lambda s: term.\ sig.known(s, arity),\\ &\lambda s: term.\ wellformed(s, arity),\\ &args(t))\,. \end{aligned}$$

This requires $sig.known(s, arity)$ to hold for each element s of list $args(t)$ (i.e., each subterm s of t) that is passed to *wellformed*. Since $sig.known(t, arity)$ by definition entails $sig.known(s, arity)$ for all subterms s of t, this verification condition is true as well and can easily be verified in √eriFun.

5 Related Work

Annotating programs with preconditions has a long history and is supported (in various ways) in several programming languages such as C, Eiffel, Haskell, and Java. In the following, we mainly consider related work that concerns programs with preconditions in the context of semi-automated theorem proving.

In ACL2 [8], procedures can be annotated by *guards* to specify preconditions. By *guard verification*, theorems are proved that ensure that a procedure satisfies the guards of all procedures that it uses in its body. Using and verifying guards is optional in ACL2, and all procedures need to be completely defined in case that guard checking mode is turned off. ACL2 has a first-order programming language, so second-order procedures such as *map* or *foldl* cannot be defined in a way that would allow procedure calls like $map(f, l)$ for concrete functions f [5,7].

In PVS [11], one can express preconditions by using specific types. For example, for the second parameter of a division algorithm on natural numbers one can use the type $\{n : \mathbb{N} \mid n \neq 0\}$. Preconditions that involve more than a single parameter can be expressed using dependent types. For instance, the type for parameter l of procedure "!!" (cf. Fig. 1) can be specified by $\{k : list[@A] \mid len(k) > n\}$. PVS generates *type-correctness conditions* to ensure that the arguments of procedure calls have the required types. Thus PVS uses type checking to verify that all preconditions are satisfied, while our approach can also be used in languages that do not support dependent types.

In Isabelle/HOL [10], developers of theories usually try to define functions "as completely as possible". For instance, *division* is completed by defining $n/0 := 0$ and function *tl* is completed by defining $tl(\emptyset) := \emptyset$. If there is no way of completing the definition of a function, the result can be left unspecified for some cases; e.g., function *hd* is defined just by $hd(x :: xs) := x$, so $hd(\emptyset)$ is a value (because all functions are total) that nothing is known about except its type (because no defining equation is applicable). This corresponds to √eriFun's concept of incompletely defined procedures [19] in its original form (i.e., without our reinterpretation as procedures with implicit preconditions).

For the programming language Haskell [12], Xu et al. present an approach to statically check contracts in programs [20]. Similarly to PVS, contracts are expressed by dependent types. Differently from PVS, ACL2, and √eriFun, however, the verification part is not tackled by a general purpose theorem prover. Instead, the term under consideration is uniformly transformed by wrapping function calls with checks that make the evaluation "crash" when a contract is violated. Then a dedicated symbolic evaluator tries to rewrite the transformed term until it is syntactically "crash-free" (i.e., it does not contain "crash" commands anymore). The symbolic evaluator is tailored to the lazy evaluation strategy of Haskell. A prototype implementation is reported to be able to "prove some simple contract satisfaction checks, but is still incomplete for more sophisticated examples involving the use of recursive functions in predicates" [20].

Regarding imperative programming languages, Eiffel [9] checks at run-time if contracts are satisfied, while Spec# [4] in addition supports static verification using the automatic verifier Boogie. According to [20], contracts that involve recursive procedures cannot be analyzed statically in Spec#. In our approach, recursive procedures pose no problem, because √eriFun is specifically designed to prove properties about recursive procedures.

As an alternative to the semantics that we considered in this paper, Sabel and Schmidt-Schauß [13] present a contextual semantics that equates undefinedness with non-termination. Thus division by zero is regarded like a non-terminating evaluation. The static analysis whether all procedure calls in a program satisfy the respective preconditions is not considered in [13].

6 Conclusion

In order to ensure that the execution of a program will never fail due to violated preconditions, one can statically analyze if all function calls in the program are safe in the sense that the arguments of each function call satisfy the precondition of the respective function. In this paper, we proposed a method to statically analyze function calls in second-order functional programs.

Our method generates verification conditions for function calls in a given term. In particular, our approach works for programming languages (and specification languages) that do not offer dependent types and the corresponding machinery for type checking. It is able to handle indirect function calls, e.g., calls of function f in $map(f, l)$, that occur when a function is passed as an argument to a second-order procedure. By analyzing the behavior of the second-order procedure with respect to its function parameter, our approach generates the weakest verification condition that ensures that the indirect function calls satisfy the precondition of the function.

We offer developers two possibilities to conveniently implement procedures with preconditions: Firstly, preconditions can be specified explicitly as a so-called context requirement of the procedure [14]. In this context requirement, any (terminating) procedure of the program can be used to specify the precondition. Secondly, preconditions can be specified implicitly by defining a procedure incompletely. In this case, a domain procedure is synthesized using the approach by Walther and Schweitzer [19] that characterizes the inputs of the procedure that do not lead to an undefined case.

In [19], the motivation for incompletely defined procedures was to model procedures with run-time exceptions in a way that does not mix up non-termination and run-time exceptions in a single notion of partiality. Thus reasoning techniques for *total* functions can be reused to reason about procedures with run-time exceptions. The absence of exceptions did *not* have to be proved, so one frequently had to reason about indetermined values. In our approach, we consider incompletely defined procedures as just another convenient way of implementing procedures with preconditions. This has the advantage that we can give a simpler definition of the semantics of first-order and second-order programs compared to [19], because the verification conditions (once proved) guarantee the absence of exceptions, so the semantics need not model indetermined values anymore.

We restricted our consideration to second-order programs to keep the semantics simple. For instance, if a call of procedure *lookup* (cf. Fig. 5) could instantiate type variable $@A$ with a function type, then the semantics would need to define when two functions are to be considered as equal. However, equality of functions is undecidable in general. By allowing the instantiation of type variables with base types only, we avoid this problem and still get a programming language where we can investigate the challenges of indirect function calls.

Our approach has been implemented in an experimental version of √eriFun. This gives us the full power of a semi-automated inductive theorem prover to verify the generated verification conditions. The proofs of verification conditions are typically relatively straightforward; often a single induction suffices to reason about recursively defined procedures that occur in the preconditions. In summary, we think that our approach effectively helps to find program errors due to violated preconditions early so that one does not need to worry about indetermined behavior once the verification conditions have been verified.

Acknowledgment. I would like to thank Christoph Walther for many discussions about incompletely defined procedures and procedures with preconditions as well as for his support in integrating the method described in this paper into √eriFun. Furthermore, I am grateful to Moritz Sinn and to Nathan Wasser for implementing the approach. I thank Simon Siegler for detailed feedback on a draft of this paper. Alexander Lux and Artem Starostin provided helpful comments on parts of this paper.

References

1. Aderhold, M.: Verification of Second-Order Functional Programs. Doctoral dissertation, TU Darmstadt (2009)
2. Aderhold, M.: Automated synthesis of induction axioms for programs with second-order recursion. In: Giesl, J., Hähnle, R. (eds.) IJCAR 2010. LNCS (LNAI), vol. 6173, pp. 263–277. Springer, Heidelberg (2010)
3. Andrews, P.B.: An Introduction to Mathematical Logic and Type Theory: To Truth Through Proof. Kluwer Academic Publishers, Dordrecht (2002)
4. Barnett, M., Leino, K.R.M., Schulte, W.: The Spec# programming system: An overview. In: Barthe, G., Burdy, L., Huisman, M., Lanet, J.-L., Muntean, T. (eds.) CASSIS 2004. LNCS, vol. 3362, pp. 49–69. Springer, Heidelberg (2005)

5. Boyer, R.S., Goldschlag, D.M., Kaufmann, M., Moore, J.S.: Functional instantiation in first-order logic. In: Lifschitz, V. (ed.) Papers in Honor of John McCarthy, pp. 7–26. Academic Press, London (1991)
6. Gries, D., Schneider, F.B.: Avoiding the undefined by underspecification. In: van Leeuwen, J. (ed.) Computer Science Today: Recent Trends and Developments. LNCS, vol. 1000, pp. 366–373. Springer, Heidelberg (1995)
7. Hunt Jr., W.A., Kaufmann, M., Krug, R.B.: Meta reasoning in ACL2. In: Hurd, J., Melham, T. (eds.) TPHOLS 2005. LNCS, vol. 3603, pp. 163–178. Springer, Heidelberg (2005)
8. Kaufmann, M., Manolios, P., Moore, J.S.: Computer-Aided Reasoning: An Approach. Kluwer Academic Publishers, Dordrecht (2000)
9. Meyer, B.: Eiffel: The Language. Prentice Hall International, London (1992)
10. Nipkow, T., Paulson, L.C., Wenzel, M.: Isabelle/HOL — A Proof Assistant for Higher-Order Logic, Springer, Heidelberg (June 2010)
11. Owre, S., Shankar, N., Rushby, J.M., Stringer-Calvert, D.W.J.: PVS Language Reference, Computer Science Laboratory, SRI International (November 2001)
12. Peyton Jones, S. (ed.): Haskell 98 Language and Libraries: The Revised Report. Cambridge University Press (2003)
13. Sabel, D., Schmidt-Schauß, M.: Reconstruction of a logic for inductive proofs of properties of functional programs. Frank report 39, J. W. Goethe-Universität, Frankfurt am Main, Germany (June 2010)
14. Schlosser, A., Walther, C., Gonder, M., Aderhold, M.: Context dependent procedures and computed types in ✓eriFun. In: Proc. of 1st Workshop Programming Languages meet Program Verification. ENTCS, vol. 174, pp. 61–78 (2007)
15. Walther, C.: Semantik und Programmverifikation. Teubner-Wiley, Leipzig (2001)
16. Walther, C., Aderhold, M., Schlosser, A.: The $\mathcal{L}$ 1.0 Primer. Technical Report VFR 06/01, TU Darmstadt (2006)
17. Walther, C., Schweitzer, S.: About ✓eriFun. In: Baader, F. (ed.) CADE 2003. LNCS (LNAI), vol. 2741, pp. 322–327. Springer, Heidelberg (2003)
18. Walther, C., Schweitzer, S.: Verification in the classroom. Journal of Automated Reasoning 32(1), 35–73 (2004)
19. Walther, C., Schweitzer, S.: Reasoning about incompletely defined programs. In: Sutcliffe, G., Voronkov, A. (eds.) LPAR 2005. LNCS (LNAI), vol. 3835, pp. 427–442. Springer, Heidelberg (2005)
20. Xu, D.N., Peyton Jones, S., Claessen, K.: Static contract checking for Haskell. In: Proceedings of the 36th ACM SIGPLAN-SIGACT Symposium on Principles of Programming Languages (POPL), pp. 41–52. ACM, New York (2009)

Author Index

GPSR Compliance

The European Union's (EU) General Product Safety Regulation (GPSR) is a set of rules that requires consumer products to be safe and our obligations to ensure this.

If you have any concerns about our products, you can contact us on ProductSafety@springernature.com

In case Publisher is established outside the EU, the EU authorized representative is:

Springer Nature Customer Service Center GmbH
Europaplatz 3
69115 Heidelberg, Germany

Batch number: 09490872

Printed by Printforce, the Netherlands